# THE
# FUTURE LIFE

*By René Pache*
*Doctor of Law*

*Translated by*
HELEN I. NEEDHAM, M.A.
*The Moody Bible Institute, Faculty,*
*French and English*

MOODY PRESS
CHICAGO

*Printed in the United States of America*

# THE
# FUTURE LIFE

"The immortality of the soul is a matter which means so much to us and which touches us so profoundly that we must have lost all feeling to be indifferent to it. All our actions and thoughts must take such different directions, according as there are or are not eternal joys to hope for, that it is impossible to pursue any course with sense and judgment unless we regulate it by our view of this point which ought to be our ultimate object."

Pascal

# PREFACE

WE PRESENT to the public this book, a sequel to our work entitled *The Return of Jesus Christ,* in which we treat prophecy up to the end of the millennium.

The vision of the future would be of very little concern if it were limited to the culmination, however glorious, of the earthly drama. God has "set [the thought of] eternity" in our hearts, so that nothing but His immediate and perpetual presence can satisfy us.

The present volume has no other aim than to seek to group together and to explain if possible the numerous Bible texts —at once marvelous and formidable—which speak to us of the world to come. If we are to live forever in another world, it would be insane to neglect the revelations and the warnings of the Scriptures on that subject.

The Psalmist exclaims: "A day in thy courts is better than a thousand!" (Psalm 84:10). One hour of serious meditation which carries us by faith within the palace of the great King will do more for our salvation and our testimony than will years devoted to transitory things, even the most beautiful of them.

> "Search me, O God, and know my heart ...
> And see if there be any wicked way in me,
> And lead me in 'the way everlasting!"
> (Psalm 139:23, 24)

# CONTENTS

PART THREE

# THE WORLD OF SPIRITS

PART FOUR

THE RESURRECTION

PART FIVE

ETERNAL PERDITION

# PART ONE

# INTRODUCTION

## *Chapter I*

# THE IMPORTANCE OF THE FUTURE LIFE

IS IT WORTH THE TROUBLE to devote a book to the study of "the future life?" To seek to become acquainted with the other world—is that not engaging in dangerous speculations? Moreover, some would say, exactly what can we know about this mysterious subject? Is not the earth sufficient for us for the moment? The hour of death will be soon enough to worry about the hereafter, if it exists! For now, let's not dwell on such gloomy topics!

This language, very common today, reveals a profound ignorance of the importance of eternity, of the extent of the Biblical revelations, and of the danger to such as have not accepted those revelations. What can we reply to the above arguments?

1. *Life is much too short to satisfy us.* When we reflect on it, we might wonder how long man is allowed to live. The very most that God allows is a hundred and twenty years, according to Genesis 6:3. But very few there are who live to be a hundred. We are more likely obliged to sigh with the psalmist: "Jehovah, make me to know mine end and the measure of my days, what it is; let me know how frail I am. Behold, thou hast made my days as handbreadths; and my life-time is as nothing before thee; surely every man at his best estate is altogether vanity" (Ps. 39: 4, 5). Before the God of eternity, "we bring our years to an end as a sigh. The days of our years are threescore years and ten; or even by reason of strength fourscore years; yet is their pride but labor

17

and sorrow; for it is soon gone, and we fly away . . . So teach us to number our days, that we may get us a heart of wisdom" (Ps. 90: 9-12). The Scriptures say with reason: "What is your life? For ye are a vapor, that appeareth for a little time, and then vanisheth away" (James 4:14). "All flesh is as grass, and all the goodliness thereof is as the flower of the field. The grass withereth, the flower fadeth; because the breath of Jehovah bloweth upon it . . . but the word of our God shall stand forever" (Isaiah 40: 6-8).

Not only is our individual life of short duration, but what about the several millenniums of human history? Before a recent past event, where were we? And in a few years, where shall we be? Isn't it worth the trouble to know whether or not something awaits us after death? And if we are to spend almost the whole of our existence elsewhere, isn't it urgent that we be concerned about it? For what are seventy or eighty years as over against eternal life?

2. *God has set in our heart the thought of eternity,* according to Ecclesiastes 3:11. God has created us in His image and has given to us the sense of that which is eternal and perfect. Nothing transitory or incomplete can satisfy us. We should like to love and to be loved without reservation; therefore, earthly love always disappoints us. Artists passionately strive for perfection and sometimes destroy splendid works because they see them still coming short of their ideal. Youth supposes that it has infinite time to live and considers a year as interminable; the aged see time running out, and they cling all the more to the existence which is flying from them. How many there are who spend enormous amounts caring for their skin and their beauty, but who despair as inescapably they see decrepitude catching up with them. The drama is that the human heart is insatiable: the gay blade is carried away by a frenzy of pleasure; the business man can never make enough money; the dictator doesn't know enough to stop, and he pushes on until the pride of his conquests leads

him to ruin; the slave for work goes so far as literally to die in the harness; the scholar struggles endlessly toward making new discoveries; and the aviator always wants to fly faster and higher. If many men vegetate in a more colorless existence, they are not happy; and they have in them the bitterness of unrealized ambitions.

God destines us for all the glories of eternal life; that is why nothing on earth will ever be able really to fill our hearts. Jesus said to the Samaritan woman who had gone the limit in riotous living: "Every one that drinketh of this water shall thirst again; but whosoever drinketh of the water that I shall give him shall never thirst; but the water that I shall give him shall become in him a well of water springing up unto eternal life" (John 4: 13, 14). The words of St. Augustine are true: "The heart is restless until it finds its rest in God."

3. *If another world does not exist, nothing in this life makes any sense.* Our existence has significance only in terms of eternity. If everything ends at the tomb, what is the use of all our exertions and all our enjoyments? The author of Ecclesiastes expresses this in a disillusioned frame of mind: "Vanity of vanities; all is vanity. What profit hath man of all his labor wherein he laboreth under the sun? One generation goeth, and another generation cometh . . . I have seen all the works that are done under the sun; and behold, all is vanity and a striving after wind" (Eccles. 1:2-4, 14). More than any other, this man had determined to taste every cup: pleasure, drink, houses, lands, riches, love, glory, and knowledge. His conclusion is that there is "no profit under the sun . . . of the wise man, even as of the fool, there is no remembrance for ever; seeing that in the days to come all will have been long forgotten . . . So I hated life . . . I hated all my labor wherein I labored under the sun, seeing that I must leave it unto the man that shall be after me. . . . Therefore I turned about to cause my heart to despair . . . For what hath a man of all his labor, and of the striving of his heart . . . For all his days are

but sorrows, and his travail is grief; yea, even in the night his heart taketh no rest . . . There is nothing better for a man than that he should eat and drink, and make his soul enjoy good in his labor. This also I saw, that it is from the hand of God" (Eccles. 2: 11-24. See also 3:19; 4:8; 6:3; 6:9, etc.)

Thus it is that a materialist thinks. Since nothing remains and he must soon leave it all, he says, "Let us eat and drink, for tomorrow we die!" (I Corinthians 15:32). This existentialist philosophy now so fashionable is the expression of revolt and despair. For if it is easy to eat and drink when one is young, possessing money and good health, what can a person do when he becomes sad, ruined, and sick, or when the infirmities of age make him a human wreck? If there is no belief in a better life, this means simply a dark hole and a depression of spirit; for the most desperate, it means suicide, the "solution" which solves nothing, but which only hastens judgment.

4. *Earth comes short of satisfying our sense of justice* if it does not quench our thirst for permanence and for perfection. How many crimes are never punished, and how many wrongs are never made right down here! (See Eccles. 4:1-3; 7:15). This problem even troubled the psalmist: ". . . My steps had well nigh slipped, for I was envious at the arrogant, when I saw the prosperity of the wicked. For there are no pangs in their death . . . They are not in trouble as other men . . . Therefore his [God's] people return hither . . . these are the wicked; and, being alway at ease, they increase in riches . . . When I thought how I might know this, it was too painful for me, until I . . . considered their latter end. Surely thou settest them in slippery places . . . How are they become a desolation in a moment! They are utterly consumed with terrors! As a dream when one awaketh, so, O Lord, when thou awakest, thou wilt despise their image" (Ps. 73:2-20). "Fret not thyself because of him who prospereth in his way, because of the man who bringeth wicked devices to pass . . . Yet

a little while, and the wicked shall not be . . . The Lord will laugh at him; for he seeth that his day is coming" (Ps. 37:7-13). Certain sins are punished immediately, but the great settling of accounts will take place in the other world. God leaves man free to go his own way. Thus, He holds back His judgment in the hope that the sinner will repent. But it would be immoral and supremely unjust if there would not be a day of general retribution. We recognize also that good men are not always recompensed here below. Trials and even persecutions are not spared them. The number of martyrs and innocent victims surpasses reckoning. Isn't there ever to be a just turning of the tables for them? The Bible says that God permits these trials to educate and to sanctify them; but that would not make any sense if death ended all. Then believers themselves would be the most unhappy of men, and many would be tempted to say with the materialists: "Let us eat and drink, for tomorrow we die" (I Cor. 15:19, 32).

5. Finally, after having known mourning and separation here below, we must have the consoling assurance that we shall *see again our loved ones that have died in the faith.* Before an open tomb, we need to know that we shall meet again the one who has departed. At all times and in all places throughout the world, humanity has been sustained by an immense hope that there will be life after death and a reunion. What happiness the Bible brings us on this point, as on all others, in the promises of the Word of truth!

6. *The purpose of man's creation is that he may see God face to face and be like Him.* God has not made us simply for eternal things: for justice and perfection; He has created us for Himself. On earth, we are separated from Him by the veil of matter and the chains of sin. How limited our horizon would be if we did not have the glorious certainty that we shall spend eternity in the very presence of the Author of all things!

But the affirmation of the necessity of a future life is not enough. It exists, God tells us so, and we are to eagerly ponder His revelations about it. We have only to study all the various religions to establish the fact that humanity, left to itself, is in the dark in regard to this great problem. How many absurd and dangerous things men have said on these subjects! The confusion, even in the so-called Christian world, is greater today than ever before. When one departs from the clear message of the Scriptures, one can only arrive at a faulty conception of the other world, of our "rapport" with the dead, and of possibilities of salvation after this life. People no longer take seriously the solemn declarations of the Bible; they deny perdition and have a false notion of the whole perspective of eternity. Bizarre sects take advantage of this confusion to make poorly established souls believe the most unrealistic and unscriptural things. That is why we want here to put ourselves with humility and submission before the Scriptures alone. With Peter we exclaim, "Lord, to whom shall we go? Thou hast the words of eternal life" (John 6:68). We propose to gather together as much as possible the Bible texts which deal with this great subject. With the help of the very numerous clear passages, we shall try to understand the less obvious ones, remembering that if "the secret things belong unto Jehovah our God . . . the things that are revealed belong unto us and to our children for ever . . ." (Deut. 29:29).

## Chapter II

## MAN AND HIS DESTINY

IN ORDER TO UNDERSTAND what awaits man in the next world, we must be acquainted with his nature and his eternal destiny.

### 1. MAN CREATED IN THE IMAGE OF GOD

"God said, Let us make man in our image, after our likeness . . . God created man in His own image, in the image of God created He him; male and female created He them" (Gen. 1:26, 27). In these two verses, God states four times that He made man by a distinct creative act; and He also states four times that He made him in His own image (see also 5:1 and 9:6).

If then the physical constitution of man sometimes resembles that of animals (thinking of comparative anatomy), his personality is entirely another thing. God has given him:

a *spirit* which can have fellowship with Him;
a *mind* which can understand His works and His revelation;
a moral *conscience* which guides him in the good way;
a *will* which permits him to use his liberty;
an *artistic sense* which makes him appreciate beauty;
and, finally, a *heart* which is capable of loving his Creator.

To the question: why did God create man? we might answer this: God, who is love, desired to have a "fellow," a being like unto Himself, who could receive and reciprocate His love. The Lord placed His creatures in Paradise so as to maintain with them the closest of ties. When the fall of man

23

had broken those ties, God's whole redemptive effort centered on reestablishing them by the cross and on making them permanent in heaven. The future life, then, is not a sort of appendix added after a fashion to life on earth, to improve it or to complete it. It is, on the contrary, the purpose which determines our whole existence. A being that has come from the hands of God and that was created in His image can do no less than to return to Him: "The spirit returneth unto God who gave it" (Eccles. 12:7).

## 2. MAN A LIVING SOUL

Man, above all, is destined to life: having formed him from the dust of the earth, God breathed into his nostrils the *breath of life* and made him a *living soul* (or, a living being); then He placed in the midst of the Garden of Eden *the tree of life* which would permit him one day to *live eternally* (Gen. 2:7, 9; 3:22). Death and perdition were not intended for Adam; they are simply the result of the fall. If it had not been for sin, it seems that after a certain time spent in the garden, man would have been allowed to partake of the fruit of the tree of life and then to enter at once into the presence of the Lord. The example of Enoch, caught away without dying, after having walked down here in communion with God, seems to indicate the way in which men would normally have been transferred from earth to heaven (Gen. 5:24; Heb. 11:5).

## 3. BODY, SOUL, AND SPIRIT

The passage in Genesis 2:7 distinguishes in man:

the *body,* taken from the dust
the *breath* (or spirit) of life that God gives him
the living *soul* which he then becomes.

Two other passages mention separately either two or three of these elements: "May your *spirit* and *soul* and *body* be

preserved entire, without blame" (I Thess. 5:23). The Word
of God pierces "even to the dividing of *soul* and *spirit* . . . to
discern the thoughts and intents of the *heart*" (Heb. 4:12).

1. It is easy to understand the role of the *body* in life. Instrument of the will, it lends itself more easily to evil than to
good; when we have become regenerated, we are to offer it
as a sacrifice to God, since it is the temple of His Spirit (Rom.
12:1; I Cor. 6:19). Paul says that our present body is "natural"—in the Greek, "psychic" (I Cor. 15:44); that is, it is
animated above all by the soul, the psyche. In the resurrection, we receive "a spiritual body."

2. As for the terms *soul* and *spirit,* it is not always easy to
distinguish them in Scripture. Let us see first the different
meanings that are given to the word *soul* (in Hebrew: *neph-
esh;* in Greek: *psyche*).

a. *The soul, breath and vital principle:*

Genesis 2:7: He "breathed into his nostrils the breath of
life, and man became a living soul."

Genesis 9:4, 5: "But flesh with the life thereof, which is the
blood thereof, shall ye not eat. And surely your blood, the
blood of your lives will I require: at the hand of every
beast . . ." (In this sense the animals themselves have "souls";
that is, they are animated by a vital principle, are not inert
like material things. In Latin the word *soul* is *anima*.)

Lev. 17.11: "The life of the flesh is in the blood . . . for it
is the blood that maketh atonement by reason of the life."
(That is, the vital principle is in the blood; whoever sheds
anyone else's blood takes away his life; to prove that the life
of the expiatory victim had been offered, one had only to
bring the blood into the sanctuary.)

I Kings 17:22: "The soul of the child came into him again,
and he revived." (Here, it is not a question of blood, which
was not shed, but of the vital breath.)

b. *A soul, meaning a person.*

This sense clearly appears in the original language, as in the American Standard Version:

Exod. 1:15: "All the souls [R.S.V., *persons*] that came out of the loins of Jacob were seventy souls . . ."

Exod. 12:4: They were to take the paschal lamb "according to the number of the souls," that is, of the people.

Lev. 4:2: "If anyone [A.V., *a soul*] shall sin unwittingly . . ." (See also Lev. 5:1-12, etc.)

Lev. 21:11 is even more significant: it prohibits a priest from going in "to any dead body"—literally, to any dead "soul"—and yet he could touch only the lifeless body.

It is in this same sense that we also say: a city of a hundred thousand souls.

c. *The soul, the seat of the emotions:*

Gen. 34:3: "His soul clave unto Dinah, the daughter of Jacob; and he loved the damsel and spake kindly unto the damsel."

Ps. 42:2, 5: "My soul thirsteth for God . . . Why art thou cast down, O my soul: and why art thou disquieted within me?"

Ps. 131:1, 2: "My heart is not haughty, nor mine eyes lofty . . . Surely I have stilled and quieted my soul . . . like a weaned child is my soul within me." (Here, *soul* and *heart* are used in the same sense.)

Luke 2:35: "A sword shall pierce through thine own soul."

Matt. 26:38: "My soul is exceeding sorrowful, even unto death . . ."

d. *The soul, in some passages, equivalent to the spirit:*

Some authorities, seeking to distinguish, in principle, between the soul and the spirit, have thought that they could pick out the following differences:

The *soul* is the vital principle which animates the body. It exists even in the unregenerate man. It is also the seat of the emotions, of the intelligence, of the will, and of purely human desires.

The *spirit,* on the other hand, is the highest part of our being, that which can communicate with God. This spirit is "dead" in the unconverted sinner. After regeneration, the Spirit of God, breaking in, gives it life and makes it capable of communicating with the Divine; the spirit of man thus becomes the depository of the supernatural life and of the presence of the Lord. It is the spirit which survives the death of the body and which goes to be with God; that also is the part which will inhabit the "spiritual body" of the resurrection.

In our practice of religion, that which comes from the soul is still human and carnal; for example, sentimental religious emotions, personal desires, a purely intellectual comprehension of the truth, a will not yet yielded: all these come from our own nature. On the other hand, the religion acceptable to God has its seat in the new nature, the regenerated spirit, animated by the divine Spirit and capable of walking in newness of life.

This distinction between *soul* and *spirit* is interesting, and we believe that there is a real difference. But we must admit that the Scriptures, both the Old and New Testaments, often use the term interchangeably:

Eccles. 12:7: "And the dust returneth to the earth as it was, and the spirit returneth unto God who gave it." (Here it is clearly the spirit which goes into the other world, into God's presence.)

Ps. 16:10: "Thou wilt not leave my soul to Sheol; neither wilt thou suffer thy holy one to see corruption." Peter explains that this is a prophecy referring to Jesus Christ, whose soul was not to stay in the abode of the dead and whose body would be raised again (Acts 2:24-31). The psalmist and the apostle could also have spoken of the spirit that the Saviour gave up on the cross (Matt. 27:50).

Luke 1:46, 47: "My soul doth magnify the Lord, and my

spirit hath rejoiced in God my Saviour." It is difficult here
to see any difference between the two terms.

Matt. 10:28: "Be not afraid of them that kill the body, but
are not able to kill the soul." The soul here does not mean
the breath of life, which ceases at the death of the body. It
means what is in other places called the spirit, the non-
material part of our being, which passes into the other world.

Acts 7:59: Stephen cried: "Lord Jesus, receive my *spirit!*"

Heb. 12:23: In the heavenly Jerusalem are "the spirits of
just men made perfect."

Rev. 6:9, 10: Still, what John saw in the other world were
the *souls* of the martyrs speaking with God. Those souls will
be raised up at the beginning of the millennium (Rev. 20:4).

Finally, Peter speaks of the soul as the spiritual part of our
being, which God sanctifies and keeps for eternity: "Receiving the end of your faith, even the salvation of your souls . . .
seeing ye have purified your souls in your obedience to the
truth . . . love one another . . . fervently . . . I beseech you
. . . abstain from fleshly lusts, which war against the soul . . .
Let them also that suffer . . . commit their souls in well-doing
unto a faithful Creator" (I Peter 1:9, 22: 2:11; 4:19). But
the same apostle declares that it is the *spirits* of the wicked
which are now in prison (I Peter 3:19).

In short, we cannot be too dogmatic about this distinction
between soul and spirit. The essential is that we retain in our
thinking the general and perfectly clear teaching of Scripture:
namely, that one part of our being is spiritual, destined to
know God and to survive the death of the body.

4. IS THE SOUL IMMORTAL?

From certain Bible texts some have wondered whether,
after all, the human soul is not perhaps mortal. According to
Paul, God "only hath immortality" (I Tim. 6:16); immortality would not be, then, the prerogative of man. Moreover,
the Scripture says "The soul that sinneth, it shall die" (Ezek.

18:4).* "The wages of sin is death" (Rom. 6:23). Just as the body becomes decomposed, the soul, some think, is annihilated at death. Then it would not be immortal; and the doctrine of the immortality of the soul, far from being Biblical, would be just a carry-over from pagan influences, especially the Greek. For the "conditionalists" our immortality would be entirely dependent on faith: man, mortal by nature, is only a candidate for immortality, and his "immortalization" would itself be the object of redemption. The life of the wicked, prolonged past the tomb, would be only transitory and would finally end. We shall consider conditionalism again in regard to the discussion about hell. Let us give at this place some words of explanation about the Greek theories, particularly those of Plato.

The Greeks (along with many other pagan peoples) believed in the survival of the soul, but not in the same sense as that of the Scriptures. Plato considered matter as evil. According to him, the soul exists before the body, being by nature divine and immortal. In the sensual body, it is a prisoner, like a foreign being. "Salvation" is summed up in deliverance from corporality. If the soul had been entirely purified, it would live through all eternity without a body. Such theories are obviously the negation of the Biblical view of the resurrection of the body, which is tied in with the regeneration of the soul. Besides, the Bible does not despise matter and does not say that the body is evil in itself, since it was created perfect by God and can be sanctified by the Holy Spirit who inhabits it; finally, the soul is neither existent before birth nor

*This passage from Ezekiel (18:4) calls for a special explanation. It is always quoted by those who believe in the annihilation of the soul. They interpret it as saying, essentially, that not only will the body of the sinner die, but also his soul. Now the text has a different emphasis. We have just seen that the word "soul" is often taken in the sense of "person." That is exactly the case here. Ezekiel speaks throughout the chapter of the respective responsibility of parents and children, insisting that each, father and son, will have to answer for his own sin. "As the soul of the father, so also the soul of the son is mine: the soul that sinneth [that is, the *person* who sins, the one responsible] it shall die" (vs. 4). So this text indicates nothing as to the fate of the sinner in the other world.

divine in itself. That these Platonic ideas have influenced certain theologians and Church Fathers is an historical fact. But they do not appear in the New Testament; and one cannot, in rejecting them, refuse the wholly different testimony of the Revelation.

Let us come back again to the question: Does the Bible teach the immortality of the soul? We have seen that God only hath immortality, for He is the source of life; He is "the life" Himself, and in essence He alone is eternal (John 1:4; 14:6; Ps. 90:2). But Paul does not say that only God *is* immortal. He possessses immortality and disposes of it as a Sovereign, granting it as a gift to His creatures. The Bible texts seem, indeed, to affirm clearly the following:

1. There is a survival in the other world, for the just and for the unjust. As for the just, let us simply cite Christ's word, when He says that all the patriarchs are living, though they passed away hundreds or even thousands of years before (Luke 20:37, 38). As for the unjust, they continue to live in Hades (Isa. 14:9, 10 and Ezek. 32:21-31). Jesus teaches us that, fully conscious, they have been suffering ever since their departure from this world (Luke 16:19-31). All the wicked will leave the abode of the dead to submit to the last judgment and to the torment of hell (Rev. 20:12-15).

2. This survival, for both groups, is without end. It goes without saying that eternal life for believers will last forever. We shall see later on that the torment of the lost will have the same duration, since the first go to eternal life and the latter to eternal punishment (Matt. 25:46); in the bottomless pit of fire and brimstone the wicked are tormented day and night for ever and ever (Rev. 14:10, 11; 20:10).

3. The term "immortality" is applied by Scripture only to the raised body, not to the soul. (See I Cor. 15:53b). It is the corruptible body which decomposes and disappears; it is the body which needs to become incorruptible and immortal. As for the soul, if it undergoes "spiritual death," it does not at

all cease to exist, either in this world or in the other. That is what we shall have ample occasion to point out.

As a suggestion, one can set up the following table: man receives

| | | |
|---|---|---|
| at his birth, | in his soul, | endless existence |
| at the new birth, | in his spirit, | eternal life |
| at the resurec-<br>tion, | in his body, | immortality. |

4. Let us notice that immortality of the angels is never spoken of either. They are created spirits and without any doubt are destined to an endless existence. The fact that the Bible does not call them "immortal angels" does not signify that they will not live forever in the other world.

5. Although they are called to an eternal existence, impenitent sinners are, at the same time, deprived of true life, which is living communion with God. "This is life eternal, that they should know thee, the only true God, and him whom thou didst send, even Jesus Christ" (John 17:3). "This [Jesus Christ] is the true God and eternal life" (I John 5:20). Even now on earth the ungodly are spiritually dead. (See later the definition of this term, p. 37): he is separated from God, dead in his trespasses and sins, according to Ephesians 2:1, at the same time dead while living, according to I Timothy 5:6. To sum it up, in Biblical language:

life is existence with God, and
death is existence without God.

Life draws its worth and its happiness from God, the source of life. "Death" consists of the privation of love, of joy, and of peace, these proceeding from God alone. We can say with the Scripture that even here below the believer *has* eternal life; he already has a taste of heaven on earth, he has God in his heart, even before he goes to be with Him forever above. On the other hand, the ungodly man is now already dead (see also I John 3:14, 15) . He knows something of hell on earth, a state in which the Lord is constantly being driven out more and more; soon, in the other world, the ungodly will realize all the suffering that eternal separation from God implies.

6. Since the Bible does not do it, we shall not use the expression "the immortality of the soul." But we shall affirm emphatically, as does the Bible, the endless existence to which man, created in the image of God, is called. Vinet has written: "I do not believe in the immortality of the soul, but in the immortality of the man, who is both body and soul" (Letters, Volume IV, p. 77, Payot 1949) . That is true for the just as for the unjust, since there will be a bodily resurrection of both (John 5:28, 29) .

# PART TWO

# DEATH AND THE DEAD

# Chapter III

## DEATH

### 1. THE ORIGINAL PLAN OF GOD

THE LORD is a God of love and of life. He intended for humanity—as for all His creatures— a wonderful lot, one of happiness and of constant communion with Him.

Man, created in His image and become "a living soul," was not meant for either death or perdition. We have seen that one day he could have eaten of the tree of life so as to live forever and that he would have been carried up to heaven as Enoch was without going through the tomb (Gen. 3:22; 5:24; Heb. 11:5).

Even after the fall, God shows that His primary purpose is still to save all men: "As I live, saith the Lord Jehovah, I have no pleasure in the death of the wicked: but that the wicked turn from his way and live: turn ye . . . why will ye die, O house of Israel?" (Ezek. 33:11). "God our Saviour . . . would have all men to be saved" (I Tim. 2:3, 4). If then we must talk of death and of eternal perdition, it is because a tragedy has come to overthrow the original plan of God.

### 2. WHY DID DEATH COME?

The fact that man was created in the image of God implies that he is endowed with free will and liberty. The God of love wants to be joyously loved and voluntarily served by His creatures. He does not force them to become His slaves, but lets them go another way if they choose. The angels, Adam and Eve, and even Jesus Himself—all were tempted. God had no intention of making out of Eden a gilded prison, from which there could be no escape. He half-opened a door, but in the hope that man, duly warned and, moreover, showered with blessings, would freely choose to continue in obedience and in communion with his Lord. Adam and Eve, after sinning deliberately, lived to see the terrible threat carried out on them: "Of the tree of the knowledge of good and evil, thou shalt not eat of it, for in the day that thou eatest thereof, thou shalt surely *die*" (Gen. 2:17).

### 3. PHYSICAL DEATH

The very day of the fall, God said to man: "In the sweat of thy face shalt thou eat bread till thou return unto the ground, for out of it wast thou taken: for dust thou art, and unto dust shalt thou return" (Gen. 3:19). Paul confirmed this when he wrote: "Through one man . . . death passed unto all men, for that all sinned" (Rom. 5:12). From henceforth the law of death is inescapable: all men, being sinners, are making their way toward the grave. The tomb becomes the king of terrors, and the conclusion of the most beautiful of earthly careers sounds like a death knell: "And he died" (Gen. 5:5, 8, 11, etc.)

So then death will catch up with us some day; and our great concern ought to be to prepare ourselves to die well, since "it is appointed unto men once to die and after this cometh judgment" (Heb. 9:27).

"Jehovah, make me to know mine end and the measure of my days, what it is; let me know how frail I am . . . every man at his best estate is altogether vanity" (Ps. 39:4, 5).

"Prepare to meet thy God!" (Amos 4:12).

However, physical death is not the end, for there will be for believers a glorious resurrection in the image of Jesus Christ and for the unjust the resurrection that is unto judgment.

## 4. SPIRITUAL DEATH

Adam (as in our case) was not struck dead in a physical sense the day of his first sin. But, on that very day, he was struck with spiritual death; that is, he was sent out from the presence of God, out of the Garden of Eden (Gen. 3:22-24). *For spiritual death, that which touches the soul, is not annihilation, but the deprivation of communion with God.* (Likewise, "life eternal," said Jesus, is "that they should know Thee, the only true God, and him whom thou didst send, even Jesus Christ," John 17:3.)

Thus, since the fall, we see sinners existing, bustling about, enjoying life, even having a religion, but all the time plunged in spiritual death. Paul said to the Ephesians that they were dead through their trespasses and sins; and he added: "Remember that ye were at that time separate from Christ . . . having no hope and without God in the world" (Eph. 2:1, 11, 12). Speaking to Timothy of the widows whose behaviour was reprehensible, the same apostle wrote: "She that giveth herself to pleasure is *dead while she liveth*" (I Tim. 5:6).

Such is the terrible state of all unregenerated men: they are dead while they live. Dead in spirit; and, as for the body, candidates for the grave! Is that still our condition? At any rate, that was the condition of the prodigal son, even when he was merrily throwing away his money on riotous living. The father, upon his return, exclaimed: "This my son was dead, and is alive again!" (Luke 15:24) "To be dead" for him meant: to exist, but to be plunged in sin, far from the father's house.

## 5. THE PASSAGE FROM DEATH TO LIFE

All sinners, headed toward spiritual and physical death, need regeneration for the soul and resurrection for the body.

The Scriptures proclaim, throughout, the necessity of the new birth; that is, of the spiritual resurrection of the sinner, dead in God's sight. Jesus said to Nicodemus, a devout and

scholarly man, though still not regenerated: "Except one be
born anew, he cannot see the kingdom of God . . . Except one
be born of water and the Spirit, he cannot enter into the
kingdom of God. That which is born of the flesh is flesh, and
that which is born of the Spirit is spirit. Marvel not that I
said unto thee: Ye must be born anew . . . So is every one
that is born of the Spirit" (John 3:3-8). Later, the Lord explains how, simply by man's faith and the operation of the
Spirit, this new birth is possible: "He that heareth my word
and believeth him that sent me hath eternal life and cometh
not into judgment, but hath passed out of death into life . . .
It is the spirit that giveth life; the flesh profiteth nothing"
(John 5:24; 6:63).

John further emphasizes this marvelous experience which
gives us eternal life and makes us children of God: "As many
as received him [the true light, Jesus] to them gave he the
right to become children of God, even to them that believe on
his name: who were born, not of blood, nor of the will of the
flesh, nor of the will of man, but of God" (John 1:12, 13).
"He that hath the Son hath the life . . . These things have I
written unto you, that ye may know that ye have eternal life,
even unto you that believe on the name of the Son of God . . .
Whosoever believeth that Jesus is the Christ is begotten of
God . . . Behold what manner of love the Father hath be-
stowed upon us, that we should be called children of God!
We know that we have passed out of death into life because
we love the brethren. He that loveth not abideth in death"
(I John 5:12, 13, 1; 3:1, 14).

Paul also develops the theme of the spiritual resurrection
of the believer: "You . . . were dead through your trespasses
and sins . . . among whom we also all once lived . . . But God
. . . for his great love wherewith he loved us, even when we
were dead through our trespasses, made us alive together with
Christ . . . And raised us up with him" (Eph. 2:1, 3-6).
"Buried with him in baptism, wherein ye were also raised

with him through faith in the working of God, who raised
him from the dead. And you being dead through your trespasses and the uncircumcision of your flesh, you, I say, did
he make alive together with him" (Col. 2:12, 13). Essentially,
the baptism spoken of here is that of the Spirit, received by
faith, of which the baptism by water is the symbol and the
witness. Whoever sincerely believes, then, is rescued from
spiritual death, "immersed" in Christ, raised again with Him.
The same thought reappears in Romans: "We were buried
therefore with him through baptism into death: that like as
Christ was raised from the dead through the glory of the
Father, so we also might walk in newness of life . . . But if
we died with Christ, we believe that we shall also live with
him . . . Present yourselves unto God, as alive from the
dead . . ." (Rom. 6:4, 8, 13).

We want to mention Peter, from whom we learn that we
have been born again by the living and permanent Word of
God and have been made partakers of the divine nature
(I Peter 1:23 and II Peter 1:4).

The point of all these texts is clear: regeneration is the
only remedy for that spiritual death into which all sinners
are plunged. This new birth is produced by the Spirit at the
very instant when, by faith, we accept Christ as our personal
Saviour. Since it comes about by faith, it can take place only
in this world. Finally, it is the indispensable prerequisite for
the glorious bodily resurrection. Only the children of God
will be raised up unto eternal life. All unregenerated sinners,
whose souls continue in the state of spiritual death, can be
raised again only for judgment and hell.

This being said, we reserve for the chapters that follow all
that concerns the resurrection of the two groups; and we go
on here with our study of death as such.

## 6. THE DEATH OF THE WICKED

All men, believers and unbelievers, are making their way

to the end of their earthly existence. But what a vast difference there is between the death of the child of God, who goes to his Father, and that of the wicked, who suddenly has to appear before his Judge!

That which is infinitely tragic is that, by definition, the unbeliever comes up to death without being prepared for it. He finds himself inevitably in one or the other of these situations:

He has lived for the world, seeking to amass all the wealth possible. And God says to him: "Thou foolish one . . . the things which thou hast prepared, whose shall they be?" (Luke 12:20). The disillusioned Preacher cried out: "How doth the wise man die even as the fool! So I hated life . . . for all is vanity and a striving after wind. And I hated all my labor wherein I labored under the sun, seeing that I must leave it unto the man that shall be after me. And who knoweth whether he will be a wise man or a fool?" (Eccles. 2:16-19). The ungodly man has attempted above all to enjoy himself and to stop his ears to any warnings: "Let us eat and drink, for tomorrow we die!" Now the careless life is over, and eternal torment begins.

"The fool hath said in his heart: There is no God" (Ps. 14:1). Right up to the end he would like to persuade himself that there is nothing after death. Then, too late, trembling, he hears for the last time the solemn warning that he made fun of on earth: "Prepare to meet thy God!" (Amos 4:12).

The worldly man dies the way he lived. Jezebel, after a life of licentiousness and unbridled egoism, puts on her make-up and dolls herself up, just like any old flirt, "to repair the irreparable ravages of time." She who had coldly condemned Naboth to death is thrown out of a window and is eaten by dogs near her victim's vineyard (II Kings 9:30-37).

The rebels, whose conscience is tormented, see with horror the hour of the regulation of accounts approaching. Having learned from Samuel that he would die in battle, Saul, filled with terror, falls to the ground (I Sam. 28.20). Seeing the hand that wrote on the wall "Thou art weighed in the balances, and art found wanting," King Belshazzar changes color, his thoughts troubling him, his knees shaking. He is killed that same night (Daniel 5:6, 25-30).

Others remain indifferent right up to the fateful moment: "I was envious at the arrogant, when I saw the prosperity of the wicked. For there are no pangs in their death, but their strength is firm. They are not in trouble . . . Therefore pride is as a chain about their neck; violence covereth them as a garment . . . their tongue walketh through the earth . . . Being alway at ease, they increase in riches." The believer is troubled that these people can "get away with it," for this seems an incentive to do evil. But, after reflexion, he realizes "their latter end." "Surely, thou settest them in slippery places; thou castest them down to destruction. How are they become a desolation in a moment!" (Ps. 73:3-19). "The Lord will laugh at him [the wicked], for he seeth that his day is coming" (Ps. 37:13).

Without any question the most tragic situation is that of the self-deceived person, of "the honest man" who lives in a false security, having convinced himself that he is right with God when he is not. How numerous they are, these religious men, sure that they are better than others, but not justified (Luke 18:11-14); the foolish virgins mingling with the wise, claiming to be awaiting the Bridegroom, but having no oil in their lamps (Matt. 25:1-12); the Ananiases and the Sapphiras, baptized and members of the best churches, but at last struck down for having tried to deceive God and men (Acts 5:1-11); those who have prophesied, cast out demons, and done many mighty works in the name of Christ, but before whom the gates of heaven are nonetheless shut (Matt. 7:22, 23).

To all those who refuse to believe on Him, the Lord addresses these terrible words:

*"Ye shall die in your sins!"* (John 8:24).

This threat is illustrated in a moving way in the well-known account of Lazarus and the rich man (Luke 16:19-31). This is thought to be a true story, for Jesus gave the name of the poor man—a thing He never did in telling a parable. Be that as it may, in this passage Jesus Himself gives us very exact details about the state of the soul immediately after death. He brings out clearly in this text that immediately after leaving this world:

> the wicked suffer, vss. 23, 24;
> they are fully conscious, vss. 23, 24;
> they are in entire possession of their memory, vs. 25;
> no one can comfort them, vs. 26;
> there is no possibility of their leaving the place of torment, vs. 26;
> they are entirely responsible for not having listened in time to the warnings of the Scriptures, vss. 27-31.

Who would not shudder before such a horrible fate as this?

## 7. The death of the righteous

A more complete contrast can scarcely be imagined. The believer has merited the same condemnation; but, having humbled himself before God, he has put his confidence in the One whose death delivers him from the consequences of sin. For him, then, death is no longer the king of terrors. Moreover, his escape from that dominion was the very day of his new birth:

"He that heareth my word and believeth him that sent me hath eternal life and cometh not into judgment, but hath passed out of death into life" (John 5:24). "This is the bread which cometh down out of heaven, that a man may eat thereof and not die . . and I will raise him up at the last day . . . he that eateth this bread shall live for ever . . . He that eateth me, he also shall live because of me . . Not as the fathers ate and died; he that eateth this bread shall live for ever" (John 6:50-58).

"If a man keep my word, he shall never see death . . . I give unto them [to my sheep] eternal life; and they shall never perish . . . I am the resurrection and the life. He that believeth on me, though he die, yet shall he live: and whosoever liveth and believeth on me shall never die" (John 8:51; 10:28; 11:25, 26). "I will build my church, and the gates of Hades shall not prevail against it" (Matt. 16:18). Death indeed cannot hold those who are part of the church, the body of the Lord. The believer can leave this world; that is of no importance. He already has eternal life; and by his departure from this earth, he takes possession of it in a greater measure; for him, then, it is not really a question of death at all. Even his body will be raised up at the last day.

The poor man Lazarus died, and he was "carried by the angels into Abraham's bosom"; that is, into the abode of the blessed dead. There, he was comforted (Luke 16:22, 25).

"There is therefore now no condemnation to them that are in Christ Jesus . . . For I am persuaded that *neither death* nor life . . . nor things present nor things to come . . . nor any other creature, shall be able to separate us from the love of God, which is in Christ Jesus our Lord" (Rom. 8:1, 38, 39).

"For whether we live, we live unto the Lord; or whether we die, we die unto the Lord. Whether we live therefore or die, we are the Lord's. For to this end Christ died and lived again, that he might be Lord of both the dead and the living" (Rom. 14:8, 9). Why then fear an experience which simply brings us close to our Divine Lord?

Stephen, surrounded by enemies who were gnashing their teeth at him, did not fear death. His face shone like the face of an angel; filled with the Holy Spirit, he saw the glory of God and prayed for his tormentors. He cried out: "Lord Jesus, receive my spirit"; then, he fell asleep as the stones were hurled at him (Acts 6:15; 7:54-60).

Paul wrote: "I know that . . . with all boldness as always, so now also Christ shall be magnified in my body, whether by life or by death. For to me to live is Christ, and to die is gain" (Phil. 1:19-21). What a triumph of faith: to be able to consider death a gain, since it takes us into the presence of Christ! And the apostle continues: "But if to live in the flesh, if this shall bring fruit from my work, then what I shall choose I know not. But I am in a strait betwixt the two, having the desire to depart and be with Christ; for it is very far better: yet to abide in the flesh is more needful for your sake. Yea, and if I am offered upon the sacrifice and service of your faith [if I am martyred] I joy and rejoice with you all: and in the same manner do ye also joy, and rejoice with me" (Phil. 1:22-24; 2:17, 18).

This is far from the gloomy ideas and the foolish terror which death generally brings! But this is not all:

Paul goes on to explain to the Corinthians that the body is like a temporarily raised tent that we shall soon exchange for an eternal home. "In this we groan, longing to be clothed upon with our habitation which is from heaven . . . For indeed we that are in this tabernacle do groan, being burdened; not for that we would be unclothed, but that we would be clothed upon, that what is mortal may be swallowed up of life" (II Cor. 5:2-5). For the believer, remaining in this body is simply something to be endured, as the outer man is in the process of being destroyed; thus he sees death and the resurrection, not as an unclothing, but as a clothing upon, something infinitely to be desired. And the apostle continues: "Being therefore always of good courage, and knowing that whilst we are at home in the body, we are absent from the Lord (for we walk by faith, not by sight); we are of good courage, I say, and are willing rather to be absent from the body, and to be at home with the Lord. Wherefore also we make it our aim, whether at home or absent, to be well-pleasing unto Him" (II Cor. 5:6-9).

That is clear, and it is wonderful. Ever since, by His resurrection and His ascension, Jesus took with Him into heaven
the believers till then held captive in the place of the dead
(Eph. 4:8-10), the children of God are brought at the very
instant of their death into the presence of the Lord. With
Paul, they consider their departure a gain—for to depart and
be with Christ is far better; they prefer to leave this body of
suffering and to live in the presence of the Lord, to walk no
longer by faith, but, at last, by sight.

The same apostle continued his career without a moment's
anxiety about the tomb. He declares: "But I hold not my life
of any account as dear unto myself, so that I may accomplish
my course, and the ministry, which I received from the Lord
Jesus, to testify the gospel of the grace of God . . . I am ready
not to be bound only, but also to die at Jerusalem for the
name of the Lord Jesus" (Acts 20:24; 21:13). And when the
fatal hour sounded, Paul seemed even more serene, if that
were possible: "For I am already being offered, and the time
of my departure is come. I have fought the good fight, I have
finished the course, I have kept the faith. Henceforth there is
laid up for me the crown of righteousness . . ." (II Tim.
4:6-8).

In this spirit of quiet assurance, we might repeat the words
that the Preacher intended as pessimistic: "The day of death
[is better] than the day of one's birth" (Eccles. 7:1). When
a child comes into the world, he has ahead of him bright
prospects of life and of happiness; but also there are uncer-
tainties, dangers, possibilities of sin, misfortunes, and even
eternal loss. On the contrary, for the believer who arrives
victoriously to the port, there is nothing more to worry about:
the battle is won, and he is at the entrance to glory. What
Christian, about to depart into the presence of his God, would
prefer to begin his life's course down here all over again? And
who would want to call back a loved one who has just entered
into the presence of the Lord?

O thou whose face made bright my dwelling place:
To hasten the happy day of our reunion,
Suppose God, in His goodness, would bring thee back ...
What have I said? Come back to this poor earth?
Leave, for our night, the ineffable light?
Along our miry paths to walk with trembling steps,
When thou already art robed in those white garments?
Come back, when Jesus, along the verdant banks,
Leads thee and quenches thy thirst at the source of the
    living waters?
No, no! Come not thou back! . . . I shall await in faith
The hour of spreading my wings to fly to thee.

—THEODORE MONOD

The one who has given himself wholly to Christ has lost
his own life—he has already accepted and experienced death
with his Lord—but he has received at the same time life everlasting. He is then ready for any eventuality; neither the fact
nor the form of physical death can frighten him any more.
He is of that number who "loved not their life even unto
death" (Rev. 12:11). He fears him who can make soul and
body perish in gehenna; but he has no fear any longer of those
who can kill the body without being able to touch the soul
(Matt. 10:28).

Then, in certain tragic cases, the departure from this life
according to the will of God becomes a deliverance: "The
righteous hath a refuge in his death" (Prov. 14:32).

At any rate, a believer never has to take the last voyage
alone: "Though I walk through the valley of the shadow of
death, I will fear no evil, for thou art with me; thy rod and
thy staff, they comfort me" (Ps. 23:4).

"Precious in the sight of Jehovah is the death of his saints!"
(Ps. 116:15).

## 8. WHICH DEATH SEEMS THE MORE DESIRABLE?

To sum up the two pictures of death—that of the just and

that of the unjust—let us set down in parallel columns the points which seem the most striking as to the fate of each.

| That which awaits the just man | That which awaits the unjust man |
| --- | --- |
| 1. His many sins, confessed to God, have been washed in the blood of Christ (I John 1:7, 9). | "Your sin will find you out" (Num. 32:23). |
| 2. "He . . . cometh not into judgment" (John 5:24). | "Know thou, that for all these things God will bring thee unto judgment" (Eccles. 11:9). |
| 3. "He entereth into peace"— he shall "rest" (Isa. 57:2). | "Tribulation and anguish upon every soul of man that worketh evil" (Rom. 2:9). |
| 4. Carried by the angels to Abraham's bosom, Lazarus is comforted (Luke 16:22, 25). | "In torments" the rich man cries out: "I am in anguish in this flame" (Luke 16:23-29). |
| 5. "Come, ye blessed of my Father!" (Matt. 25:34). | "Depart from me, ye cursed" (Matt. 25:41). |
| 6. "Thou wilt guide me with thy counsel, and afterward receive me to glory" (Ps. 73:24). | "Many . . . shall awake . . . to shame and everlasting contempt" (Dan. 12:2). |
| "Ye shall receive the crown of glory that fadeth not away" (I Peter 5:4). | |
| 7. "The Lord . . . will save me unto his heavenly kingdom" (II Tim. 4:18). | "His angels . . . shall gather out of his kingdom . . . them that do iniquity and shall cast them into the furnace of fire" (Matt. 13:41, 42). |
| "Inherit the kingdom prepared for you" (Matt. 25:34). | |

8. "Enter thou into the joy of thy lord" (Matt. 25:21).

"Without are the dogs" (Rev. 22:15).

"Cast ye out the unprofitable servant into the outer darkness: there shall be the weeping and the gnashing of teeth" (Matt. 25:30).

9. He "begot us again . . . unto an inheritance incorruptible, and undefiled, and that fadeth not away, reserved in heaven for you" (I Peter 1: 3, 4).

"This ye know of a surety, that no fornicator nor unclean person, nor covetous man, who is an idolator, hath any inheritance in the kingdom of Christ and God" (Eph. 5:5).

10. When he dies, the believer is not "unclothed," but is "clothed upon, that mortality might be swallowed up of life" (II Cor. 5:4).

The unbeliever stands naked before God (II Cor. 5:3); a man has to leave everything and go back naked into the earth (Job 1:21).

11. "He that soweth unto the Spirit shall of the Spirit reap eternal life" (Gal. 6:8).

"He that soweth unto his own flesh shall of the flesh reap corruption" (Gal. 6:8).

12. To "be with Christ . . . is very far better" (Phil. 1:23).

Now, for ever "separate from Christ . . . having no hope, and without God in the world" (Eph. 2:12).

"I know you not!" (Matt. 25: 12).

13. For Paul, death was gain; he desired to depart (Phil. 1: 21, 23).

They "sit in darkness and the shadow of death" (Luke 1: 79).

We are "willing rather to be absent from the body, and

The devil has "the power of death"; he oppresses all those

to be at home with the Lord" (II Cor. 5:8).

who "through fear of death were all their lifetime subject to bondage" (Heb. 2:14, 15).

14. When he dies, the believer says: "At last! Here I am!" "Lord Jesus, receive my spirit" (Acts 7:59).

The wicked man cries out: "What ... already? Too late!" "It is a fearful thing to fall into the hands of the living God" (Heb. 10:31).

Yes, "blessed are the dead who die in the Lord!"

As for us, our choice is made; and we say to God with all our heart: "Let me die the death of the righteous, and let my last end be like his!" (Num. 23:10).

### 9. CONSOLATION IN THE PRESENCE OF DEATH

No matter how triumphant has been the faith of a believer who has departed victoriously to be with his Saviour, his death is, nevertheless, heart-rending for the loved ones he leaves behind. We firmly believe in a reunion; but "the flesh is weak," and we are all the same crushed by the brutality of the separation. Let us not think that God is not touched by our sorrow. Seeing Mary's tears, Jesus shuddered in His spirit; He was deeply moved; and He wept at the tomb of Lazarus, even though he was a few minutes later going to raise him to life again (John 11:33-35). He Himself knew suffering, death pangs, and death itself; He experienced more than any of us death's atrocious power; and "in that he himself hath suffered being tempted, he is able to succor them that are tempted" (Heb. 2:18). God, the psalmist says, is "nigh unto them that are of a broken heart, and saveth such as be of a contrite spirit" (Ps. 34:18). He sends us the Holy Spirit, whom Jesus calls by the lovely name of "the Comforter" (John 14:15). "Blessed be ... the God of all comfort, who comforteth us in all our affliction that we may be able to comfort them that are in any affliction, through the comfort

wherewith we ourselves are comforted of God" (II Cor. 1:
3, 4).

In our mourning, then, let us lay hold on the supernatural
help of Him who "abolished death and brought life and
immortality to light through the gospel" (II Tim. 1:10).
And may that consolation help us to understand, in our turn,
the grief of others and permit us to lead them to the only
source of victory and peace. We shall find, with them, that
the testing never surpasses our strength; and the hope of
eternal salvation will sustain us until that moment when all
tears shall be wiped away from our eyes.

### 10. THE HOUR OF DEATH

a. *God has determined the length of our lives.*

No one knows the hour of his death; that is a secret which
belongs to God alone. "For everything there is a season . . .
a time to be born, and a time to die . . . there is no man that
hath power over the spirit to retain the spirit; neither hath
he power over the day of death; and there is no discharge in
war . . . For man also knoweth not his time: as the fishes that
are taken in an evil net. . ." (Eccles. 3:1, 2; 8:8; 9:12).

"Man that is born of a woman is of few days, and full of
trouble. He cometh forth like a flower, and is cut down . . .
Seeing his days are determined, the number of his months is
with thee; and thou hast appointed his bounds that he cannot
pass; look away from him, that he may rest, till he shall accomplish, as a hireling, his day; I shall go the way whence I
shall not return" (Job 14:1-6; 16:22).

"For what is the hope of the godless, though he get him
gain, when God taketh away his soul?" (Job 27:8).

After having said "Into thy hand I commend my spirit,"
the psalmist adds: "My times are in thy hand" (Ps. 31:5, 15).
"Thine eyes did see mine unformed substance; and in thy
book they were all written, even the days that were ordained
for me, when as yet there was none of them" (Ps. 139:16).

For each of us, whether we know it or not, the fateful hour arrives when God says to us:

"This night is thy soul required of thee" (Luke 12:20). This very night!

What would it be if suddenly, even today, I were to appear before God? Would I really be ready?

We see, in the life of Jesus, that on several occasions the Pharisees could not arrest Him to put Him to death because "his hour was not yet come" (John 7:30; 8:20). Then the moment came when Christ knew that "his hour was come" ... to go "unto the Father" (John 13:1).

What joy to think that if we sincerely seek to live in His will, nothing can come to us outside the time and plan foreseen by God for us! Sometimes truly spiritual believers have a sort of presentiment of the approach of their death; for example, Elijah (II Kings 2:1-11) and Paul (II Tim. 4:6). Peter also was warned, not of the time of his death, but of the sudden manner by which he would be martyred (John 21:18, 19; II Peter 1:14). Those exceptional believers whom God warns like this can prepare themselves somewhat for their departure and can also prepare their loved ones. But, whether or not we are so privileged, the important thing is that we should be ready and submitted to the perfect will of God.

b. *What about suicide?*

The act by which a man hastens God's hour by taking his own life is disapproved by the Bible. Saul (I Sam. 31:4), Ahithophel (II Sam. 17:23), and Judas (Matt. 27:5) are examples. The sorrow of the world brings death; godly sorrow produces repentance and salvation, which there will never be occasion to regret (II Cor. 7:10). The Lord plainly says to us: "Thou shalt not kill" (Exod. 20:13). The one who commits suicide is a murderer, and "no murderer hath eternal life abiding in him" (I John 3:15). Not only does he put an end to his life in a moment of rebellion or despair, but also he deprives himself of any chance of receiving God's deliverance from his sorrows and, more important, the grace of repentance and of faith. What folly to cast oneself into the abyss that God would like to save us from!

Some people, even some believers, are haunted by the idea of suicide. It must be recognized that this is a special form of temptation. The devil, our sworn enemy, is a "murderer from the beginning" (John 8:44). Since he is never more happy than when he can destroy one of God's creatures, we are to resist him with a firm faith (I Peter 5: 8, 9); and we must constantly go in prayer to God, asking Him to keep our hearts and thoughts in Jesus Christ (Phil. 4:6, 7).

Murderers, such as the thief on the cross, have found grace (Luke 23:41-43). Likewise, by the marvelous goodness of God, there have been people who have attempted suicide and who have failed in it, and who at last have been thoroughly converted. Others, on their death beds, have had a few minutes of lucidity to cry out to God and to receive His pardon by faith.

That is why we must refrain from judging: the Lord alone knows what takes place the last moment between a soul and Himself; but let us repeat strongly that, according to the Bible, suicide is a crime—and that it is senseless to finish one's life by provoking God like this.

c. *Is it permitted to hasten the death of another, in the name of love?*

We shall not at all discuss murder itself, which is denounced by the Bible all the way through. But in our day there is the increasing claim that it is right and just to hasten the end of a sick person's life by "euthanasia," that is, by producing a gentle death to spare him great sufferings. What are we to reply to this?

First of all, to inflict death is always murder, whatever the beautiful Greek name given to it. God does not permit anyone voluntarily to touch the life of his neighbor: "Thou shalt not kill" is still in force. "At the hand of man, even at the hand of every man's brother, will I require the life of man . . . for in the image of God made he man" (Gen. 9:5, 6). Murderers are numbered with those who go to hell (Rev. 21:8; 22:15).

Moreover, in shortening someone's life, one perhaps deprives him of a last chance to repent and to be saved for all eternity.

Finally, who knows whether the sick person in question cannot be cured? Doctors are mistaken in their prognoses and sometimes say it is the end for someone when it is not. And even if that is so from the human and scientific point of view, isn't a miracle of God always possible? "While there's life, there's hope" goes the proverb.

If we are not allowed to touch anyone else's life, ought we to consent to it if he expressly asks for it? Actually there are invalids or wounded men who beg others to "end it all" for them. For the reasons that we have just set down, we do not believe that this is permitted either. We ought not to help someone steal if he begged us to help him to get out of poverty in that way. But our response will be double: we shall do all we can to alleviate the sufferings of the sick person; and at the same time and above all, we shall see to it that we bring him, as God enables, all the spiritual help he needs. Who knows, again, if the Lord in His omnipotence will not intervene—and if the prayer of faith will not save the sick? (James 5:15). Anyway, the trial has a spiritual significance (Heb. 12:5-11); and in His goodness, God plainly promises that no trial will be beyond our strength (I Cor. 10:13) — even if that strength must be augmented in some supernatural way at a given moment.

d. *What about capital punishment?*

If the individual cannot put an end to his life, can society condemn a criminal to be executed?

First, let us notice that the death penalty was current in

Old Testament times. God declared even to Noah, "Whoso sheddeth man's blood, by man shall his blood be shed: for in the image of God made he man" (Gen. 9:6).

According to the law of Moses, such a penalty was inflicted for a great many kinds of cases, for example:

homicide (Lev. 24:17)
adultery (Lev. 20:10)
magic and spiritism (Exod. 22:18; Lev. 20:27)
blasphemy (Lev. 24:16)
revolt in regard to parents (Lev. 20:9; Deut. 21:21)
disobedience to a priest (Deut. 17:12)
violation of the Sabbath (Exod. 35:2)
idolatry (Deut. 17:2-6, etc.)

In Deuteronomy we read: "Thou shalt put away the evil from Israel" (17:12); and the epistle to the Hebrews says "A man that hath set at nought Moses' law dieth without compassion on the word of two or three witnesses" (10:28).

In the New Testament, punishments are no longer primarily corporal or temporal, but spiritual and eternal; that is, they are infinitely more serious, according to the same passage, Hebrews 10:28-31. However, although divine retribution—the only just and universal one—takes place in another world, not only does God sometimes directly strike a proud man like Herod (Acts 12:23), but He can also delegate to earthly judges the power to inflict the death penalty. "He [i.e. an earthly ruler] is a minister of God to thee for good. But if thou do that which is evil, be afraid; for he beareth not the sword in vain: for he is a minister of God, an avenger for wrath to him that doeth evil" (Rom. 13:4). Evidently it is not a question here of the Church, which, filled with the love of Christ, must act according to Matthew 5:38-48: i.e. not resist the evil one, love its enemies, and do good to its persecutors. (And this is not the spirit of the Inquisition.) The passage in Romans 13:4 refers to the world and to the State, which, not Christian, have the responsibility, as much as possible, to command respect for law and morality, as a deterrent to crime. Otherwise, life would be impossible in our corrupted society.

It is certain that, from the ideal point of view, it is much better that the State uphold the law without having recourse to the death penalty: such is the case in those countries most thoroughly impregnated with the Gospel. What is repugnant to Christians in the death penalty is not simply the blood poured out. There is also the thought that in shortening the life of the guilty person, one perhaps deprives him of the time needed to repent for the salvation of his soul. Under the influence of Christian concepts, the whole notion concerning infliction of punishment has recently made great strides: punishment should be not only a deterrent to crime, but also a sort of reeducation. The worst criminal can be changed and by regeneration can become a new man. The thief on the cross is an outstanding example of this (Luke 23:42, 43). But for any such results Christians would have to be characterized by an increasing awareness of their responsibility in constantly setting the Gospel before criminals. Another grave objection to the death penalty is this: an error in justice cannot be made right if an innocent person has been executed.

e. *Can anyone unwittingly hasten the hour of his own death?*

Certainly. A debauchee who ruins his health and a sportsman who tempts God in risking his life foolishly can by their wrong doing bring on death prematurely. But there can be spiritual causes which produce the same result, and we have many examples of them in the Bible:

"Er, Judah's first-born, was wicked in the sight of Jehovah; and Jehovah slew him . . . The thing which he [Onan, his brother] did was evil in the sight of Jehovah: and he slew him also" (Gen. 38:7, 10).

Eli's sons, after having gravely sinned, "hearkened not unto the voice of their father, because Jehovah was minded to slay them." This is what the Lord said to Eli: "All the increase of thy house shall die in the flower of their age. And this shall be the sign unto thee, that shall come upon thy two sons, Hophni and Phinehas: in one day they shall die both of them" (I Sam. 2:25, 33, 34).

Let us cite also some texts from the Old Testament: "Bloodthirsty and deceitful men shall not live out half their days" (Ps. 55:23). "He [the wicked] . . . shall not depart out of darkness; . . . and by the breath of God's mouth shall he go away . . . vanity shall be his recompense. It shall be accomplished before his time" (Job 15:30-32). "Be not overmuch wicked, neither be thou foolish: why shouldest thou die before thy time?" (Eccles. 7:17).

It is terrible to think that even Christians can shorten their lives. Speaking of the Lord's Supper, Paul writes: "He that eateth and drinketh, eateth and drinketh judgment unto himself if he discern not the body. For this cause many among you are weak and sickly, and not a few sleep [have died]. But if we discerned ourselves, we should not be judged. But when we are judged, we are chastened of the Lord, that we may not be condemned with the world" (I Cor. 11:29-32). If the apostle wrote that to one of the early churches, so full of vitality and faith, what would he say in our days!

He expresses himself even more strongly about the scandal caused by a member of the same church: "To deliver such a one unto Satan for the destruction of the flesh, that the spirit may be saved in the day of the Lord Jesus" (I Cor. 5:5).

If a believer refuses to mend his ways, the Lord, then, sometimes strikes him in his body and even takes away his life, so as to stop him on his way to perdition and at least to save his soul. And hypocrites, such as Ananias and Sapphira, He sometimes even strikes dead on the spot (Acts 5:1-11).

f. *On the other hand, can a person prolong his life?*

Yes, since the Bible says so: not only in caring for his body, the temple of the Holy Spirit, but in respecting certain spiritual principles: "And thou shalt keep his statues, and his commandments, which I command thee this day, that it may go well with thee, and with thy children after thee, and that thou mayest prolong thy days in the land which Jehovah thy God giveth thee forever" (Deut. 4:40). And the content of Deuteronomy 5:16 is repeated in Ephesians 6:2, 3: "Honor thy father and mother, which is the first commandment with promise, that it may be well with thee, and thou mayest live long on the earth." "The fear of Jehovah prolongeth days; but the years of the wicked shall be shortened" (Prov. 10:27).

Also, in answer to prayer, God sometimes heals a person who is at death's door and prolongs his life. The typical example is Hezekiah, to whom the Lord accorded fifteen more years of life in response to his tears and his supplications (II Kings 20:1-6). Unfortunately, the king did not use his new lease on life as he should have. He let himself be carried away by pride when visitors came from the king of Babylon (vss. 12-19). And, especially, during those fifteen years he had the son who was to succeed him when the boy, Manasseh, was twelve years old. This Manasseh was so wicked that because of him God refused to pardon Jerusalem any more and consequently destroyed it (II Kings 21:1; 24:3, 4). May we not conclude that it would have been better for Hezekiah and for his people if he had let God take him at the time marked out for him?

Then there is the case of Epaphroditus, of whom Paul says: "For indeed he was sick nigh unto death: but God had mercy on him; and not on him only, but on me also, that I might not have sorrow upon sorrow" (Phil. 2:27). This encourages us to pray in faith, and in entire submission, to allow God to accomplish His always perfect will.

11. VICTORY OVER DEATH

"The last enemy that shall be abolished is death" (I Cor. 15:26).

The reign of death will not last forever, and we have already had a glimpse of its permanent end.

*Jesus Christ conquered death at the time of His first coming.*

The grace of God "hath now been manifested by the appearing of our Saviour Christ Jesus, who abolished death, and brought life and immortality to light through the gospel" (II Tim. 1:10).

Jesus became flesh "that through death he might bring to nought him that had the power of death, that is, the devil; and might deliver all them who through fear of death were all their lifetime subject to bondage" (Heb. 2:14, 15).

*The resurrection will set believers free from death's last hold on them.* When, at the return of Christ, they shall have been clothed with their new and glorious bodies, then shall be accomplished the word that was written: "Death is swallowed up in victory. O death, where is thy victory? O death, where is thy sting?" (I Cor. 15:54, 55).

*During the millennium, physical death will have only a limited dominion over the subjects of the kingdom.*

We have seen that God, because of sin, not only permitted death, but also limited life to a hundred and twenty years (Gen. 6:3) —even, for all practical purposes, to only seventy or eighty years (Ps. 90:10).

During the glorious reign of Christ down here, Satan will be bound, and human life will again be considerably prolonged. There will be no more premature death, and a man of a hundred years will be a young man: "They shall not . . . bring forth for calamity; for they are the seed of the blessed of Jehovah, and their offspring with them . . . There shall be no more thence an infant of days, nor an old man that hath not filled his days; for the child shall die a hundred years old

. . . for as the days of a tree shall be the days of my people"
(Isa. 65:23, 20, 22). But this will be only the last step before
the final triumph.

*In the end, the first death itself shall cease to exist.*

After the two resurrections and the destruction of the earth,
no one will have to undergo physical death. That is why
John, after having described the last judgment, added: "And
death and Hades were cast into the lake of fire," as having no
longer any need for existing (Rev. 20:14). God in heaven
"shall wipe away every tear from their eyes; and death shall be
no more; neither shall there be mourning, nor crying, nor
pain, any more: the first things are passed away" (Rev. 21:4).
As for the elect, they will have put on immortal bodies (I Cor.
15:53). What a glorious triumph that will be!

Unfortunately, though physical death shall be no more, it
gives place to the lake of fire and brimstone for the condemned, which is the second death (Rev. 20:14; 21:8).

For deliverance from death, now and forever, is only by
Jesus Christ, our eternal life!

## 12. Preparing to die well

Rather, let us live well now, so that we can face death without any fear whatsoever. Man's destiny is decided here below.
It is therefore of prime importance that we decide today
where we are going to spend eternity.

"So teach us to number our days, that we may get us a heart
of wisdom" (Ps. 90:12).

"For this God is our God for ever and ever: He will be our
guide even unto death" (Ps. 48:14).

Let us remember at all times Him who has vanquished
death, and let us live each day according to His eternal life.
Then when we have to leave this world, it will not be death
for us. Did not Adele Kamm say this: "I love life; I enjoy it
fully; but I also welcome the thought of death, of going to
be with God. For me, to live and to die are alike a joy."

"All things are yours . . . whether . . . life, *or death,* or things present or things to come; all are yours; and ye are Christ's; and Christ is God's" (I Cor. 3:21-23). If even death is "ours," the meaning is that we are, by faith, its masters. May we truly know that by experience!

## Chapter IV

# THE PLACE OF THE DEAD

### 1. Before the first coming of Christ

BEFORE THE FIRST COMING OF CHRIST, where did the souls of the dead go; and where is it they go since His coming, while awaiting His glorious return and the last judgment? Let us try to examine these questions one at a time.

a. The place of all the dead, both the saved and the lost, was called by the Jews "sheol." (The corresponding word in the Greek New Testament is "hades.") "There is one event unto all . . . and after that they go to the dead . . . For who is exempted?" (Eccles. 9:3, 4). When a patriarch died, it was said that he was "gathered unto his people" (Gen. 25:8, 17; 35:29; 49:33). Samuel, called back from the other world, said to Saul: "Tomorrow shalt thou and thy sons be with me" (I Sam. 28:19). David, bereaved of his child, said, "Now he is dead . . . can I bring him back again? I shall go to him, but he will not return to me" (II Sam. 12:23). At the end of his life a king "slept with his fathers," the current expression in the book of the Kings (I Kings 2:10; 11:43; 14:20, etc.)

b. The place of the dead is considered in the Old Testament as the place of oblivion and of rest—especially for the believer. Job longed for death with these words: "For now should I have lain down and been quiet; I should have slept; then had I been at rest, with kings and counsellors of the earth; there the wicked cease from troubling; and there the weary are at rest. There the prisoners are at ease together . . .

and the servant is free from his master . . ." (Job 3:13-19).
In that place the dead were obviously separated from all
earthly activity; they no longer had a worship service, or
sacrifices, or any of the festivities of the living. That is the
way the Preacher puts it, from an earthly and disillusioned
point of view. For him, everything goes back to the dust,
man as well as beast (3:19-21); the dead know nothing, they
are forgotten and will never again have anything at all to do
with what goes on under the sun; for there is no work, or
thought, or science, or wisdom (human and earthly) in the
sojourn of the dead. A person carries nothing into the
tomb (5:14), and it is heart-breaking for the worldly man
when he dies to have to leave everything that has made up
his pride, his wealth, and his whole life on earth.

c. Still it is evident that, according to many other texts,
souls continue to exist in the place of the dead. Samuel, already cited, came back and spoke with Saul (I Sam. 28).
Moses and Elijah, absent a long time from this world, appeared with Jesus on the Mount of Transfiguration (Matt.
17:3). God said to Moses: "I *am* the God of Abraham, the
God of Isaac, and the God of Jacob." Jesus' argument, recorded in Matthew 22:31, 32 rests on the tense of the verb:
"God would have said "I *was*" if the patriarchs had ceased
to exist. But, the Lord adds, God is not the God of the dead,
but of the living, for "all live unto him" (Luke 20:38).
Moveover, the wicked keep their personality in the sojourn of
the dead. Isaiah 14:9, 10 and Ezekiel 32:21-31 show us the
dead greeting and speaking together in that sinister place. We
have already seen, in Luke 16:19-31, that the blessed dead
and the wretched dead keep their personality in the other
world, as well as their memory and the consciousness of their
state. Lazarus is comforted, the wicked rich man suffers, and
Abraham exhorts him with perfect lucidity.

d. During the time preceding the coming of Christ, the
Jews came to distinguish two separate parts in the place of

the dead: one reserved for the wicked, tormented from the moment of their departure from the world, and the other prepared for the blessed dead. The latter is what was known as "paradise" or "Abraham's bosom." Jesus Himself used these two expressions and confirmed this teaching. He showed us Lazarus and the wicked rich man in totally different situations, separated by a great uncrossable gulf (Luke 16:22, 23); further, He promised the thief on the cross a meeting with Him that very day in paradise (Luke 23:43).

2. AFTER THE DESCENT OF CHRIST INTO THE PLACE OF THE DEAD

Christ, the sinless Son of God, of course did not descend into the part of "sheol" where the wicked are in torment. No change took place there, and the above passages—especially Luke 16:19-31—depict the present state of all the impenitent dead.

On the other hand, Christ did descend among the blessed dead, with the repentant thief with whom He had arranged that glorious rendezvous: "Today shalt thou be with me in paradise."

After three days, "God raised up [Jesus], having loosed the pangs of death: because it was not possible that he should be holden of it" (Acts 2:24). The victorious Christ defeated the great enemy and broke down the gates of the tomb. "When he ascended on high, he led captivity captive, and gave gifts unto men" (Eph. 4:8-10). Commentators have believed for a long time that, at the time of His glorification, Christ liberated the believing dead from "sheol" and took them with Him into heaven. From then on, all those who have died in the faith, instead of going down into the place of the dead, go directly into the presence of the Lord. We have just seen that Paul cries out: "To me to live is Christ, and to die is gain . . . I desire to depart and be with Christ, for it is very far better" (Phil. 1:21-24). "Whilst we are at home in the body, we are absent from the Lord . . . We . . . are willing rather to be absent from the body and to be at home with the Lord" (II Cor. 5:6-8) .

Still it is clear that the present state of the dead, both believing and unbelieving, is only provisional. The former, even now, are at rest and are happy in the presence of God, awaiting the resurrection and His eternal kingdom. The latter, the condemned, are in a place of temporary detention, as it were, awaiting the last judgment and final hell.

Do we know where we shall be one instant after our death?

# Chapter V

## OCCUPATION OF THE DEAD

AFTER LEAVING THIS WORLD, the dead are not annihilated. But can we know anything more than that about them? The way our loved ones are snatched away from us is so tragic that it is not surprising that people and religions everywhere beat anxiously on the stony wall of the other world, trying to keep contact with them, or at least to know what has become of them. So many hearts in mourning are full of bitterness and rebellion. Many cry out as David did: "O my son Absalom! my son, my son! Would I had died for thee!" (II Sam. 18:33). With the Shunammite they are tempted to ask: "Did I desire a son . . . ?" (II Kings 4:28). In the midst of such sorrow, looking forward only to a reunion in some far-distant future seems too hard. We should like, in any case, that the contact would not be interrupted, that the reunion might be immediate. God knows this desire of our hearts; He knows too in His love what is best for our loved ones and for us; and He has not failed to reveal it to us. Let us then listen once more to what the inspired Book tells us, but let us be ready also to respect its silence where it does keep silence.

### 1. WHERE ARE THE DEAD?

The answer of the Scriptures is clear: unbelievers are in the place of the tormented, awaiting the last judgment and hell; believers are in the Lord's presence, at rest, awaiting the glorious resurrection.

All the same, let us examine the theory, upheld, for example, by the Adventists, that the dead person, both body and spirit, is in the grave, where it sleeps until the resurrection.

It is certain that the body is in the grave, that is, in the dust of the earth (John 5:28; Daniel 12:2). But the spirit is not there, and we shall shortly see that it is far from asleep. According to Luke 16:22, 23, the poor man, Lazarus, was carried by the angels to Abraham's bosom, whereas the wicked rich man was in the place of torment. The converted thief departed to find himself at once with Jesus in paradise, which certainly is not in the tomb. After the great resurrection victory, Paul prefers to depart to be with Christ and to abide in his Lord's presence (Phil. 1:23; II Cor. 5:8). Now Christ is not in the ground, but at the right hand of the Father, in the glory of heaven.

It is clear, moreover, that physical death consists precisely in the separation of the soul from the body. According to the Preacher, the body returns to the dust, and the spirit returns to God who gave it (Eccles. 12:9). We read that the soul of the child that Elijah raised up came back into him and that he was brought back to life (I Kings 17:22). Likewise, when the daughter of Jairus was raised from the dead, "her spirit returned" (Luke 8:55). Jesus Himself committed His spirit into the Father's hands and stayed for a short time in the place of the dead, while His body remained in the sepulchre (Luke 23:46; John 19:30; Acts 2:27). Stephen too cried out as he was dying: "Lord Jesus, receive my spirit!" (Acts 7:59). How much more comforting is this perspective than that of sinking into decomposition and unconsciousness until the end of time!

## 2. ARE THE DEAD SLEEPING?

Let us look more closely at the texts which speak of the "sleep of death" (Ps. 13:4) and of "them that fall asleep" (I Thess. 4:13), etc. We believe that they have to do with the body (the eyes closed to the light of earth), which sleeps in the tomb awaiting the resurrection. Thus Stephen, having given up his spirit to the Lord Jesus, "fell asleep" (Acts 7: 59, 60). Daniel 12:2 speaks of the resurrection of "them that sleep in the dust of the earth." Now, as we were saying, it is the body which returns to the dust, while the spirit returns to God (Eccles. 12:9).

The authors of the Old Testament, sometimes taking an earthly point of view, call the place of the dead the "land of forgetfulness" (Ps. 88:12), "silence" (Ps. 115:17), "the pit of nothingness" (Isa. 38:17). The Preacher, we have seen, says that "the dead know not anything . . . the memory of them is forgotten . . . neither have they any more a portion for ever in anything that is done under the sun . . . there is no work, nor device, nor knowledge, nor wisdom, in Sheol..." (Eccles. 9:5, 6, 10). Some of the Psalms declare that it is the living who praise God and who hope in Him, that in the place of the dead there is nothing like that (Ps. 6:6; 88:11-13; 115:17; see also Isa. 38:18, 19). This is the way that anyone, from the point of view of this world, can picture the destiny of those who leave the community of the living: they have no longer anything to do with the worship or the sacrifices of the people; they are forever withdrawn from any activity here below.

But let us not forget the other texts, according to which the souls in the other world are far from being asleep. Samuel, fully conscious, comes back to speak to Saul (I Sam. 28:12-19). Moses and Elijah, having come from that other world, converse with Jesus on the Mount of Transfiguration (Luke 9:30). The wicked rich man undergoes his torment in full possession of his lucidity and of his memory, while Abraham answers him and Lazarus is comforted (Luke 16:23-31). The "paradise" promised immediately to the repentant thief would be a very curious name for the unconsciousness of sleep or for annihilation (Luke 23:43). Paul considers death a gain, something which would not be so if he were to sleep in the tomb. Furthermore, "to go to be with Christ" or "to be absent from the body and present with the Lord"— these words do not by any stretch of the imagination imply sleep (Phil. 1:21-23; II Cor. 5:6-8). For would one really be "with Christ" and would one be "present with the Lord" if he were to sink—perhaps for thousands of years—into total unconsciousness? and what would be an eternal life interrupted by centuries of non-existence? Finally, John saw the souls of the martyrs before God: they claim the intervention of the great Judge, although it is told them to wait quietly for the final deliverance (Rev. 6:9-11).

So then, it cannot at all be, as some claim, that the believer's soul sleeps in the grave with the body until the day of the resurrection. Further, that theory has never been widely accepted in the Church. It is at the opposite pole from Catholic concepts, and it was vigorously attacked by Calvin in his tract, *De Psychopannychia (On Soul Sleep.)* For the writers of the Reformation, as for us, the soul, immediately after death, experiences joy or misery. The final resurrection will be only the final consummation of that glory or that suffering.

### 3. THE REST OF THE BLESSED DEAD

Believers gone on before are not yet enjoying either the activity or the reign which will follow the resurrection. On the contrary, ever since their arrival in the other world, they are enjoying a rest from the struggles and suffering here below. Samuel, coming back to speak to Saul, reproached him thus: "Why hast thou disquieted me, to bring me up?" (I Sam. 28:15). The poor man Lazarus, when he died, was taken at once by the angels to "Abraham's bosom," which represented to the Jews the height of happiness. Abraham adds that Lazarus, after having had so much trouble in his lifetime, was then comforted (Luke 16:22, 25). When the thief converted on the cross entered that same day into Para-

dise ( the place of the blessed dead), he found there both
rest and joy. The Revelation also shows us that the souls of
the martyrs "rest yet for a little time" until the day of judgment and the end of the persecutions. Then we read this
most comforting word: "Blessed are the dead who die in the
Lord from henceforth: yea, saith the Spirit, that they may
rest from their labors; for their works follow with them"
(Rev. 6:10, 11; 14:13).

Ths rest is granted by the pure grace of God to all those
who have been saved. How sweet it is to realize that our
beloved who have died in the faith are enjoying it in the
presence of the Lord!

### 4. DO THE DEAD SEE US?

Many people derive much comfort from the thought that
the loved ones they have lost continue to see them and to
follow them in the intimacy so suddenly interrupted. However appealing this thought may be, what is there actually
to it? We are obliged to say that the Bible is absolutely silent
on this point. There must be good reasons for this.

We have just spoken of the "rest" of our believing dead.
Now, it seems certain that they would not have any rest at all
if they had to look down on what we are doing. Saul was
Samuel's great favorite; nevertheless, Samuel reproached Saul
for troubling him in an attempt to obtain help. How dis-
tressing it would be for some of the dead if they could see the
subsequent behavior of those who have just been lamenting
over them with a loud noise! What concern there would
also be if they could see us exposed to countless dangers and
temptations! Furthermore, our dead are not omniscient so
as to take in from heaven everything that goes on, in so many
different places, in the hearts and lives of those they have
left behind.

There is nothing in the account of Lazarus and the wicked

rich man, either, to let us believe that the souls of the dead see what is going on here on earth.

If the dead do not see us, that does not mean that they have forgotten us. We have just alluded to the wicked rich man, who was concerned about the indifference of his brothers, although unable to do anything about it (Luke 16:27-31). The blessed, as well, retain their memory with perfect clarity.

## 5. DO THE DEAD SURROUND US WITH THEIR PRESENCE?

Without going into the subject of spiritism (a matter which we shall look at in the next paragraph), some people in mourning frequently express this thought: "I am certain that my mother [for example] has not actually left me, that she is constantly with me." Even if we understand what human consolation such a thought might bring, we must again state that the Scriptures do not confirm any such idea as that. We have already said that if it were like this, our loved ones would not have any true rest. But let us emphasize again that they are not omnipresent. The texts plainly declare that the dead are either in the Lord's presence or else in the inescapable place of torment. So how could they be at the same time on earth—everywhere at once, wherever the members of their families happened to be scattered?

Then what is the explanation of Hebrews 12:1: "Therefore let us also, seeing we are compassed about with so great a cloud of witnesses, . . . run with patience . . ."? Does this mean that the believers gone on before surround us and see us? Reading again the context of the whole chapter (11), we do not believe so. The author has just spoken about all the heroes of the Old Testament who have preceded us in the noble arena of faith. Challenged by their experiences and upheld by their example, we ought in our turn to push forward in the way of victory, our eyes fixed on Jesus. But this text does not at all say that our own loved ones who have died continue to share our day-by-day life.

On the subject of contact with the dead and with spirits, we must, in the interest of the truth, say that Sadhu Sundar Singh in some of his books sets forth some things which honestly seem to us untenable from the Biblical point of view. This is surprising in a man otherwise so thoroughly evangelical.

6. WHAT IS ONE TO THINK OF SPIRITISM?

In pagan religions the attempt to establish contact with the dead is very common, so as to obtain revelations, help, or consolation from them. In our days a disturbingly large number of so-called Christians (and even of spiritual leaders) call up spirits, either because they insist at any cost on maintaining contact with their dead or because they are determined to learn what the Bible does not tell them. They would especially like additional light on the future, decisions to be made, love affairs, or business matters, the mysteries of the other side of the grave, etc. Is it really possible to enter into contact with spirits through mediums, tilted tables, Ouija boards, pendulums, rappings, etc.? And especially, what does the Bible teach about all this?

a. Let us note first that in spiritism there is mingled a great deal of fraud. As in anything occult, temptation is great on the part of charlatans to take advantage of the immeasurable credulity of the public. What is easier than to take advantage of the uneasiness that surrounds the mysterious by making spirits say what one might wish them to say? Anyway, two things are curious: when famous men, such as Shakespeare or Milton, are supposedly made to speak, why are their "revelations" so trite, not at all like what they wrote when they were alive? Then, if the spirits communicate, for example, to the medium the best tips on gambling on the stock market, why doesn't the so-called medium take advantage of this informa-

tion himself rather than hand over to his clients such a secret?
And how is it that judicial law so often mentions mediums
and diviners who have been condemned for swindling?

Charles Nordmann, an astronomer of the Paris Observa-
tory, speaks of the exploits of mediums during their trances:
physical projections, part of the organism which projects and
manifests itself outside the body, filaments of a vaporous substance—all that in the vague light of spiritist seances. He
adds that it is said that those things are due principally to an
"inflammation of the imagination." A certain Miss Bessinet
is mentioned and the projections and manifestations outside
her body. Now, she was surprised by magnesium, far from
the chair where she supposedly was tied, illuminating her face
by means of an electric lamp! (*L'Au-Dela, The Future Life*,
Hachette, Paris, 1927).

b. The spiritists (Allan Kardec, for example) recognize that
sometimes *certain evil spirits make fun of them* by respond-
ing in the place of souls called up; or they reveal themselves
in a bizzare and dangerous way. How many people have
even lost their minds through these pernicious contacts!
Camille Flammarion, in a book entitled *Après la mort (After
Death)*, writes as follows: "The Duchess of Pomar, known by
all the occultists, had lost the necessary orientation in the
continuance of those studies, for she believed herself to be
Mary Stuart reincarnated, and yet called up the spirit of the
unfortunate Queen of Scotland!" Flammarion speaks also of
the dead who, by rappings, ask for masses and rosaries—but
only in Catholic families! (pp. 187, 224). By whom then
are such requests inspired?

c. *Still, there is in spiritism an indisputable reality.*

The Bible alludes in unequivocal terms to those who
"turn unto them that have familiar spirits," who "consult
with a familiar spirit" (Lev. 19:31; 20:6; Deut. 18:11). It
speaks of "a man . . . or a woman that hath a familiar spirit
or that is a wizard"; that is, it speaks of mediums (Lev. 20:

27) ; of people who predict the future by calling up the dead, such as the one that King Saul went to consult (I Sam. 28:3, 7, 8) . Even in the book of the Acts, there is the question of a medium animated by " a spirit of divination," who "brought her masters much gain by soothsaying" (Acts 16:16) . That woman was what we would call one of those "extra-lucid clairvoyants," whose activity today is still extremely lucrative.

d. *Under penalty of death, the Old Testament forbade the giving of oneself over to spiritism or occultism.* Every time that the Scriptures touch on this subject, they point out its mortal danger. The calling up of the dead was in widespread practice by the Canaanites, and Israel was solemnly exhorted to have absolutely nothing to do with it. "Turn ye not unto them that have familiar spirits, nor unto the wizards; seek them not out, to be defiled by them . . . And the soul that turneth unto them that have familiar spirits, and unto the wizards, to play the harlot after them, I will even set my face against that soul, and will cut him off from among his people . . . A man also or a woman that hath a familiar spirit, or that is a wizard, shall surely be put to death . . . their blood shall be upon them" (Lev. 19:31: 20:6, 27) . "When thou art come into the land which Jehovah thy God giveth thee, thou shalt not learn to do after the abominations of those nations. There shall not be found with thee any one that . . . useth divination, one that practiseth augury, or an enchanter, or a sorcerer, or a charmer, or a consulter with a familiar spirit, or a wizard [fortune teller] or a necromancer. For whosoever doeth these things is an abomination unto Jehovah; and because of these abominations Jehovah thy God doth drive them out from before thee. Thou shalt be perfect with Jehovah thy God" (Deut. 18:9-13) . One of the crimes that Israel was reproved for is having eaten "the sacrifices of the dead" and having thus provoked the Lord (Ps. 106: 28, 29) .

These texts show that:

1). spiritism is a defilement, a prostitution, an abomination in the sight of God;

2). because of that and because of their occultism, the Canaanites were exterminated;

3). the calling up of the dead and spirits was punished by death in Israel;

4). the consulting of spiritists and mediums was prohibited, as was being a medium oneself;

5). the believer belongs wholly to God; spiritism for him would be infidelity and idolatry and would interrupt his communion with the Lord;

6). occultism, divination, and astrology are just as pernicious as spiritism, for they likewise come from contact with the seduction of the enemy. Let us remember this in these times when any kind of "occult science" is held in such unprecedented favor.

e. *How are we to understand I Samuel 28?*

To establish a basis for their practices, the spiritists often cite Saul's adventure in questioning Samuel when he was dead. Actually this example absolutely condemns them, as shown by the following considerations:

1). First of all, was it really Samuel who came out of the tomb to speak to Saul? We believe so, because of the explicit words of the text. The king said: " 'Bring me up Samuel.' And when the woman *saw Samuel,* she cried with a loud voice . . . Saul perceived that *it was Samuel,* and he bowed with his face to the ground and did obeisance. And *Samuel said* to Saul: 'Why hast thou disquieted me to bring me up? . . . Tomorrow shalt thou and thy sons be *with me . . .*' Then Saul fell straightway his full length upon the earth, and was afraid because of *the words of Samuel"* (I Sam. 28:11-20). There is nothing in this passage to allow the interpretation that another personality—for example, a demon—had taken on the appearance of Samuel to deceive Saul. Rather, we would think the opposite: that is, that ordinarily, in response to incantations, it was not a dead person who used to appear, but none other than an evil spirit. The woman was stupefied when she saw Samuel; she realized at once that something unexpected had happened and that the king had deceived her; then she described the apparition of the old man wrapped in a mantle (vss. 12-14). She then abandoned at once her habitual role of a medium, while Samuel spoke directly to Saul.

Let us recognize, at any rate, that throughout the whole Bible this is the only example of a dead man's coming back that way to speak to a living man. It seems to us that God has permitted this single miracle, as the exception which proves the rule, doubtless to show us all the tragic consequences of such an attempt.

2). Saul and the woman knew very well that they were disobeying God. During the days when he was faithful, the king had driven out of the country those who called up the dead and those who foretold the future, thus carrying out the law of Moses (I Sam. 28:3; Lev. 20:27). The woman therefore knew that she was risking her own life too (vs. 9). What good or what light can come from such flagrant disobedience?

3). Saul turned to the dead because he knew himself to be abandoned by God. During the lifetime of Samuel, he had already been rejected as king, and he had never shown either true repentance or a change of life (I Sam. 15:10, 22, 23). Now "when Saul saw the host of the Philistines, he was afraid, and his heart trembled greatly. And when Saul inquired of Jehovah, Jehovah answered him not, neither by dreams, nor by Urim, nor by prophets. Then said Saul unto his servants, Seek me a woman that hath a familiar spirit" (I Sam. 28:5-7). Then he declared to Samuel: "God is departed from me . . . therefore I have called thee, that thou mayest make known unto me what I shall do. And Samuel said, Wherefore then dost thou ask of me, seeing Jehovah is departed from thee and is become thine adversary?" (vss. 15, 16).

This is entirely typical: when one does not feel himself to be right with God, or when one is not satisfied with His revelation, that person seeks help and light elsewhere. Saul had one thing to do: to truly repent and to seek the Lord's pardon. Since he would not do that (as his life showed), God had no further word for him. To insist at any cost on another revelation was—and still is today—to turn away increasingly from the Word of God.

4). The results of the calling up of the dead are entirely negative. Samuel refused to say practically anything different from what had already been declared to the king as from God. "And Jehovah hath done unto thee as he spake by me . . . Because thou obeyest not the voice of Jehovah . . . therefore hath Jehovah done this thing unto thee this day" (vss. 17, 18). There was no need whatsoever of risking his life and his eternal salvation to hear things he already knew.

5). There is something worse: Samuel announced only one new thing: that was that the next day Saul and his sons would themselves be among the dead (vs. 19). We read in regard to this I Chronicles 10:13, 14: "So Saul died for his trespass which he committed against Jehovah, because of the word of Jehovah, which he kept not; and also for that he asked counsel of one that had a familiar spirit, to inquire thereby, and inquired not of Jehovah: therefore he slew him and turned the kingdom unto David . . ." This text expressly states that God struck Saul down because he had called up the dead. The king might otherwise have been spared in the battle. The only thing, then, that he got out of his encounter with Samuel was condemnation to death. What a warning for us!

6). Samuel said to Saul: "Why hast thou disquieted me?" This seems to us one of the great reasons why God does not permit us to call up the dead. What would become of their rest if they were at the mercy of any and every friend or enemy who had the notion to keep after them, asking the most impossible things of them?

Recourse to the dead (as to the Virgin and to the saints, to be considered later) presents, finally, the immense danger of idolatry. The Lord constantly says this to us: "Thou shalt love God with all thy heart, thou shalt seek Him, thou shalt serve only Him, and thou shalt have no other gods before Him." To call on created beings is an outrage to the one true God.

f. *Why does God punish so severely the calling up of the dead and of spirits?*

To all we have just said, we must add this: We believe that in spiritism there is much more of demons than of the dead. According to Luke 16:26, the wicked dead are already in the place of torment, from which none can escape. As for those who died in the Lord, they would have nothing to do with a contact with the living expressly forbidden by Scripture. Thus, when people think they are causing such a dead person to speak, it is an evil spirit which answers and deceives those more-or-less naive individuals. A medium, such as the woman of Acts 16:16-18, was for all practical purposes possessed by a demon. That is why such a contact is called an abomination, a defilement, and a prostitution. To call up the dead and the spirits is essentially giving oneself over to Satan, the prince of the evil spirits; it is to jeopardize one's eternal salvation—and likewise his reason and his nervous stability. How many people we have known personally who have become completely unbalanced by spiritism and been made, so it seemed, absolutely impervious to the Gospel. And let us not forget this: since God in ancient times cut off from His people anyone who had recourse to the dead and to spirits (Lev. 20:6), He is not likely to do otherwise today.

g. *What is the "astral body" which the spirits speak of?*

Besides our physical body, they say that we have a sort of

fluid-like double called an "astral body," or "perispirit," or metaphysical body. This double could detach itself from the first body and go off to greater or shorter distances and for varying lengths of time. In a state of ecstasy, or of semi-wakefulness, the personality of the initiate would "divide" and have the strange experiences that some of the sadhus of India boast about. Similar also are the "apparitions" of the spirit seances; the habitués sometimes claim to touch the hands or other parts of such an "astral body," the vehicle of the invoked spirit. At death, this same fluid double is supposed to accompany the soul into the world beyond. We reply that the devil and his demons, according to the Scriptures, are entirely capable of working miracles to seduce and drag down to perdition those devotees of a prohibited occultism (Matt. 24:24; II Thess. 2:9, 10, etc.). Those claims of "materializations" do not prove the spiritist theory on this point. Moreover, it is easy to see that II Corinthians 12:14, often quoted on this subject, does not allude to a so-called "astral body" in which Paul went up to the third heaven. The apostle says that he was carried away into paradise, without his knowing whether he was "in the body, out of the body, or without a body," that is, without being conscious of his body. There, in an ecstasy, he heard ineffable words in the presence of God. According to this passage (and others, too, such as Acts 10:10 and 22:17, for instance), ecstasy is certainly a possible experience, which God uses sometimes for revealing Himself to His servants. But let us state that there is a world of difference between such an encounter with the Lord and the strange theory of the spiritists.

Moreover, when Paul mentions the parts that make up our personality, he gives "body, soul, and spirit" (I Thess. 5:23). He does not speak as do the occultists, who claim that man is a triad: having 1) the physical body 2) the soul-spirit; and 3) the metaphysical body, something without weight or mass, probably made of ether or some similar element. One is honestly put to it to know where people go, to dream up such revelations!

h. *The extreme platitude of spirit revelations*

The reading of spiritist books leaves a disconcerting impression. Whole volumes are filled up to provide "scientific" proof of the reality of spirits by the monotonous and interminable enumeration of the same insignificant things: rappings, more-or-less uncontrollable apparitions, dreams of premonitions, and messages transmitted in various ways.

For Christians who believe anyway in the supernatural and the life beyond, there comes out of this very little except that spirits do actually exist and that they can manifest themselves, certainly if anyone gives himself over to them.

The content of the so-called revelations is also noteworthy for its triteness. In one of his books, the master spiritist Allan Kardec tries to give a summary of the religion supposedly taught by the spirits. What is curious is that this system contains exactly the ideas that a bourgeois French deist, imbued with notions about evolution and progress by man's efforts, might have had fifty years ago. A hundred of those pages teach us far less about God, Jesus Christ, perdition, and the salvation of mankind than do a few lines of the Gospels or the Epistles. Further, the spiritists are often, by their own confession, the dupes of evil spirits which take pleasure in mystifying them. One must have completely lost the sense of the perfection and the sufficiency of the Biblical revelation to go seeking for light in such an abyss. To enroll oneself in the spiritists' school is simply to lose confidence in the Holy Spirit.

i. *Is there at the present time a growing interest in spiritism?*

We believe, unfortunately, that there is. But our old enemy, true to his usual tactics, is trying again to disguise himself as an angel of light (II Cor. 11:13-15). Dressed up as wonderfully evangelical, he presents to us a growing number of "messages" from the beyond, which purport to have nothing to do with spiritism. One is overwhelmed at seeing the ready acceptance accorded to such laboriously contrived absurdities.

For example, people made a great deal of certain *Letters of Peter;* this young officer, who fell at the front in France in 1915, had supposedly dictated the letters to his mother, one a day for about twenty years (an accumulation of seven big volumes). Under the pretext that these revelations were received spontaneously and in privacy rather than in spiritist seances, it is claimed that they do not come from the spiritism so strongly forbidden by the Bible. Now one has only to read these *Letters of Peter,* and other similar works, to affirm that their teaching, in spite of a language which in places is evangelical, is the same as that of the spiritists: the medium must yield to the spirit in a state of complete passivity, so as to allow free course to the message that he is receiving. The astral body can sometimes become separated from the physical body in this world, and it accompanies the soul into the life beyond. In the other world the dead endure purifying and expiatory sufferings, and they must be prayed for. As the soul rises from one sphere to another, its spiritual body passes from brown to grey, or blue, or mauve, then through all the shades of rose, finally to become the purest white. There is a possibility of reincarnation. "Peter" declares that in the lower spheres of the other world, the spirits, still near the earth, have as a mission the guiding of humanity along the paths of righteousness; when they are lifted up higher, the distance becomes wider and the contact is broken. Their message must be listened to: "Not a word is addressed to you which is not inspired by God for us." The same spirit goes so far as to say: "Like God, the creation is eternal"; and further: "When humanity resolutely sets out on this laborious and sorrowful way, it can be called a 'Christ of God';

it has received the unction which consecrates it . . . it is CHRIST" (Vol. 5, p. 371, etc., etc.) .

Does not Scripture speak of a generalized offensive warfare of the seductive spirits at the end of time? (I Tim. 4: 1; II Thess. 2:9, 10; Rev. 16:14). We can easily see the prelude to this, and we ought to be more than ever on our guard against it.

"And when they shall say unto you, Seek unto them that have familiar spirits and unto the wizards that chirp and that mutter: should not a people seek unto their God? On behalf of the living should they seek unto the dead? To the law and to the testimony! If they speak not according to this word, surely there is no morning for them" (Isa. 8:19, 20) .

7.  WHAT DOES THE BIBLE SAY ABOUT THE INVOCATION OF THE
    SAINTS AND OF THE VIRGIN?

In the Roman and Orthodox Churches, the worship of the saints and of Mary holds a great place. What does the Bible say about this?

a. *First, the "saints" are dead.*

None of them are raised yet, and consequently any effort to establish contact with them falls under the condemnation of Leviticus 20:6 and Deuteronomy 18:11. For Saul and for Israel, Samuel was unquestionably a "saint." Still, God caused the death of the king for having sought his help instead of that of the Lord Himself.

b. *The Virgin herself is still among the dead.*

We believe with all our heart that Jesus, conceived of the Holy Ghost, was born miraculously of the Virgin Mary. We have a deep respect for her, but we see in the Gospels that she was not conceived without sin. She herself called God her Saviour (Luke 1:47) , a thing that Jesus never did. After the birth of Christ, she did become the wife of Joseph and had other children by him (Matt. 1:25; 13:55, 56) . Her presence is mentioned for the last time in the midst of the primitive Church, in Acts 1:14, that is, before Pentecost. So she did not play the role attributed to her as distributor of the Spirit and of the divine graces. The Scriptures have nothing to say about the end of her life, much less about the "assumption" by which, right after her death, she is supposed to have been raised and carried up to heaven. On the contrary Paul definitely declares that for the time being Christ alone is raised again, as the first-fruits of those who are dead; those who belong to Him—including His mother—will be raised again at the time of His glorious return (I Cor. 15:20, 23). Mary, then, is still among the blessed dead; her spirit is in the Lord's presence, but her body is still in the dust. It is no more permitted to us to address her than to address any other dead person now in the other world.

c. *The saints, like the rest of the dead, are neither omniscient nor omnipresent.* How could they hear and answer, in so many different places, the prayers that supposedly reach them? The Lord alone can do that, because He is at once omniscient, omnipresent, and omnipotent.

d. *The problem is further aggravated by the fact that the invocation of the saints and of the Virgin is constantly linked to the worship of statues.* Not only is it forbidden to pray to the dead, but it is also forbidden by the Decalogue to make any image or statue to use in any worship whatsoever. "Thou shalt not make unto thee a graven image, nor any likeness of anything that is in heaven above, or that is in the earth beneath, or that is in the water under the earth: thou shalt not bow down thyself unto them, nor serve them; for I, Jehovah, thy God, am a jealous God . . . Take ye therefore good heed unto yourselves; for ye saw no manner of form on the day that Jehovah spake unto you in Horeb out of the midst of the fire; lest ye corrupt yourselves, and make you a graven image in the form of any figure, the likeness of male or female . . . Take heed unto yourselves, lest ye forget the covenant of Jehovah your God, which he made with you and make you a

graven image in the form of anything which Jehovah thy
God hath forbidden thee. For Jehovah thy God is a devouring fire, a jealous God" (Deut. 5:8, 9; 4:15, 16 and 23, 24).

Just as strict a prohibition is tied in with the first commandment: "Thou shalt have no other gods before me."
The Lord jealously claims all our adoration; He desires that
our worship be for Him alone. Moreover, "God is a Spirit,
and they that worship him must worship in spirit and truth"
(John 4:24). He does not want us to materialize our worship by fixing it on statues or images. For this reason, He forbids us to make any sort of representation of the things which
are in the heavens, or of a man or of a woman, etc. That is
to say that images and statues of Christ, of the Sacred Heart,
of the Virgin, and of the saints, of the cross, and of medals,
are proscribed. They inevitably become idols, to which some
magic power is attributed; otherwise why would one say that
the statue of the Black Virgin of Chartres works miracles, that
the statue of the Virgin of Boulogne is supposed to bring
peace, and that one statue of a given saint is much more
powerful than another? The Church of Rome tries to excuse
itself by saying that it worships God alone and that it merely
honors the Virgin and the saints. (This is still entirely without proof.) But the Decalogue forbids not only the adoration
of statues, but also the prostrating of oneself before them and
the serving of them. Then it is absolutely forbidden to put
them up on altars, burn candles to them, kneel before them,
and address prayer to them. The popular Roman catechism
passes over in silence this second commandment, to go directly to the third (consequently called the "second"), on
the prohibition of taking the name of God in vain. The
tenth commandment, on covetousness, is then divided in two
(Exod. 20:17; Deut. 5:21).

e. *What is the greatest danger linked to the worship of
statues?* At the time of the apostles the Greeks sacrificed to
idols, at the same time claiming that the statues represented

the great Olympian gods. For the Christians, these gods did
not exist, and the statues were nothing but a little marble or
metal. But listen to what Paul says about this: "What say I
then? that a thing sacrificed to idols is anything, or that an
idol is anything? But I say, that the things which the Gentiles
sacrifice, they sacrifice to demons, and not to God: and I
would not that ye should have communion with demons. Ye
cannot drink the cup of the Lord and the cup of demons . . .
Or do we provoke the Lord to jealousy?" (I Cor. 10:19-22).
The forbidden worship of idols, addressed to non-existent
gods, is in reality a worship of demons. This thought is terrible in its modern implications. The worship of statues of the
saints is twice prohibited: the saints are dead, and the graven
images are forbidden. The worship rendered to them, then,
cannot please God or be addressed to Him, directly or in-
directly. To whom is it addressed then? We would not dare
say it ourselves, but our text does it for us: these statues are
nothing in themselves; but people make objects of worship
of them, thus idols; and therefore their worship borders on
idolatry and on spiritism. Many people, naive and sincere
in the faith that they were brought up in, are not aware of
this. In His infinite mercy, God can doubtless even answer
some of their prayers, in spite of the involuntarily supersti-
tious form of them. It is none the less true that such worship
is an immense obstacle to a personal acquaintance with the
Savior.

f. *The invocation of other mediators provokes the jealousy
of the Lord.*

In forbidding other gods and the rendering of worship to
their images, the Lord adds: "For I, Jehovah, thy God, am
a jealous God" (Exod. 20:5). He is also jealous for His
Son, the only Bridegroom to whom the Church has been
promised (II Cor. 11:2, 3). And "Doth the spirit which he
made to dwell in us long unto envying?" (James 4:5). He
gives neither His glory nor His place to another.

We have an example of this in the way in which the Lord intervened to uphold the sole priesthood of Aaron ( Numbers 16). Korah, son of Levi, and two hundred fifty princes of the congregation murmured against Aaron, declaring themselves to be priests also and claiming their share in the supreme priesthood (vss. 3, 10, 11). Moses answered: "The man whom Jehovah doth choose, he shall be holy" (vs. 7). Korah and his men presented themselves with censers to offer the consecrated incense before the Lord (a symbol of the intercession which Jesus, our High Priest, offers without ceasing on our behalf, Exod. 30:7-9, 37, 38; Lev. 16:12, 13). They were punished at once for their audacity: the earth swallowed up some, and fire devoured the others (Num. 16: 18, 32-35). After that, among the princes of the twelve tribes, Aaron was solemnly designated, by the miracle concerning his rod, as the only high priest; this rod, a dramatic symbol of the resurrection, produced in one night blossoms and almonds (Num. 17:1-9). It is thus that God first designated His Son, giving to Him the sovereign priesthood: "This is my beloved Son, in whom I am well pleased; hear ye him" (Matt. 17:5; 3:17). The Jews became indignant against that designation and claimed to get along without the mediation of Christ: were they not all holy, the sons of Abraham and the disciples of Moses; and were not their priests enough to lead them to salvation? Then the Lord intervened and declared Jesus to be the Son of God with power by His resurrection from the dead (Rom. 1:4). Since then, "in none other is there salvation: for neither is there any other name under heaven, that is given among men, wherein we must be saved" (Acts 4:12). Jesus, then, "because he abideth for ever, hath his priesthood unchangeable. Wherefore also he is able to save to the uttermost them that draw near unto God through him, seeing he ever liveth to make intercession for them (Heb. 7:24, 25). "For there is one God, one mediator also between God and men, himself man, Christ Jesus" (I Tim. 2:5).

How miserable then are those who, exposed to divine judgment, direct pious souls to other mediators than to Jesus only!

## 8. Do the dead pray for us?

The invocation of the Virgin and of the saints is founded on the belief that those personnages, for their part, efficaciously intercede with God for the faithful. The Lord is represented as being excessively holy, severe, and formidable. If one addresses His all-powerful Mother, "mediatrix of all the graces," he will be more sure of being understood and accepted. The Lord can refuse nothing to that one whose maternal heart is so very tender. Or, God seems too distant, too busy, to be interested in all our little affairs; it is good, then, to have different saints that one can go to with small requests. Thus, in Belgium, for example, there is a special saint (with his particular statue and place of pilgrimage) for every circumstance of life: Saint Anne for prolificness, Saint Mary of Augnies for safety in childbirth, Saint Cloud for carbuncles and boils; Saint Claire for eye troubles, Saint Blaise for afflictions of the throat, Saint Lambert for paralysis, Saint Apollonia for toothache, Saint Job for ulcers, Saint Lawrence for burns, Saint Erasmus for stomach trouble, Saint Gummarus for hernias, and Saint Rita for critical cases. Saint Anthony helps one find lost articles and brings prosperity in business. Our Lady of the Woods helps a student pass his examinations. Saint Eligius protects the metallurgists; Saint Barbara, the miners; Saint Joseph, the carpenters; Saint Cecelia, the musicians; Saint Christopher, the travelers; and Saint Hubert, the hunters. Saint Gertrude protects against rats and mice. Saint Feuillen assures good harvests, etc., etc. It is the same thing in Italy and in Spain, as in South America and in all other strongly Catholic countries. One very dis-

concerting thing is that in the large Congo Museum at Ter-
vueren, near Brussels, huge rooms are filled with native
fetiches which serve exactly the same ends.

What does the Bible say about this intercession of the
saints and of the Virgin—in other words, of the dead? The
truth is that it says nothing about it. The wicked rich man
(who was not a "saint") tried hard enough to beg Abraham
to intervene in the interest of his brothers who were still on
earth; but the response was negative: "They have Moses and
the prophets; let them hear them!" (Luke 16:29). When
God offered to men Christ and the Scriptures, He could give
them no more. Some have thought that they have found in
the Revelation texts in favor of the intercession of the saints.
What do these texts say? "The four and twenty elders fell
down . . . having golden bowls full of incense, which are the
prayers of the saints . . . And another angel came . . . there
was given unto him much incense that he should add it unto
the prayers of all the saints, upon the golden altar which was
before the throne. And the smoke of the incense with the
prayers of the saints went up before God out of the angel's
hand" (Rev. 5:8; 8:3, 4). Let us note first of all that in the
New Testament the word "saint" signifies all believers, not
the "canonized saints" of the Roman Church. In such passages as II Corinthians 1:1, Ephesians 1:1, I Timothy 5:10,
etc., the saints mentioned are on the earth. In the Revelation,
chapters 5 and 8, the twenty-four elders and the angel, already in heaven, simply present to God the prayers uttered
to Him by believers from the earth. In the sacred Scriptures
we have not one example of a prayer of intercession which a
believer already in heaven might offer to God on behalf of
the men in this world. When the Reformers began to question where in the Bible the intercession of the saints could be
found, the Roman Church became singularly embarrassed.
At the Council of Trent, in 1546, it was obliged to admit into
the canon of the Holy Scriptures the apochryphal books of

the Old Testament, which neither the Jews nor the early Church had ever considered as inspired. This is because it thought it had found in II Maccabees 15:11-16 grounds for that doctrine. There Jeremiah and the high priest Onias are seen interceding in heaven for the persecuted Jewish people. Needless to say, the apochryphal books, of such an inferior quality and put into the canon from necessity, hold no authority for us.

If the Scriptures themselves say nothing about the intercession of the saints, they constantly repeat that we have but one Mediator, a sole and all-sufficient Intercessor. "There is one God, one Mediator also between God and men, Himself man, Christ Jesus, who gave himself a ransom for all" (I Tim. 2:5, 6). He is the only Saviour. The love and compassion of any other creature could not be compared to His. He Himself declares: "I am the way, and the truth, and the life; no one cometh unto the Father but by me . . . I am the door: by me if any man enter in, he shall be saved . . . He that entereth not by the door into the fold of the sheep, but climbeth up some other way, the same is a thief and a robber" (John 14: 6; 10:9, 1). Peter cries out emphatically: "In none other is there salvation: for neither is there any other name under heaven that is given among men wherein we must be saved" (Acts 4:12).

To claim that to go to God one needs other intermediaries than Jesus Christ is to fail to understand also His perfect and sufficient intercession. "Wherefore it behooved him in all things to be made like unto his brethren, that he might become a merciful and faithful high priest . . . For in that he himself hath suffered being tempted, he is able to succor them that are tempted . . . For we have not a high priest that cannot be touched with the feeling of our infirmities; but one that hath been in all points tempted like as we are, yet without sin. Let us therefore draw near with boldness unto the throne of grace, that we may receive mercy, and may find grace to help us in time of need . . . He, because he abideth for ever, hath his priesthood unchangeable. Wherefore also he is able to save to the uttermost them that draw near unto God through him, seeing he ever liveth to make intercession for them" (Heb. 2:17, 18; 4:15, 16; 7:24, 25) . Paul strengthens this further as follows: "If God is for us, who is against us? . . . It is Christ Jesus that died, yea rather, that was raised from the dead, who is at the right hand of God, who also maketh intercession for us" (Rom. 8:31, 34) . Many people know only that Christ died for them on the cross. According to Paul He does far more than that: alive and glorified, He is interceding for us. What more could we want?

If Christ perfectly saves us by His constant intercession, we need no other intercessors. As the proverb has it: "It is better to go to God Himself than to His saints." Since we have the Lord, He is fully sufficient for us.

## 9. IS IT NECESSARY TO PRAY FOR THE DEAD?

The Biblical answer to this question will seem clearer when we treat the subjects of purgatory and of hell. But it is proper to mention it briefly here. We have seen what takes place at the death of the just and of the unjust. For the believing dead we have nothing to ask for, because they are already in the place of bliss. They are with Christ, which is far better than anything in this life. They are resting, awaiting the glorious resurrection. It is not at all necessary to beg God, in endless litanies, to "give them eternal rest." Indeed they entered into that rest when they were still on earth, the day when they put all their confidence in Jesus Christ, who purified them from all their sins (Heb. 4:9-11). As for the wicked dead, they are already in torment. Jesus teaches us that the wicked rich man called out in vain for comfort. It was impossible for anyone to come to give it from the heights of heaven and likewise impossible for the condemned one to leave that place of suffering (Luke 16:

23-26). We shall see later on that purgatory is a totally non-existent place, not mentioned at all in the Bible. There is therefore for impenitent sinners nothing but the prospect of eternal hell. In that case, what good would it do to pray for them? The only thing we can do is commit them entirely to the perfect justice of God. The Lord has manifested His love toward all His creatures, and He will do nothing inconsistent with His absolute perfection.

On what, then, does the Roman Church base its prayers for the dead, a practice which has such a large place in its system? Once more, for lack of a better, it has principally taken a text from the apocryphal books, proclaimed canonical after the Reformation. According to the Maccabees, the Jews prayed for the dead soldiers in a certain battle and offered for them an expiatory sacrifice for the pardon of their sins (II Maccabees 12:39-46). Thus, they declare, this prayer is legitimate and useful; the expiatory sacrifice of the mass can be offered for the dead, and there must indeed exist some place—purgatory—where souls finish their purification. It is strange that ideas as unbiblical as these are being infiltrated little by little into some Protestant circles. That proves to what point the wholly inspired Scriptures cease to be for many people the only and final authority.

## 10. WHAT IS BAPTISM FOR THE DEAD?

Only one passage speaks of this: "Else what shall they do that are baptized for the dead? If the dead are not raised at all, why then are they baptized for them?" (I Cor. 15:29). More than thirty interpretations have been given to this obscure text, for actually nothing exact is known of the custom that Paul speaks of. Two attempts at an explanation may well be brought to our attention:

a. Admission to the early Church was normally marked by the baptism of those who had believed (Acts 2:41; 10:47, 48, etc.). They knew that at His return the Lord would raise

again and would take unto Himself all those who had been
part of His Church. Now some Christians, because of illness or persecution, had not had time to be baptized. Therefore, brethren had themselves baptized in their place, so that
the reception of these into the Church might be according to
the rules and so that they would not risk being left behind
at the resurrection. Paul did not say that he approved of this
practice; he saw it only as a proof that those people firmly believed in the resurrection.

b. Another interpretation, given by F. Godet (Commen-
tary on I Cor. vol. II, p. 389) seems to us personally to be less
probable. The expression "to be baptized for the dead"
would have to do, not with a water baptism, but with a blood
baptism, by martyrdom. Twice Jesus employed the term
"baptism" in this sense; first, in speaking of His own death:
"I have a baptism to be baptized with" (Luke 12:50). Then,
on announcing the bloody death of some of His disciples:
"With the baptism that I am baptized withal shall ye be baptized" (Mark 10:38, 39). In Paul's writings the term "for
the dead" would mean: not a baptism with water to enter
the Church of the living, but a "baptism" (by blood) to enter
that of the dead. Now if there were no resurrection, what
would those "baptized" ones have to gain in getting themselves numbered with the dead for the love of Christ and of
the heavenly Church? That explanation, according to Godet,
would make natural the passage with the following question,
found in verse 30 of I Corinthians 15: "Why do we also stand
in jeopardy every hour?" since Paul himself constantly had
before him the possibility of martyrdom. Another advantage
to this interpretation would be that Paul would not seem to
be emphasizing a practice which he himself could not ap-
prove.

Let us note, finally, that the apostle does not say that the
dead themselves benefit at all from the baptism in question.
Otherwise, he would have written: "Else what would the

dead do that others are baptized for?" (vs. 29) Nothing that
the living do down here can change the fate of the dead.

## 11. IS THERE A POSSIBILITY OF REINCARNATION?

From India the idea of reincarnation is being introduced
again into our western world. All sorts of philosophies and
sects find it appealing, and we ought to know what the Bible
says about it.

It is clear that, according to the Scriptures, man has only
one existence to spend here below: "It is appointed unto men
once to die, and after this cometh judgment" (Heb. 9:27).
"The wages of sin is death" (singular number), not an indefinite number of deaths. Indeed there is only one physical
death, after which comes in the other world the *second* death,
which is eternal perdition (Rev. 20:14). Finally, Jesus
teaches us that the wicked are, from the moment of death, in
a place of judgment surrounded by an uncrossable gulf (Luke
16:23, 26). The righteous, in the Lord's presence, are resting
as they wait for the glorious day of the resurrection.

The whole theory of reincarnations is based on the pagan
notion of the slow amelioration of man by his own efforts and
of the expiatory value of his sufferings. From one existence
to another, man purifies himself so as to save himself. But
the utter absurdity is that he has no memory of his past
lives; thus, he suffers without knowing why. Moreover, if he
wants to behave ignobly, he is always under the delusion that
he will be able to make up for such behavior in a future life.
For some, man can be reborn only as a man; for others, he appears under the form of all kinds of animals. That almost
infinite repetition of reincarnations (six hundred thousand
times, they say in India) becomes so exhausting and desperate that man's principal concern is to be liberated from
it: salvation is the nirvana, or the absence of desire and sensa-
tion and thus the end of suffering, an abandonment to the
great whole. It is difficult to find a more ridiculous doctrine,

one more inimical to life and more contrary to all the teachings of the Bible. The favor that it enjoys, along with its entire procession of Hindu doctrines and practices, is a proof of the apostasy of our formerly "christianized" world.

All that is very true, say some. But isn't there in the Bible at least one example of reincarnation: isn't John the Baptist a reappearance of Elijah? Let us look closely at the texts concerned:

The last verses of the Old Testament announce that Elijah will come back before the day of the Lord, to touch the hearts of fathers and of children ( Mal. 4:5, 6). The angel, announcing the birth of John the Baptist, declared: "He shall go before his face in the spirit and power of Elijah, to turn the hearts of the fathers to the children . . . to make ready for the Lord a people prepared for him" (Luke 1:17). However, when they asked John the Baptist at the beginning of his ministry: "Art thou Elijah?" he replied firmly: "I am not" (John 1:21). Then what is the meaning of Jesus' words: "And if ye are willing to receive it, this [John the Baptist] is Elijah, that is to come" (Matt. 11:14)? And especially the following passage: "And his disciples asked him, saying, Why then say the scribes that Elijah must first come? And he answered and said, *Elijah* indeed *cometh*, and shall restore all things; but I say unto you, that *Elijah is come already,* and they knew him not, but did unto him whatsoever they would . . . Then understood the disciples that he spake unto them of John the Baptist" (Matt. 17:10-13). Jesus affirms two things here:

a. *Elijah has come already.* Christ, in His first coming, had John the Baptist as a forerunner, who appeared "in the spirit and power of Elijah." In this sense John was like Elijah.

b. *Elijah is to come.* Indeed, the true return of Elijah is still future and is to precede the return of the Lord. John the Baptist himself said that he was not Elijah in person (John 1:21). And Jesus made this clear: "Elijah indeed cometh and shall restore all things." It is evident that this part of the prophecy is not yet realized. It will be accomplished immediately before the great day of the Lord, according to Malachi 4:5, 6. Elijah will have, we believe, a special ministry in the conversion of Israel at that time, which will mark the beginning of the "restoration of all things," that is, the inauguration of the millennium. (See Acts 3:19-21; Rom. 11:12, 15). We also believe that Elijah will be one of the two witnesses of Revelation 11:1-12, whose task will be specifically to prophesy with power in Jerusalem (the holy city, where their Lord had been crucified, vss. 2, 8), during the great tribulation. The second of those witnesses seems to us to be Enoch, for the following reason: Enoch and Elijah were the only men, who, although sinners, did not go through death. They will be kept for that special ministry until the end of time, at the end of which they also will submit to death, vs. 9.

In conclusion, one can draw from all that story of Elijah no argument in favor of the theory of reincarnation. One might better realize that that idea is totally contrary to the letter and the spirit of the Scriptures. Apart from any other consideration, it would be the complete negation of the resurrection, as well as of the whole work of Jesus Christ. For such a lamentable perspective as that we shall not abandon the glorious certainties of salvation!

## 12.  THE MEMORY OF THE RIGHTEOUS A BENEDICTION

The chapter that we are finishing has perhaps seemed disappointing to some. On this subject of contact with our dead, the Bible has seemed to them negative and silent. That impression, if it exists, cannot, human as it may be, make us doubt in any respect the wisdom and truth of the Scriptures. But do we mean that, from the instant of their death, we totally lose our loved ones and must even banish their memory? Not at all.

The Bible affirms first of all that "the memory of the righteous is blessed" (Prov. 10:7) and even that "the righteous shall be had in everlasting remembrance" (Ps. 112:6). It adds: "Remember them that had the rule over you, men that spake unto you the Word of God; and considering the issue of their life, imitate their faith" (Heb. 13:7). What an encouragement and what a comfort we find in the memory of many beloved ones, whose example and testimony does us so much good! We shall not cease to bless God for it to the end of our days. Being surrounded by such a great cloud of witnesses we are strongly encouraged to walk faithfully as they did, in the Savior's footsteps (Heb. 12:1, 2).

Moreover, those righteous ones whom we remember are in Christ, as we are by faith. They, the same as we, are members of the body of the Lord, in which reigns an eternal unity which nothing can destroy. Let no one misunderstand us: after all we have said up to this point, it is clear that the dead are in another world and have no direct communication with us. But we commit them to God with an extra confidence, knowing that, in His arms, they are marvelously kept and comforted. It is to Him alone that we can go at all times to pour out our sorrow, our desires, and our need of communion and consolation. It is not told to us what the Lord makes known to those who are now in His presence, awaiting the reunion and the resurrection. But it is enough for us to feel kept and united together by the powerful hand of the One who is all and in all.

It is in this sense that we understand the passage in Hebrews 12:22-24. We have come by faith, not to Mount Sinai, kindled by the fire of the divine justice, but to the mountain of the heavenly Jerusalem, made accessible by the blood of sprinkling. Found there, with the myriads of the angels, are "the general assembly and church of the firstborn who are enrolled in heaven and . . . the spirits of just men made perfect." It is a great consolation to us to know that the believers gone on before are already in glory in the heavenly places to which we ourselves are carried away with the Lord even now in spirit and by faith (Eph. 2:6). And we rejoice in the thought that the present period of separation and of silence will not last long. Soon we shall all be in the perfection and eternity of heaven.

# PART THREE

# THE WORLD OF SPIRITS

# Chapter VI

# THE ANGELS

## 1. WHAT ARE THE ANGELS?

THE ANGELS ARE MENTIONED one hundred and eight times in the Old Testament and one hundred and sixty-five in the New. There could be no doubt of their existence, although some today deny it, even as the Sadducees did in their day (Acts 23:8). If there is the world of physical bodies—vegetable, animal, and men—why would there not be heavenly spirits too?

According to the definition of Hebrews 1:14, the angels are "ministering spirits, sent forth to do service for the sake of them that shall inherit salvation." The word "angel" actually means "sent one." (It is sometimes used for men, for example in Luke 7:24 and James 2:25.)

The angels were created, as were all the heavenly hosts, by a simple command of God (Ps. 148:2-5). They were already present at the creation of the physical world (Job 38:4, 7). Paul makes it clear that they were created by Christ and for Him. Being spirits, they are part of the invisible things in the heavens (Col. 1:16). Job 4:18, 19 indicates that the angels have not, as we have, "houses of clay," bodies made out of dust.

## 2. THE CHARACTERISTICS OF ANGELS

### a. *Power*

They are superior in *strength* and in *power* (II Peter 2:11). They are mighty in strength (Ps. 103:20). In connection with Christ, they are called the "angels of his power" (II Thess. 1:7).

### b. *Wisdom*

They possess very great *wisdom*. The Bible mentions ". . . according to the wisdom of an angel of God" (II Sam. 14: 20) . But they are not omniscient; they do not know, for instance, the day of Christ's return (Mark 13:32) .

They are learning, by the Church, to understand better the infinitely varied wisdom of God (Eph. 3:10) . They desire to look into the marvels announced by the prophets and proclaimed by the apostles (I Peter 1:12) .

### c. *Holiness*

The angels are *holy* (Acts 10:22) . It is evident that otherwise they could not stand before God. The white garments in which they are clothed are a symbol of holiness (Matt. 28: 3) .

### d. *Glory*

They are surrounded by a dazzling glory. Daniel depicts like this the appearance of one of them: "His body also was like the beryl, and his face as the appearance of lightning, and his eyes as flaming torches, and his arms and feet like unto burnished brass, and the voice of his words like the voice of a multitude" (Daniel 10:6) . Before this flashing manifestation, the companions of the prophet were seized with great terror; and they took flight, leaving him alone and without strength. (See again Matt. 28:2, 3; Rev. 10:1, etc.) The Son of man "cometh in his own glory . . . and [that] of the holy angels" (Luke 9:26) .

### e. *Election*

They are designated as the elect (I Tim. 5:21) . All the angels having been tempted, some rebelled to follow Satan. It is not surprising that the others were chosen of God according to His perfect foreknowledge. That election of the angels has to do with Christ, for Paul tells us this: In Christ God purposed to unite all things, "the things in the heavens and the things upon the earth" (Eph. 1:10) . "And through him [Christ] to reconcile all things unto himself, having made peace through the blood of his cross; through him, I say, whether things upon the earth, or things in the heavens" (Col. 1:25). The salvation that Christ purchased at so great a cost does not extend to demons; we shall see, in fact, that in regard to them, there is no redemption or conversion possible. What do the above verses mean then? We believe that the work of Christ had an immense repercussion in heaven, where it arrested the revolt of the angels and affirmed the fidelity and submission of these angels which had been elected. It is in this sense that the New Testament emphasizes the special sovereignty that Christ, after the cross, was given over the angels (Eph. 1:20, 21; Phil. 2:9-11; Heb. 1:3, 4, 6; I Peter 3:22).

"To sum up" or "to reconcile" the "things upon the earth and [things] in the heavens" (Eph. 1:10 and Col. 1:20) seems to us, furthermore, to mean this: the universe has been ravished because of sin; war is being waged in heaven and on earth; men, having revolted against their Creator, have lost contact with the inhabitants of paradise; the cross, which takes away the sin of the world, provides the reestablishment of peace and unity. If men remain outside the scope of redemption's work, it is, as we shall see later on, because they have of their own choice deprived themselves of it.

f. *Humility* characterizes the faithful angels. They cover their faces and their feet before the presence of God (Isa. 6:2). They refuse from men the homage which belongs to the Lord alone (Rev. 19:10; 22:8, 9). Satan and his angels have, on the other hand, only one desire: to be worshipped and to take the place of God (Isa. 14:12-14).

g. *Obedience.* When the Lord says, "Thy will be done, as in heaven so on earth" (Matt. 6:10), what obedience in heaven is meant if not that of the angels? Better than we, they do indeed know how to obey at all times, immediately, completely—and without asking why! See in this regard

Psalm 103:20: the angels, mighty in strength, carry out the orders of God, hearkening unto the voice of His word.

h. *The hierarchy and the organization.* The Bible seems to distinguish different classes of celestial spirits: thrones, dominions, principalities, and powers (Col. 1:16). See also Rom. 8:38; Eph. 1:21, and I Peter 3:22. Paul applies these last two terms, "principalities and powers," to the Satanic powers, over which Christ triumphed on the cross (Col. 2:15) and which are struggling against us in the heavenly places (Eph. 6:12). Peter and Jude speak of the "dignities" that it would be presumptuous and audacious to rail at, even though they are fallen (II Peter 2:10; Jude 8, 9).

Michael bears the title of archangel, and he is called "one of the chief princes," "the great prince" (Jude 9; Dan. 10:13; 12:1). The Revelation shows us Michael and his angels waging war on the dragon and his angels (12:7).

There is still the question of the "innumerable hosts of angels" (Heb. 12:22); of legions of angels (Matt. 26:53); of the multitude of the heavenly host (Luke 2:13) —or the host of heaven (I Kings 22:19). When God is called the Lord of hosts, the reference is of course to those celestial hosts.

Let us examine two more groups of angels. The *cherubim* are mentioned several times: they guarded with a flaming sword the "way" of "paradise lost" (Gen. 3:22-24). They were represented on the veil which barred the entrance to the holy of holies; and they were above the ark of the covenant, where without a sword they were looking at the atoning blood (Exod. 26:31; 25:17-20). They are found again in Ezekiel's vision, where the "animals" (living creatures) are expressly called "cherubim" (Ezek. 1; 10:18-22). There they seemed ready to carry away as on a chariot of fire the glory of the Lord, outraged by sin. The four "living creatures" (Rev. 4:6-8) resemble very much those of Ezekiel. They unceasingly worship the Lord and proclaim His holiness; they also participate in the accomplishment of His judgments (6:1, 3, 5, 7, etc.). Possibly Daniel, in his chapter 4, is alluding to celestial beings like the cherubim, guardians of the divine majesty. Nebuchadnezzar recounts the dream about the great tree and says: "I saw . . . and behold, a watcher and a holy one came down from heaven . . . This sentence [to fell the tree] is by the decree of the watchers, and the demand by the word of the holy ones to the intent that the living may know that the Most High ruleth in the kingdom of men . . ." (4:13, 17). Farther on, the prophet adds: "Then I heard a holy one speaking; and another holy one said unto that certain one who spake, How long shall be the vision . . .?" (8:13).

Thus the angels can raise questions about prophecy, in the sense of I Peter 1:12; they can also watch over and intervene when the august majesty of God calls for it.

The *seraphim* (that is, the "burning ones") are mentioned only in Isaiah 6:1-7. Like the living creatures of Revelation 4, they have six wings and proclaim, in adoration and humility, the holiness of the Lord.

### i. *Personality*

Each angel has a distinct *personality*. We know the names of at least three of them: Michael, already mentioned, means "Who is like God?"; Gabriel, "God is strength," stands before the Lord (Luke 1:19, 26; Daniel 8:16; 9:21); and last of all, there is Satan. The way in which the angels act, obey, revolt, and are judged shows abundantly their personality.

### j. *Individuality*

Let us establish, in conclusion, the following interesting comparisons (from F. Godet, *Studies of Creation and Life*, "The Angels," pp. 97, 98):

*The plant* is significant only in relation to its species, the individual plant being merely a specimen;
*the animal* is more developed, but the individual is still governed simply by instinct and the laws of the species;

   *man* is a person; he is no longer irrevocably bound by the
    instincts of the race;

   *an angel* is a created individual, without species. The
    heavenly spirits are sometimes called "sons of God," but
    never "sons of angels." Not having any heredity, the
    angels are fully responsible for their acts—and they have
    no redemption.

3. THE MINISTRY OF THE ANGELS

   a. *In the service of God*

"Are they not all ministering spirits?" (Heb. 1:14). We
see them constantly surrounding the Lord, doing His will,
and helping in His work:

   They assisted with cries of joy at the creation of the world
    (Job 38:4-7);

   they transmitted the law to Moses on Sinai (Gal. 3:19;
    Acts 7:53);

   they carry out the deliverances and the judgments that
    the Lord commands (Gen. 19:15-22; II Sam. 24:16—see
    also the role of the angels in the judgments of the Reve-
    lation (7:2; 8:6-12, etc.);

   they carry out God's orders (Ps. 103:20);

   they participate in the government of the nations. The
    angels sustain some peoples, such as Israel (Dan. 12:1);
    the Persians, the Medes, and the Greeks (Javan) (Dan.
    10:13, 20, 21; 11:1). They fight against the wicked spir-
    itual powers, which seek to harm those nations.

The angels are also fighting against Satan and his armies,
until the complete victory (Rev. 12:7-9). It is an angel also
which is to bind the devil in the abyss (Rev. 20:1, 2).

Reunited before the throne of God, the angels unceasingly
adore Him and glorify Him (Rev. 5:11; Dan. 7:10, etc.)

   b. *In the service of Jesus Christ*

We see, likewise, the angels accompanying our Lord in all the steps of His earthly career:

The angel Gabriel announced the birth of the Lord to *Mary,* as he had predicted that of His forerunner, John the Baptist (Luke 1:26, 19).

*Joseph* was also warned by another celestial messenger (Matt. 1:20-24).

An angel appeared to the *shepherds* on Christmas night, and a multitude of the heavenly host sounded the praises of God (Luke 2:9-15).

The flight into Egypt and then the return from that country took place in connection with new angelic interventions (Matt. 2:13, 19).

As soon as Jesus victoriously overcame the *temptation* in the desert, angels came to Him and served Him (Matt. 4:11).

During His agony in *Gethsemane,* an angel appeared to Him from heaven and rolled away the stone from the tomb (Matt. 28:2); two angels appeared to the women and proclaimed the glorious news (Luke 24:4).

At the moment of the *ascension,* the angels announced again that Jesus Christ would come as He had gone away (Acts 1:11).

The Lord *will descend from heaven* to take away His Church at the "voice of the archangel" (I Thess. 4:16).

He will send His angels to *regather His elect* from the four winds (Matt. 24:31).

He will appear from heaven "with angels of His power," *to punish the wicked* (II Thess. 1:7, 8). He will come in His glory, "with all the angels," and will sit down to judge the nations (Matt. 25:31).

The *last judgment* also will be held by Christ in the presence of the angels: those who have denied Christ will then be denied before the angels of God (Luke 12:9; 9:26).

The impenitents cast into *eternal hell* will be "tormented

with fire and brimstone in the presence of the holy angels and in the presence of the Lamb" (Rev. 14:10).

Finally, in *heaven* Jesus will confess before His Father and before His angels the names of the overcomers (Rev. 3:5).

Are we not overwhelmed to see with what faithfulness and what adoration the angels follow step by step their Master and ours? What an example for our own service! "And without controversy, great is the mystery of godliness: he who was manifested in the flesh, justified in the spirit, seen of angels, preached among the nations, believed on in the world, received up in glory" (I Tim. 3:16).

If the angels exert such a ministry in regard to Christ, it is because they are particularly subordinated to Him. Like all other creatures, they were made by Him and for Him (Col. 1:16). They all adore the Son, "having become by so much better than the angels [after His incarnation] as he hath inherited a more excellent name than they" (Heb. 1:4, 6). Since Jesus has gone back to heaven, "angels and authorities and powers" are "made subject unto him" in an even more direct way (I Peter 3:22; Eph. 1:21). In the Gospels, Christ speaks several times of *His* angels (Matt. 13:41; 24:31, etc.).

The twelve legions of angels that He chose not to call upon that He might avoid the cross (Matt. 26:53) have been given back to Him and infinitely multiplied. The complete subordination of the angels to the Lord makes it so that believers could not in any eventuality be separated by them from the love of God manifested in Jesus Christ (Rom. 8: 38, 39). That is true of the faithful angels, but equally of the demons and of Satan himself, who cannot ever go farther than the bounds fixed by God.

c. *In the service of the believers*

According to Hebrews 1:14, the angels are "sent forth to do service for the sake of them that shall inherit salvation." The ladder of Jacob's dream, by which angels ascended and descended between heaven and earth, is a beautiful picture of their incessant activity in our behalf (Gen. 28:12). Indeed in the Bible examples abound where we see the angels:

*provide* for physical needs of believers, as in the case of Hagar (Gen. 21:15-19) and of Elijah under his juniper tree (I Kings 19:5-7);

*preserve* from danger, by taking Lot out of Sodom (Gen. 19:15, 16), by watching over the three Hebrews in the furnace, and by watching over Daniel in the lions' den (Dan. 3:24, 25; 6:22);

*deliver* Peter from prison and from the hand of Herod (Acts 12:7-10; see also Acts 5:19);

*direct* the servants of God, as Philip, when he was to go to speak to the Ethiopian (Acts 8:26);

*reveal* the Lord's plans, for example to Daniel (9:21-23), to Cornelius (Acts 10:3-6); or again to John (Rev. 1:1);

*announce* happy events, such as the birth of John the Baptist and that of the Lord (Luke 1:11-13; 2:10-12);

*encourage* Paul in the midst of the anguish of the shipwreck (Acts 27:23, 24);

*take* the soul of poor Lazarus and carry it into Abraham's bosom (Luke 16:22);

*reassemble* the elect at the return of Christ (Matt. 24:31).

To summarize, the Lord, by means of His servants, watches without ceasing over the steps of His beloved: "For he will give his angels charge over thee in all thy ways. They shall bear thee up in their hands, lest thou dash thy foot against a stone" (Ps. 91:11). "The angel of Jehovah encampeth round about them that fear him and delivereth them" (Ps. 34:8). One might even wonder, according to Matthew 18:10, if each child—or each of these "little ones" before God—has not an angel which sees constantly the face of our Father which is in heaven. But the Bible says nothing more which might lead to any further development of the idea of a "guardian angel."

Still, a text speaks to us of the role of intercessor that an angelic spirit can have in behalf of a man tested in the face of death: "If there be with him an angel, an interpreter, one among a thousand to show unto man what is right for him; then God is gracious unto him and saith, Deliver him from going down to the pit: I have found a ransom!" (Job 33:23, 24).

## 4. THE NUMBER OF THE ANGELS

To accomplish so many tasks, the angels are extremely numerous. When Daniel saw the Lord on His throne, "thousands of thousands ministered unto him, and ten thousand times ten thousand stood before him" (7:10). John wrote: "I heard a voice of many angels round about the throne . . . and the number of them was ten thousand times ten thousand [one myriad=ten thousand] and thousands of thousands (Rev. 5:11). We have already spoken of the multitude of the heavenly host which the Christmas shepherds heard (Luke 2:13). Elisha said to his servant appalled at the crowd of enemies: "Fear not, for they that are with us are more than they that are with them . . . And Jehovah opened the eyes of the young man, and behold the mountain was full of horses and chariots of fire round about Elisha" (II Kings 6:16, 17). On this point, Psalm 68 verse 17 adds: "The chariots of God are twenty thousand, even thousands upon thousands. The Lord is among them." Jesus Christ mentions as an entirely natural thing the asking for twelve legions of angels. Now, if a legion is six thousand men, that would make seventy-two thousand. And the epistle to the Hebrews mentions "the innumerable hosts" which form the choir of the angels (12:27).

All these expressions lead us to cry out with the book of Job: "Is there any number of his armies?" (25:3).

Still one question comes up: is there a fixed number of angels, or does the Lord continue to create them? Nothing in the Scriptures would permit us to answer in this latter sense. The angels do not reproduce themselves, and it seems that they were all called forth at one time: "He commanded, and they were created" (Ps. 148:2, 5).

## 5. HAVE THE ANGELS SEX?

Since they do not reproduce themselves, they do not constitute a race. Angelic apparitions in the Bible never have a feminine form. Jesus especially declares clearly that " in the resurrection, they [the believers] neither marry, nor are given in marriage, but are as angels in heaven" (Matt. 22: 30). They "neither marry, nor are given in marriage . . . being sons of the resurrection" (Luke 20:35, 36).

What is one to make then of Genesis 6:1-4, according to which the "sons of God," immediately before the flood, took the "daughters of men" as wives and brought forth giants? Some have thought this a question of rebellious angels, which, according to Jude 6, did not keep "their own principality, but left their proper habitation." We are not prepared to say whether or not this verse in Jude applies to anything but the fall of the angels from heaven. Furthermore, to multiply on earth, those angels would have had to be incarnated.

We know that evil spirits can take hold of men at times and possess them. But this is never a question of a real incarnation; the miracle of the creation of a body apart from natural means belongs solely to the Creator and took place only in the case of Jesus Christ. The "sons of God" mentioned in Genesis 6 seem to us rather to be the devout descendants of the faithful line of Seth, mentioned in chapter 5. When even that good line allowed itself to be led astray by the beauty and perversion of the "daughters of men" (the descendants of Cain), the whole race was contaminated and the judgment of the flood became inevitable (vss. 5-7). It might be said that this does not explain why giants were born of those unions. Let us note first that verse 4 simply says that the giants were in the earth in those days, *after* the sons of God "came in unto the daughters of men and they bare children to them." Thus it is after those marriages that the giants appeared. Without being actually able to explain the reason for the giants, those "mighty men that were of old," let us state that they really did exist, as attested to by different passages in the Bible. Even after the deluge, there were giants in Palestine ( Numbers 13:33; Deut. 2:10, etc.) Traces of truly Cyclopean constructions have been found in that country. Several other people, the Greeks, for instance, have also retained accounts of particularly tall and wicked men; they claim, for example, that the Titans attempted to scale heaven to snatch the thunderbolts from the Most High God. Then let us note that even today there are pygmies, abnormally small people; and we cannot lay their change in stature to any direct intervention of infernal powers.

## 6. The dwelling place of the angels

A very great many passages name heaven as the dwelling place of the angels. At the birth of Christ, a multitude of the heavenly host appeared to the shepherds; then the angels left them to go back to heaven (Luke 2:13-15). On Easter Day an angel of the Lord descended from heaven and rolled away the stone from the tomb (Matt. 28:2). Paul uses the term "an angel from heaven" (Gal. 1:8). He locates in the heavenly places the principalities and powers that today, through the Church, are acquainted with the manifold wisdom of God (Eph. 3:10). The book of Job brings in twice "sons of God" that came before God (1:6; 2:1). Another passage represents Jehovah as sitting on His throne and all the host of heaven standing by Him on His right hand and on His left (I Kings 22:19). Jesus Himself declared that in heaven the angels of the little ones continually behold the face of the Father

(Matt. 18:10). He adds that we too shall soon be like the angels of God in heaven (Matt. 22:30). So the angels hold such an exalted place that God will judge very severely those who have "kept not their own principality, but left their proper habitation" (Jude 6).

## 7. THE ANGELIC APPEARANCES

These are frequent in the Bible. The angels are spirits; but in order to communicate with men, they clothe themselves with a human aspect. Sometimes when they appear, they are even taken for men at the beginning; then they reveal their identity as they accomplish their mission. Thus it is that in showing hospitality believers have "entertained angels unawares" (Heb. 13:2). Let us mention, for example, the three "men" received by Abraham, then again the two who were given lodging by Lot (Gen. 18:2; 19:3, 10-12).

At other times, although still in human form, their appearance is heavenly and glorious. Those who see them have been left terrified and trembling (Dan. 10:5-9; see also Rev. 10:1-3). When the angel stopped Balaam, it was at first only the ass that saw him standing with his drawn sword in his hand. God had to open Balaam's eyes before he could see him (Num. 22:23, 31). Also Elisha alone recognized the heavenly host that had come to help him. He had to pray to God to reveal them also to his frightened servant (II Kings 6:16, 17). How many times we are surrounded by heavenly spirits to help us and even to serve us—without our knowing anything about them! Many of God's servants of indubitable character have recounted stories of unexpected presences which have delivered them from great dangers. Some day we shall surely comprehend all that we owe to this blessed ministry.

But, after all, how is it that angelic apparitions—like all that is supernatural—are so rare during the church era? There seem to be several reasons for this. God meant to

authenticate the Old covenant, then the New, at their begin-
nings, by a great many miracles which were not always re-
produced later. Moreover, throughout the Old Testament,
the Lord Himself was still far from men and often sent them
His messengers in a perceptible way. Since the incarnation,
especially since Pentecost, the Holy Spirit lives in the Church
and in the heart of every believer. It is He who directly
leads, convicts, protects, and illumines. Remarkably enough,
it seems that no text makes any allusion to angels during the
millennium, during which time the glorious presence of the
Lord will be manifested directly. See for example Isaiah 24:
23.

One more thing, somewhat subordinate. In their appearances, *do the angels have wings?* Painters uniformly picture
them that way, but what does the Bible have to say? At least
twice it speaks of the flight of a heavenly messenger: "Gabriel
... being caused to fly swiftly, touched me ... " (Dan. 9:21).
"And I saw another angel flying in mid heaven" (Rev. 14:
6). Moreover, there is the description of the six wings of
the seraphim and of the four living creatures (Isa. 6:2 and
Rev. 4:8). There is mention of the four wings of the extraordinary creatures that Ezekiel calls cherubim (1:6; 10:
19, 20). Finally, there were at the two ends of the ark of the
testimony in the tabernacle, also in Solomon's temple, two
cherubim, each having two wings (Exod. 25:18-20; II Chron.
3:10-12). What do these wings represent? Nothing material,
since angels are spirits and can move about without them.
But they are doubtless the symbol of the astonishing rapidity
and precision of the intervention of the angels. In Isaiah 6:2
four wings out of six serve, moreover, to hide the feet and
faces of the seraphim, beings which consider themselves unworthy of appearing uncovered before the absolute holiness of
God.

8. THE ANGEL OF JEHOVAH

One of the most striking apparitions in the Old Testament

is that of the angel of Jehovah. It is distinguished from the others by the fact that this angel seems in reality to be the Lord Himself manifesting His presence to men. He spoke to Hagar in the first person singular, when He said to her, "I will greatly multiply thy seed" (Gen. 16:7, 10).

One of the three angels that appeared to Abraham promised him a son in these words: "I will certainly return unto thee when the season cometh round; and lo, Sarah thy wife shall have a son . . . And Sarah laughed . . . and Jehovah said unto Abraham, Wherefore did Sarah laugh . . .? At the set time I will return unto thee . . ." (Gen. 18:10, 13-15). The other two angels went away (19:1). The third, which was Jehovah Himself, remained with Abraham and heard his plea in behalf of Sodom (18:22). The angel of Jehovah stayed the arm of the patriarch when he was about to slay his son. Then he cried: ". . .Thou hast not withheld thy son . . . By myself have I sworn, saith Jehovah . . . that in blessing I will bless thee and in multiplying I will multiply thy seed . . . thou hast obeyed my voice" (22:11-18). The angel with which Jacob wrestled said to him, "Thou hast striven with God . . ." And Jacob answered: "I have seen God face to face" (32:28-30). In blessing Joseph, the patriarch identified as God the angel which had delivered him from all evil (48:15). The angel of Jehovah appeared to Moses in the burning bush (Exod. 3:2); and he revealed Himself to him, speaking as being God Himself (vss. 4-6; see also Exodus 13:21 and 14:19). Two more striking examples appear in the book of Judges: The angel of Jehovah called Gideon, who responded in a discouraged spirit. Then the text continues: "And Jehovah looked upon him, and said, Go in this thy might . . ." Gideon exclaimed, "Show me a sign . . . Depart not thence . . ." And Jehovah said: "I will tarry until thou come again" (Judges 6:12-22). In a final example, Samson's parents, after having seen the angel of Jehovah, said: "We shall surely die, because we have seen

God" (Judges 13:13-22). From all the above, it is clear that it is entirely correct to call such manifestations "theophanies," that is, appearances of God.

One has wondered whether, in those cases, the Lord simply took on an angelic—or a human—appearance, in order to manifest Himself; or whether it was already a question of temporary appearances of that One who one day would become completely incarnate for our salvation. There is no doubt but that Christ was active all the way through the Old Testament. He participated in creation (Heb. 1:2); Paul declared that He was like a spiritual rock, which followed the Israelites, at which they could quench their thirst (I Cor. 10:4). The prophets spoke by the Spirit of Christ which was in them (I Peter 1:11). Since this is true, it is perfectly plausible to think that the angel of Jehovah, identified as God, was made the manifestation of Christ Himself. No one has seen God, but it is His only Son who makes Him known to us (John 1:18). This seems to us to be confirmed by the following passages, among others: in Exodus 23:20, 21 God said to Israel: "Behold, I send an angel before thee to keep thee by the way . . . Take ye heed before him . . . provoke him not, for he will not pardon your transgression: for *my name is in him.*" Isaiah, alluding to the painful pilgrimage of Israel, wrote: "In all their affliction he was afflicted, and the angel of his presence saved them" (Isaiah 63:9). The angel of Jehovah answered Samson's father: "Wherefore askest thou after my name, seeing it is wonderful?" (Judges 13:18). The Hebrew word employed here is the same as in Isaiah 9:6, where it speaks of Jesus: "His name shall be called *Wonderful.*"

A magnificent passage referring to the angel of Jehovah representing Jesus, our Advocate before God, is found in the scene where Joshua is accused by Satan. (Compare Zech. 3:1-5 with Rev. 12:10 and I John 2:1, 2.)

9. THE POSITION OF THE ANGELS

After this brief study of the angelic theophanies, let us come back to the angels themselves. Let us see what their position is in relation to Christ and to believers.

a. *In relation to Christ.* It is clear that the Lord is their Creator and that in heaven they adore Him as Creator (Col. 1:16). By the incarnation, which makes Him like unto us, Christ made Himself for a little time lower than the angels (Heb. 2:6, 7, 9). Still, we have seen with what devotion those angels accompanied Him in His earthly ministry. After the cross, Jesus was highly exalted, "having become by so much better than the angels, as he hath inherited a more excellent name than they" (Heb. 1:4). When the Father, by the resurrection and glorification, "again bringeth in the first-born into the world, he saith, And let all the angels of God worship him" (Heb. 1:6). That is what they will continue to do throughout eternity.

b. *In relation to believers.* From what we have just said, as well as from the preceding paragraphs, it is clear that the angels are now, from many points of view, superior to us in holiness, strength, wisdom, and glory (Heb. 2:6, 7). However, the Lord has conferred on men a unique nobility and position. It is they who are to profit by redemption, since it is written of Christ: "For verily not to angels doth he give help, but he giveth help to the seed of Abraham" (Heb. 2: 16). If in the Old Testament the angels are several times called "sons of God" (Job 1:6 and 38:7; Ps. 89:7, etc.), in the New Testament they are presented principally as ministering spirits, sent forth to do service for the sake of believers, the children of God (Heb. 1:14). There is even more than this, since, according to Paul, we shall judge the angels (I Cor. 6:3). It seems difficult for us to grasp how such a role could be given to sinners like us. But that is one consequence of the inconceivable manner in which the Lord regenerates us, communicates to us His divine nature, and transforms us into His image (II Peter 1:4; Rom. 8:29; I John 3:2). He makes of us His bride, seated with Him on His throne, destined with Him to govern the universe (Eph. 5:25, 26; Rev. 3:21 and 22:5b). Before such affirmations one can understand what the Epistle to the Hebrews adds: "For not unto angels did he subject the world to come" (2:5). Thus we can say that if we are now lower than the angels, our position will soon in an extraordinary way be higher than theirs.

Paul had such a consciousness of the unique value of his "Gospel" that he dared to write: "Though we, or an angel from heaven, should preach unto you any gospel other than that which we preached unto you, let him be anathema" (Gal. 1:8). The revelations of the Holy Spirit transmitted by the inspired and faithful apsotle are, then, above everything that an angel could say. Perhaps Paul also envisages in this passage the possibility of the intervention of a fallen angel, disguised as an angel of light, to turn souls away from the true message (II Cor. 11:14).

## 10. ANGELS AS SPECTATORS

The angels that participate in so many of the Lord's works are only spectators of creation and redemption. They well realize the superior revelation that God grants to the earth. Even heaven itself has never seen anything so marvelous as the incarnation and the suffering and death of the Creator; nothing so inconceivable as the complete redemption of rebels made to become the Church of the Lord. That is why the prophets describe the predicted sufferings of Christ and the glories that would follow; they reveal things into which the angels desire to look (I Peter 1:12).

In an imaginary and prophetic way, this thought was expressed in the Old Testament. After having driven man from the garden of Eden, God had the way of the tree of life guarded by cherubim armed with a flaming sword (Gen. 3:

24). They would have killed without mercy any sinner bold enough to go back into paradise. Jesus was destined to present Himself; and, in order to make a way for us, He would cast Himself voluntarily on that sword, by His death disarming the defenders of the divine justice. That is why the cherubim in the tabernacle are pictured at the two extremities of the ark containing the law that had been violated by sinners. When once a year the high priest, representing sinners, appeared, the cherubim normally would have pierced him through. But they no longer have a sword: fascinated, they have their faces turned "toward the mercy seat," which they cover with their wings; they are looking at the place where the high priest will place the blood of the victim that has died in the place of the guilty ones. And God adds, speaking to Moses: "And there I will meet with thee, and I will commune with thee from above the mercy-seat [the top of the ark, where the atoning blood is put], from between the two cherubim which are upon the ark of the testimony, of all things which I will give thee in commandment unto the children of Israel" (Exod. 25:18-22). Thus, when the psalmist exclaims, "Thou that sittest above the cherubim, shine forth" (Psalm 80:1), he is addressing the One whose holiness has been satisfied because of grace, and that in the sight of the angels. Truly, the great mystery of godliness has been "seen of angels," who have followed the unfolding of it with wonder and adoration (I Tim. 3:16). It took the revelation of this mystery which for ages was hid in God for "the principalities and the powers in the heavenly places" to know "through the church the manifold wisdom of God" (Eph. 3:10).

On the other hand, the angels, given such a great ministry on the earth, observe what goes on among men. Before all the assembled "sons of God," the Lord asked Satan, "Hast thou considered my servant Job?" (Job 1:6). There is likewise joy in the presence of the angels of God over one sinner that repents (Luke 15:10). Doubtless it is in a similar sense that the enigmatical word of Paul can be understood: "For this cause ought the woman to have a sign of authority on her head, because of the angels" (I Cor. 11:10). Since the angels are watching us, they must not see a Christian woman wearing immodest apparel. The apostle also writes to Timothy: "I charge thee in the sight of God, and Christ Jesus, and the elect angels, that thou observe these things without prejudice, doing nothing by partiality" (I Tim. 5:21). It is thus a question of properly fulfilling one's ministry because of the angelic powers which watch us. Paul trembles before the thought that everything he does is thus scrutinized and brought to light: "For, I think, God hath set forth us the apostles last of all, as men doomed to death: for we are made a spectacle unto the world, both to angels and men" (I Cor. 4:9). When a gladiator dies before the public eye, the crowd avidly observes all the grimaces of his suffering and the last gasps of his death struggle. It is indeed disconcerting for the Christian warrior to know that he is laid open to inspection like this. But does not God make us always to triumph in Christ? (II Cor. 2:14).

And let us not forget that the angels are the most benevolent and the most discerning of spectators and that the Lord commands them not only to watch us, but also to keep us in all our ways (Ps. 91:11).

## 11. THE WORSHIP OF ANGELS

It is not surprising that man is tempted to worship these celestial beings, which are endowed with so much power and glory. Twice the apostle John, even though such a spiritual man, fell in adoration at the feet of the angel that was instructing him (Rev. 19:10; 22:8, 9). But both times the angel stopped him. "See thou do it not! I am a fellow-servant with thee and with thy brethren that hold the testimony of Jesus: worship God"! If the angels are fellow-servants with us, ministering on our behalf, how could we worship them? Paul's warning is just as explicit: "Let no man rob you of your prize by a voluntary humility and *worshipping of angels,* dwelling in the things which he hath seen, . . . not holding fast the Head [Christ]" (Col. 2:19). The worship of angels, then, is absolutely forbidden. Moreover, the simple fact that they are created beings ought to suffice to remind us of the Decalogue, according to which we are to worship God alone.

In spite of these very clear principles, the Roman Church instituted the invocation of angels, just as it did that of the saints. It makes a great point of the doctrine of the "guardian angel"; and, according to the catechism, the believer is to love his guardian angel, pray to him devoutly each day, follow his suggestions faithfully, and remember that he sees him everywhere. *(A Catholic Catechism,* Herder and Herder, 1959, p. 44.) In the "confiteor," or formula of confession, the believer confesses his faults to God, to the Virgin, to *Saint Michael the archangel,* to John the Baptist, to the apostles Peter and Paul, and to all the saints. Then he calls on all these individuals to pray to God on his behalf. *(A Catechism for Inquirers,* Rev. Joseph I. Malloy, C.S.P., The Paulist Press, N. Y., 1958, p. 88.) In the citation of the case of Daniel, an attempt is made to justify this worship of angels: when a particularly glorious angel appeared to Daniel, he fell down in astonishment, his face to the ground (Dan. 10:5-9). It is claimed then that we ought to do as he did: bow down before the angels. But we have already seen that the two passages from the Revelation (19:10 and 22:8) clearly refute this idea. For if one starts to honor and venerate celestial beings, who can say where adoration begins? Revelation 8:3, 4 is also cited, which shows us an angel in heaven over the altar. "There was given unto him much incense, that he should add it unto the prayers of all the saints upon the golden altar which was before the throne. And the smoke of the incense, with the prayers of the saints, went up before God out of the angel's hand." This passage, which we have already alluded to, is the only one of its kind in the Bible; and it does not at all indicate that the saints in question (living believers, on the earth) addressed their prayers to the angel or to angels in general. We can draw no example from this. They prayed to God Himself; and that is what we are to do, whatever may be the role of the angels in the invisible world. In conclusion, let us add that the Roman Church bases a large part of its teachings regarding this subject on the apocryphal books, especially on that of Tobias, in which the angels play a very special role.

In conclusion, we believe that in general the angels remain invisible (especially to us down here) for this reason particularly: that they may not attract the attention of believers to themselves. Paul declares that that would amount to snatching away the prize for the race, in getting us to give ourselves over to visions and to the pride of our fleshly minds. On the contrary, our worship is always and exclusively to be directed toward Him who is the Head, even Christ (Col. 2: 18, 19).

## Chapter VII

## SATAN[1]

### 1. WHO IS SATAN?

THE SCRIPTURES GIVE at least forty different names to the enemy of God and of men. Here are some of the most striking, which teach us a great deal about this redoubtable personnage:

    a.  Satan (from a Hebrew word meaning "to be the enemy") : the one who hates, who resists, an opponent.

    b.  the tempter, Matt. 4:3.

    c.  the devil, Matt. 4:5: the slanderer

    d.  the enemy, Matt. 13:25, 39.

    e.  the evil one, Matt. 13:38.

    f.  the dragon, Rev. 12:9.

    g.  the old serpent, Rev. 12:9 (in Hebrew "nahash" means "the shining one") ; the swift and crooked serpent, Isa. 27:1.

    h.  the accuser, Rev. 12:10.

    i.  the deceiver, Rev. 12:9.

    j.  the adversary, I Peter 5:8.

    k.  the liar, John 8:44.

    l.  the father of lies, John 8:44.

    m.  the murderer, John 8:44.

    n.  the oppressor, Isa. 14:4.

    o.  the day-star, Isa. 14:12.

[1]In our book, *The Return of Jesus Christ*, we have spoken at length of Satan, the Prince of this world; and we advise our readers to refer to what we have said about him there on pages 165 to 176. In taking up some essential points now, let us attempt to complete the picture begun there.

p.  the son of the morning, Isa. 14:12.

q.  the one that laid low the nations, Isa. 14:12.

r.  leviathan, the monster that is in the sea, Isa. 27:1.

s.  the anointed cherub, Ezek. 28:14.

t.  Beelzebub, Matt. 12:24 (literally: "the Lord of Flies," that is, of evil spirits) .

u.  Belial, II Cor. 6:15, which means "wickedness."

v.  Apollyon: in Greek, "Destroyer," Rev. 9:11.

w.  Abaddon: in Hebrew, "destruction," Rev. 9:11.

x.  the angel of the abyss, Rev. 9:11.

y.  the prince of this world, John 14:30.

z.  the prince of the power of the air, Eph. 2:2.

aa. the prince of the demons, Matt. 12:24.

bb. the god of this world, II Cor. 4:4.

cc. the angel of light, II Cor. 11:14.

dd. the strong man, Luke 11:21.

ee. the thief, John 10:10.

ff. the wolf, John 10:12.

gg. the roaring lion, I Peter 5:8, etc.

Satan is mentioned in the Bible as many times as are all the other angels together, from the first to the last page of the history of man and of the universe. He plainly possesses all the attributes of personality: the names given above show that fact, and the actions which are attributed to him will prove it even more abundantly. The rationalists claim that the devil is only a metaphor, the pictured personification of the idea of evil. But how could such a metaphor speak; act; tempt Christ, angels, and men; struggle against God with incredible cunning and strength; and at last be tormented throughout eternity?

Let us note that there is in the Bible nothing of the grotesque representations of the devil and of hell familiar to the Middle Ages. Indeed, the great impostor alternately uses two methods to deceive souls in regard to his person: either he makes himself appear so laughable and absurd that people do not fear him; or he persuades them that he does not exist, so that they are incapable of resisting his assaults.

The one who makes fun of the devil is but a step away from making fun of the Lord and of His Word, for both constantly warn us against him. According to Jude 8-10, the Archangel Michael himself refrains from bringing a railing judgment against Satan. Let us then not be among those presumptuous ones who "rail at whatsoever things they know not, set at nought dominion, and rail at dignities." For the sake of our eternal salvation, let us be intelligent enough to understand both that we have a fearful enemy and that God has given us the victory over him.

## 2. THE CAREER OF SATAN

A fact unique in Scripture, the enemy's career is described to us from his creation until his place in eternity. Here is what we learn about his origin:

He is a *created being* (Ezek. 28:15).

He was *perfect* as created (Ezek. 28:12b, 15).

He once held a *very high position.* He was a (or, rather, *the*) "anointed cherub" in Eden, on God's holy mountain (Ezek. 28:13, 14). He was called by Jesus "the prince of this world" (John 14:13), and he affirms that all the power and glory of the kingdoms of earth have been given to him (Luke 4:6).

He *fell through pride* (Ezek. 28:16, 17), having sought, in his folly, to make himself equal with God and even to supplant Him (Isa. 14:13, 14).

He underwent *an initial judgment,* in which he was declared fallen. God said to him: ". . . Thou hast sinned: therefore have I cast thee as profane out of the mountain of God; and I have destroyed thee, O covering cherub, from the midst of the stones of fire" (Ezek. 28:16). Satan was denounced as having been the instigator of rebellion, the chief of the princes of this world of darkness (Eph. 2:2; 6:12). He is therefore deprived of the glorious position that he occupied in the light of the glory of God's presence.

A *second judgment,* much more terrible, was inflicted on him at the cross. Indeed, Christ "despoiled the principalities and the powers [Satanic powers]," and "he made a show of them openly, triumphing over them in it" (Col. 2:15). Jesus exclaimed, "Now is the judgment of this world: now shall the prince of this world be cast out" (John 12:31). The Lord, by His incarnation, partook of flesh and blood "that through death he might bring to nought him that had the power of death, that is, the devil" (Heb. 2:14). Thus it is that He crushed the serpent's head, at the moment when the serpent bruised His heel (Gen. 3:15). Satan is therefore, for all practical purposes, an already conquered foe; and all his victims who are washed in the blood of the cross escape his dominion.

But during the time of our testing, he can still *tempt us,* and he keeps in bondage those who continue in unbelief. He even has access to the heavenly places, right up to the very presence of God, to make accusations against us (Eph. 6:12; Job 1:6-12; Rev. 12:10). But this incomprehensible patience of God will soon come to an end.

A *third judgment* will cast him from heaven down to earth at the time of the great tribulation. "And there was war in heaven: Michael and his angels going forth to war with the dragon; and the dragon warred and his angels; and they prevailed not, neither was their place found any more in heaven. And the great dragon was cast down, the old serpent, he that is called the Devil and Satan, the deceiver of the whole world; he was cast down to the earth, and his angels were cast down with him . . . Now is come the salvation . . . for the accuser of our brethren is cast down, who accuseth them before our God day and night . . . Woe for the earth and for the sea: because the devil is gone down unto you, having great wrath, knowing that he hath but a short time" (Rev. 12:7-12). The worst horrors of the three and a half years of the reign of the Antichrist are, then, due to those last desperate outbursts of the powerless rage of the enemy.

By a *fourth judgment* the devil will be chained for a thousand years in the abyss (Rev. 20:1-3). Thus he will no longer be deceiving the nations during the Saviour's glorious reign on earth. Still, at the end of the thousand years, he will be released to tempt the men who had not yet had the freedom of choosing between God and him. A thousand years in prison will not have changed him, any more than a thousand years of bliss could transform human nature left to itself. The result of that last deception will still be immense and disconcerting. But it will be the end.

A *fifth and last judgment* will come upon the devil, when he is cast into the lake of fire and brimstone to be tormented day and night for ever and ever (Rev. 20:7-10). This fate has been long reserved for him, since it was expressly for him and his angels that the eternal fire was prepared (Matt. 25:41).

### 3. THE TACTICS OF THE ADVERSARY

As long as the enemy continues capable of harming us, the Scriptures put us on constant guard against him. Therefore it is imperative that we be acquainted with his methods of attack.

#### a. *The Tempter*

Fallen himself, Satan has no greater joy than to make others fall. Being without doubt the chief of the angels (the anointed cherub of Ezek. 28:14), he tempted *celestial spirits*. He thus became the prince of the demons, who also are called "his angels" (Matt. 12:24; Rev. 12:7).

The *first angel* also tempted and caused the fall of the *first men* (Gen. 3). What a triumph for him to have been able to depose the creation that God had just made in all its perfection! Then Satan tried relentlessly to bring the Son of God to do evil. After having tempted Him three times in the desert, he departed from Him "for a season" (Luke 4:1-13). If Jesus was tempted in all points even as we are, if He was tempted in the things that He suffered (thus infinitely more than we, Heb. 4:15; 2:18), we know very well that the enemy will not spare us either.

It is to believers that Peter wrote: "Be sober, be watchful: your adversary the devil, as a roaring lion, walketh about, seeking whom he may devour" (I Peter 5:8). Above all, the tempter will harass God's servants and the spiritual believers, as they are especially dangerous to him. He will tempt them right up to the end of their lives, because it would be a fine victory for him to ruin a testimony that had been faithful and strong up until then.

As for unbelievers, they are wholly the victims of Satan, since they are called "children of the devil" (I John 3:8-10). He has blinded their minds so that the light of the Gospel of the glory of Christ should not dawn upon them (II Cor. 4:4). It is he who deceives nations and who is leading the world to ruin (Rev. 20:3). No creature is immune to his attacks, but we cannot say that we have not been warned.

b. *The Evil One*

1). *"Deliver us from the evil one"* (Matt. 6:13). Although Satan's power is immense, it is broken for the one who puts his confidence in Christ. What we have to fear, then, is, above all, his subtlety, by means of which he tries to surprise us and to separate us from the Lord: "Put on the whole armor of God, that ye may be able to stand against the wiles of the devil" (Eph. 6:11). That subtlety is especially apparent in the best-known temptations:

*Eve* was tempted when she was alone. The serpent awakened her bodily appetites, her sense of taste and of beauty, her desire to learn. He began by a seemingly innocent question about God and His Word. Then, seeing that the woman was intrigued by this dangerous conversation, to doubt he added negation, calumny, and, finally, the undisguised invitation to pride and to rebellion (Gen. 3:1-5).

*Job* was tempted to doubt the love of God by the enemy who had sworn he would bring him to open blasphemy. That enemy made him lose his children, his goods, his servants, and his health. He destroyed his home and took from him his prosperity and his peace. Then he even made use of Job's wife to get him, in his despair, to curse God and to despise life (Job 1 and 2). In similar circumstances, how many others have not been able to discern the source of the attack and to resist it by faith!

*Jesus Christ* underwent temptations which at first seemed entirely natural: to satisfy the needs of His body after a very prolonged fast; to establish His Divinity by a dramatic miracle so as to assure Himself of immediate success; to take the promised throne, avoiding the cross (Luke 4:1-7). When Jesus spoke specifically of His sufferings, Peter, at the instigation of Satan, cried out: "Be it far from thee, Lord: this shall never be unto thee!" Indeed, how is it that a God of love would deliver up His only Son to torture? Now that is just what temptation is: to follow, not the thoughts of God, but those of man, and at last those of the enemy.

2). *The human instruments of the adversary.* One of the most terrible ruses of Satan is that of employing to tempt us those people that we would suspect the least of being his instruments. It is an elementary strategy in war to camouflage as well as possible traitors and fifth columnists.

*Eve,* given to Adam to be a help to him, became at the hands of the tempter the instrument of his fall (Gen. 2:18; 3:6).

*Job's wife,* who ought to have encouraged him in his trials, urged him to give up entirely (Job 2:9, 10).

*The prophets,* speaking by a lying spirit, succeeded in enticing King Ahab (I Kings 22:22).

*The relatives of Jesus* came to lay hold on Him to put an

end to His ministry, saying, "He is beside Himself!" (that is, He is crazy).

*The multitude,* satisfied by the multiplication of the loaves, wanted to take Jesus away to make Him a king. Those people were doubtless conniving with the *disciples,* since the Lord hastened to have the disciples go into the boat while He sent away the crowd (John 6:15 and Matt. 14:22). Many Christian leaders have succumbed to the temptation that Jesus overcame here: that is, success without the cross.

*Peter,* who had just made to Christ a magnificent proclamation of his faith, actually suggested to Him that He avoid that bloody death, the only possible means of salvation. He was given the answer: "Get thee behind me, Satan!" (Matt. 16:15-23).

*The Greeks,* who insisted on seeing Jesus, received no reply but this: "Except a grain of wheat fall into the earth and die, it abideth by itself . . . Now is my soul troubled; and what shall I say? Father, save me from this hour? But for this cause came I unto this hour . . . Now shall the prince of this world be cast out. And I, if I be lifted up from the earth, will draw all men unto myself. But this he said signifying by what manner of death he should die" (John 12:20-33). Christ had come for the salvation of the multitudes of both Gentiles and Jews; and the Greeks, in showing themselves so eager to receive Him before the cross, were renewing for Him the temptation of ruling over the nations apart from it. That is why His soul was so troubled and so desirous of strongly affirming both the necessity of His death and His imminent victory over the prince of this world.

c. *The Liar*

"He . . . standeth not in the truth, because there is no truth in him. When he speaketh a lie, he speaketh of his own: for he is *a liar, and the father thereof*" (John 8:44). Such men are false apostles, deceitful workers, fashioning themselves into apostles of Christ. And no marvel; for even *Satan fashioneth himself into an angel of light.* It is no great thing therefore if his ministers also fashion themselves as ministers of righteousness" (II Cor. 11:13-15).

The devil was formerly "the day-star, son of the morning" (Isa. 14:12). He fell for having determined to take the place of the Lord. And today he is still obsessed with the desire to imitate Him, to pose as God. The fallen angel would like, with this as his goal, to dress himself up in the cloak of his lost innocence. Being the father of lies, he excels in this work of constant deception (John 8).

He has at all times the *Word of God* in his mouth: it was his main topic of conversation with Eve (Gen. 3:1). He cited it very shrewdly to Jesus in the desert, as though he were preaching faith in God to Him in some such way as this: "Trust in Him; cast thyself down from the pinnacle of the temple, for the prophecies foretell that thou wilt do so."

We shall see that he pretends to make himself the defender of the *divine law* violated by sinners, on that basis daring to attack us even in the presence of the sovereign Judge. He persuaded the Jews that in effecting the death of Christ they would be avenging the honor of the one God and causing respect for His law, that Jesus had transgressed (John 8:44; 10:33; 19:7). According to the Lord's Word in John 16:2, men blinded by the enemy would come to believe that they were offering service to God when they killed true believers.

Saul of Tarsus, in his fanatical zeal for the Jewish law and traditions, was thus persuaded (Gal. 1:13, 14). And throughout the centuries, how many so-called Christian churches have similarly been impelled to make martyrs of God's children!

Moreover, how many times has Satan succeeded in making us take our own will to be the will of God. Indeed it is the quintessence of pride that persuades us that our own desires are the expression of absolute wisdom and truth. Let us remember in regard to this the word addressed to the prince of Tyre, who is a type of Satan: ". . . Thy heart is lifted up, and thou hast said, I am a god ... thou art man, and not God, though thou didst set thy heart as *the heart of God"* (Ezek. 28:2).

The enemy excels even in giving blinded men a zeal for God, just as long as that zeal is empty and devoid of knowledge (Rom. 10:2, 3). He gets them to perform many *works,* but "dead" works, since they are produced by unregenerate individuals (Heb. 9:14). He puts into their hearts an enormous love for outcasts, making them think only of the body rather than of their eternal salvation. He says to some "This is *the truth!"* and he flings them into some pernicious and fanatical sect. In adding slightly to the Gospel "better to honor the law" (by circumcision or to return to obsolete ordinances), he separates men from Christ and makes them fall from grace (Gal. 5:2-4).

Under the pretext of exalting the love of God, he confidently denied perdition: "Ye shall not surely die, for God doth know that ... ye shall be as God ..." (Gen. 3:5). With the same argument, he succeeds today in making people believe that there is no hell and that all the impenitent, including himself, will be saved "so that God's triumph may be truly complete."

Our world, given over to Satan, is manifestly under the insignia of a lie. Modern propaganda is always perfecting the art of deceiving the masses with the most scientific and efficacious means: by slogans, billboards, the press, statistics, films, radio, and television. Lying is common at home, in political life, in business, and in the courts. There is even deception in religion when a false Gospel is preached, in which traffic is made of holy things.

The masterpiece of lies and camouflage will be the appearance of the Antichrist accompanied by the false prophet. By the power of Satan this individual will do great miracles and will persuade a multitude of people—Jews and Gentiles alike—that he is the true Christ. He will require men to wor-

ship him and will induce them to adore the devil himself (II
Thess. 2:3, 4, 9; Rev. 13:4, 8). We see again in this the supreme ambition which has always characterized the enemy
from the beginning: to get himself accepted, not only as an
angel of light, but as one like unto the Most High (Isa.
14:14). An unheard-of thing, the god of this world (II Cor.
4:4) will succeed once and for a short time in persuading
misguided humanity that he is the true God. He will then
have come to the end of his rope, the mystery of iniquity will
have been fully accomplished, and judgment, so long delayed,
will break over his head.

d. *The Accuser*

Glimpsing the final triumph, John cried out: "Now is
come the salvation, and the power, and the kingdom of our
God, and the authority of his Christ: for the *accuser* of our
brethren is cast down, who accuseth them before our God
day and night" (Rev. 12:10).

At the *tribunal of God,* the first and the chief of sinners pre-
sumes, with unparalleled audacity, to pose as defender of the
law violated by our transgressions. On that basis he demands
that the sovereign Judge vindicate His holiness and His
righteousness. For example, Satan claimed to unmask what
there was of self-interest and hypocrisy in the piety of Job
(1:9-11). In the scene recorded in Zechariah 3:1-7, he made
accusations against *Joshua,* the high priest who appeared in
the presence of God in filthy garments—whereas the law required total purity of such a personnage. Satan's charges are,
then, only too well founded; it is the same in regard to us
when he makes a point of our disobediences and our defilement. On that basis, Joshua, in the same position as we are,
would certainly have been justly condemned. But Zechariah
adds: "And Jehovah said unto Satan, Jehovah rebuke thee, O
Satan; yea, Jehovah that hath chosen Jerusalem rebuke thee:
is not this a brand plucked out of the fire?" That is to say that
God, far from condemning us on the grounds of the law,

saves us on the grounds of election and grace, snatching us as
brands from the fire of the judgment we merit. The angel
of the Lord, here representing Jesus, our Advocate (I John
2:1) intervenes, saying: "Take the filthy garments from off
him . . . Behold, I have caused thine iniquity to pass from
thee, and I will clothe thee with rich apparel. And I said, Let
them set a clean mitre [turban] upon his head!" (This is what
was required, according to Exod. 28:36-38 and 29:6.) That
means that Jesus alone, our omnipotent intercessor, can reduce to silence the accuser, for He fulfilled the law, avenged
the divine justice, and expiated all our iniquities. And when
we are harassed by the adversary, the Lord says to us what He
said to Peter: "Satan asked to have you, that he might sift you
as wheat: but I made supplication for thee, that thy faith fail
not (Luke 22:31, 32).

It is frequently at the *tribunal of our conscience* that
Satan torments us with his accusations. What he says is often
only too true: he reminds us of all the sins we have committed, and he would like to persuade us that there is no
longer any hope for us. Moreover, we understand his tactics:
before our fall he assures us that the disobedience involved
will be slight and inconsequential; then after our succumb-
ing, he exaggerates out of all proportion that same sin as if
it could never be pardoned. That is the way he persuades
many Christians, after a momentary slip, that they have
committed the unpardonable sin. But a sinner guilty before
God and men is not to abandon himself to discouragement
or to an excess of sorrow (II Cor. 2:6-11). "Godly sorrow
worketh repentance unto salvation, a repentance which
bringeth no regret: but the sorrow of the world worketh
death [and even death by suicide]" (II Cor. 7:9, 10). If the
offender is remorseful over his sin and longs for the pardon
and grace of God, let him go to Him without fear: he has
not committed the unpardonable sin, which consists of an
obstinate refusal of pardon. (See our book on *The Person*

*and Work of the Holy Spirit, p.* 58.) The blood of Christ can thoroughly purify anyone who sincerely confesses his faults, and it will even cleanse the conscience from dead works (I John 1:7-2:2; 3:20, 21; Heb. 9:14).

Finally, it is before the *tribunal of public opinion* that the enemy flaunts our smallest peccadilloes. We ought to remember more often and to ponder Paul's words: "I desire therefore that the younger widows marry, bear children, rule the household, *give no occasion to the adversary for railing:* for already some are turned aside after Satan" (I Tim. 5:14, 15). The apostle gives more advice still for practical holiness, addressing himself to aged men, to women, to young people, and to Titus himself, "that the word of God be not blasphemed . . . *that he that is of the contrary part may be ashamed, having no evil thing to say of us"* (Titus 2:5, 8).

By his crime David had given the enemies of the Lord occasion to blaspheme (II Sam. 12:14). And the unbelieving Jews were dishonoring God's name among the Gentiles (Rom. 2:24). Indeed, who is more bent on shouting from the housetops the scandals of Christians, adding plenty of calumnies, than is our greatest enemy? Let us then be on our guard not to give him any leeway for such action.

e. *The Murderer*

Jesus said to the Jews: ". . . Ye seek to kill me . . . Ye are of your father the devil, and the lusts of your father it is your will to do. He was a murderer from the beginning . . ." (John 8:37, 44).

God the Creator and the good Shepherd give life. Satan's only ambition is to slaughter life and to destroy it (John 10:10). He has showed that bloodthirsty rage from the beginning.

*Abel* was innocent; but Cain, being of the evil one, killed him. The fall of Adam and Eve was not, then, so insignificant, as its first result was a fratricide. Since then, hatred has been the rudiment of all murders and of all wars (I John 3:

12, 15). Satan knew that of the woman's line would be born that One who would bruise his head (Gen. 3:15). Doubtless, in doing away with Abel he was trying, if not to destroy the Messiah Himself, at least to break the first link of the chain that could lead to Him.

*The first-born boys of Israel* were sought out in Egypt by Pharaoh, who wanted to kill them all (Exod. 1:22). In this king can be seen a type of Satan, the prince of this world, who severely oppresses the people of God. At any rate, the hatred of the enemy had for a goal the suppression of the chosen people to hinder them from giving to the world its Deliverer.

*Athaliah,* daughter of the wicked Jezebel, vowed in a moment of frenzy to make the whole royal race perish (II Kings 11:1-3). Once more the devil was aiming at the line which would end in the Messiah, since the promise of that line had been made to David. It was by a miracle that Joash, still a baby, was saved.

In the time of *Esther,* Haman thought he could massacre the whole Jewish race in one day (Esther 3:13). The intervention of the queen thwarted this diabolical plan, the instigator—always the same—being easily identifiable.

To harm *Job,* Satan caused death-dealing catastrophes: he made fire fall from heaven on Job's sheep and on his servants; then he stirred up a great wind, which brought the house down on his sons (Job 1:12, 16, 19).

Scarcely was *Jesus* born than Herod, thinking he could destroy Him, had all the little children of Bethlehem killed (Matt. 2:16).

After the Lord began His ministry to Nazareth, His countrymen tried to throw Him down headlong from the brow of the hill (Luke 4:29); and John recounts to us how many times the Jews manifested their desire to kill Him, because they could not endure hearing Him affirm His Divinity (5:18; 8:59; 10:31). The resurrection of Lazarus made them beside themselves and provoked their determination to do away with Christ and with Lazarus too (John 11:53; 12:10).

Finally the devil attained his goal when the Romans joined in with Jesus' enemies to crucify Him (John 19:15, 16). The Lord thus had good reason to say that the enemy is a murderer from the beginning.

Satan is shown as a murderer down through history, and he will continue to be one to the end. The false religion that he inspires is always one that persecutes and causes bloodshed. In killing believers his well-taught followers think they are doing God service (John 16:2). We have illustrations of this in the martyrdom of Stephen and of James (Acts 7:58 and 12:1-3), then in the innumerable victims of the Inquisition, the "auto-da-fés" (acts of faith!), and in the ancient and modern persecutions. All the suicides and all the wars are his doing, and one trembles at the thought of the atomic carnage that humanity will be capable of in the last days, when it is wholly given over to Satan and to his false Christ. The prince of this world, the tempter, the evil one, the liar, and the murderer can truly boast of having transformed into his sinister image the creation, all of which writhes under his power (I John 5:19). As for us, we have learned enough about all this not to let him get any advantage over us, for we are not ignorant of his devices (II Cor. 2:11).

## 4. GIVEN OVER TO SATAN

What is the meaning of the disturbing expression that Paul uses in two different places: "To deliver such a one [the incestuous man of Corinth] unto Satan for the destruction of the flesh, that the spirit may be saved in the day of the Lord Jesus" (I Cor. 5:5)? "Some . . . made shipwreck concerning the faith: of whom is Hymenaeus and Alexander; whom I delivered unto Satan, that they might be taught not to blaspheme" (I Tim. 1:19, 20).

In the first instance, it is a question of a Christian who has gone astray. Paul had sufficient authority and discernment to give this man over to Satan, the same thing that had happened to Job long before. The enemy was to be allowed to touch his body so that his spirit might be saved for all eternity. It is a terrible thing to know that God sometimes has to go to such lengths with Christians who refuse to judge themselves (I Cor. 11:30-32).

In the second case, the men had made shipwreck in regard to the faith. They were therefore not believers, and Paul delivered them to Satan "that they might be taught not to blaspheme." They remind us of Elymas, the sorcerer, whom Paul treated as a son of the devil and whom he made blind so that he could not oppose the Gospel (Acts 13:8-11).

Satan, then, in spite of himself, can be a means of judgment, to bring a believer back to the right way or to bring to an end the blasphemies of the wicked. Thus it is that even the wrath of the enemy can turn out to the praise of God. But what an awful thing it is to fall into the hands of such a villain! In any case, let us have pity on his victims and seek in all gentleness to restore them "if peradventure God may give them repentance unto the knowledge of the truth, and they may recover themselves out of the snare of the devil, having been taken captive by him unto his will (II Tim. 2:25, 26).

The adversary paces around us constantly in order to tempt us. All he asks is that we let him in (Eph. 4:27). And all that is needed for that is one guilty thought in which we delight, one wrong feeling that is not judged and forsaken, or one forbidden act or habit. The sin par excellence that Satan drives us to is the one that caused his own fall: pride and the spirit of independence of the Lord. Paul writes regarding the choice of a servant of God: "Not a novice, lest being puffed up he fall into the condemnation of the devil [that is, into the judgment pronounced on the enemy and his pride]" (I Tim. 3:6, 7). So we are duly warned. What remains for consideration is how we can keep out of the clutches of such a dangerous adversary.

## 5. DELIVERED FROM SATAN

We have seen that since the cross the devil is a conquered foe. Jesus was anticipating that victory when He said to His disciples, as they were rejoicing because even the demons were subject to them in His name: "I beheld Satan fallen as lightning from heaven. Behold, I have given you authority to tread upon serpents and scorpions . . . and nothing shall in any wise hurt you" (Luke 10:17-19).

It is by the incarnation of Christ and by His atoning death that the power of the enemy has been broken: He partook of flesh and blood "that through death he might bring to nought [might render impotent] him that had the power of death, that is, the devil; and might deliver all them who through fear of death were all their lifetime subject to bondage" (Heb. 2:14, 15). "Having despoiled the principalities and the powers, he made a show of them openly, triumphing over them in it" (Col. 2:15). "Giving thanks unto the Father . . . who delivered us out of the power of darkness, and translated us into the kingdom of the Son of his love" (Col. 1:12, 13).

Daily deliverance comes by obedience and faith: "Be subject therefore unto God; but resist the devil; and he will flee from you" (James 4:7). "Be sober, be watchful: your adversary the devil, as a roaring lion, walketh about, seeking whom he may devour: whom withstand stedfast in your faith, knowing that the same sufferings are accomplished in your brethren who are in the world" (I Peter 5:8, 9).

Since the fall of Lucifer himself came about by his proudly pitting his own will against God's, the way for us to escape from all his traps is to put ourselves resolutely in the way of a full submission to the Lord. Let us imitate Jesus, who triumphed over the severest of temptations by repeating: "Not as I will, but as thou wilt" (Matt. 26:39).

Moreover, let us always recognize the presence and power of the Holy Spirit, who can successfully undertake any offensive. "When the adversary shall come in like a flood, the Spirit of Jehovah will lift up a standard against him" (Isa. 59:19). "Ye are of God, my little children, and have overcome them: because greater is he that is in you than he that is in the world . . . the devil sinneth from the beginning. To this end was the Son of God manifested, that he might destroy the works of the devil" (I John 4:4; 3:8).

Let us never forget either that Satan is a created being. However strong he may be, he is not omnipresent, omnipotent, or omniscient. God, still his Master, has set limits beyond which he cannot go. Twice He informed Satan of the extent he could go to in attacking Job (1:12; 2:6). Satan could do nothing against Jesus Himself, as long as His hour had not yet come. Likewise not a hair of our heads can fall without God's permission. Like Paul we can know with confidence that neither angels, nor principalities (infernal powers) nor any other creature (and therefore not Satan either) shall be able to separate us from the love of God, which is in Christ Jesus our Lord (Rom. 8:38, 39).

That is why we are boldly to repulse the enemy by using the armor provided for us. "They overcame him because of the blood of the Lamb, and because of the word of their testimony" (Rev. 12:11). "Put on the whole armor of God, that ye may be able to stand against the wiles of the devil . . . Stand therefore, having girded your loins with truth, and having put on the breastplate of righteousness, and having shod your feet with the preparation of the gospel of peace; withal taking up the shield of faith, wherewith ye shall be able to quench all the fiery darts of the evil one. And take the helmet of salvation, and the sword of the Spirit, which is the word of God: with all prayer and supplication praying at all seasons in the Spirit . . . and on my behalf . . ." (Eph. 6:11-19).

Let us, like our Lord, know how to cut short the adversary's insinuations, replying to him: "It is written . . . again it is written . . ."! (Matt. 4:4, 7, 10). Let us always take as our example Jesus Christ, who fasted and prayed during the hours and days of His special temptations (eg. Matt. 4:1, 2) and who said to the disciples when they were astonished at not being able to cast out a devil: "Because of your little faith . . . This kind goeth not out, save by prayer and fasting" (Matt. 17:19, 21).

Such a seeking of the will of God will enable us increasingly to say, as Jesus did: "The prince of the world cometh, and he hath nothing in me" (John 14:30). If we at the same time keep ourselves hidden in Jesus Christ, the enemy will no more have any hold on us. "He that was begotten of God keepeth himself, and the evil one toucheth him not . . . I write unto you, young men, because ye . . . have overcome the evil one . . . I have written unto you, young men, because ye are strong, and the word of God abideth in you, and ye have overcome the evil one" (I John 5:18; 2:13, 14).

As for the final triumph, let us know how to take possession of it by faith, since it is certain and imminent: "The God of peace shall bruise Satan under your feet shortly" (Rom. 16:20).

## Chapter VIII

# THE DEMONS

### 1. ORIGIN AND FALL OF THE DEMONS

WHAT WE HAVE SAID of the origin of Satan applies equally to that of the demons. They were heavenly spirits in the first place, created perfect for the service of God. Then the revolt of Lucifer, the anointed cherub, fascinated and seduced them. They became the angels of whom Jude speaks who "kept not their own principality, but left their proper habitation" (vs. 6). Peter also calls them the angels that sinned (II Peter 2:4).

It is difficult to say just when this fall of the angels took place; at any rate, it was between the fall of Satan and the creation of man. Some put it between verses 1 and 2 of Genesis 1. According to this view God first created everything perfect. After the fall of the angels and the first judgment on Satan, the prince of this world, the earth became "without form and void." In the six days of Genesis 1, God reorganized our planet in view of the appearance of man. This interpretation explains why, among the animals, combats, suffering, and death—signs of an already existent disorder—preceded the fall of Adam and Eve. It has been observed, moreover, that the only other passage containing the expression "without form and void" (Jer. 4:23-26) also depicts the ravages produced by a judgment. Thus the chaos spoken of in Genesis 1:2 would not have been the result of a natural evolution.

However that may be, the fall of the demons shows that the Lord could not trust heavenly spirits. From this come the sad words from the book of Job: "He putteth no trust in his servants [in heaven]; and his angels he chargeth with folly . . . he putteth no trust in his holy ones; yea, the heavens are not clean in his sight: how much less one that is abominable and corrupt, a man . . ."! (Job 4:18; 15:15, 16).

## 2. ARE THE DEMONS NUMEROUS?

If there are myriads of faithful angels, the demons are also numerous, it would appear. A legion of evil spirits took possession of a single man (Mark 5:9). John shows us that Satan and his angels consider themselves powerful enough to fight openly against Michael and his angels (Rev. 12:7). According to this same passage, the tail of the great dragon—a picture of the devil—"draweth the third part of the stars of heaven, and did cast them to the earth" (vs. 4). One wonders if that signifies a third of the angels revolting, at the instigation of Satan.

One thing is sure. The Bible states in many places not only the existence, but also the power and the incessant activity of the demons. It would be senseless of us not to pay attention to its warnings.

## 3. THE KINGDOM OF DARKNESS

Like the angels, the demons have their hierarchy and their organization.

The Bible speaks of Satan and "his angels" (Rev. 12:9; Matt. 25:41) just as it says that Michael, the archangel, commands the heavenly hosts (Jude 9; Rev. 12:7). He is likewise "prince of the demons" (Matt. 9:34).

Among the rebellious angels there are what Paul calls the "principalities . . . the powers . . . the world-rulers of this darkness . . . the spiritual hosts of wickedness in the heavenly places" (Eph. 6:12). These "dignities" are now fallen; but it would be madness on our part to despise them, when the faithful angels themselves do not bring against them any railing judgment (Jude 8; II Peter 2:11). This judgment belongs to God alone. As there is a hierarchy among the fallen angels, there are also degrees in the strength of their wickedness. The spirit chased out of his house took with him seven other spirits more wicked than he, to take possession of it again. And Jesus spoke of a sort of demon that does not go out except as a result of prayer and fasting (Matt. 17:21).

The assemblage of diabolical spirits makes up the kingdom of "the prince of the powers of the air" and of "the power of darkness" (Eph. 2:2 and Col. 1:13). Set up by Jesus as against the kingdom of God, this "kingdom of Satan" is not divided against itself; and that is why its strength is so formidable. To conquer it, the Son of God first had to bind up its head, "the strong man," by the power of the Holy Ghost (Matt. 12:24-29) and by His own death on the cross (Heb. 2:14).

4. THE STRUGGLE OF THE DEMONS AGAINST GOD

Ever since Satan lifted the standard of revolt, his angels have been carrying on, with him, a fight to the finish against the Lord.

Daniel reveals to us that fearful powers are striving to impede the action of the faithful angels, even of the most glorious of them. A heavenly messenger said to the prophet: "The prince [Satanic] of the kingdom of Persia withstood me one and twenty days; but, lo, Michael, one of the chief princes, came to help me . . . Now I am come to make thee understand what shall befall thy people in the latter days . . . Now will I return to fight with the prince of Persia; and when I go forth, lo, the prince of Greece [Javan] shall come . . . There is none that holdeth with me against these, but Michael your prince" (Dan. 10:13, 14, 20, 21). The true conflict, then, takes place primarily on the spiritual plane, in the invisible sphere which Paul calls "the heavenly places": "Our wrestling is not against flesh and blood, but against . . . the spiritual hosts of wickedness in the heavenly places" (Eph. 6:12). What goes on in that higher sphere has repercussions down here, and vice versa. Being no longer able to touch the glorified Lord, the demons furiously attack His body, which is the Church. And when the believers carry away a victory, there are consequential effects of it even in the "heavenly places," where the adversary is forced to retreat.

The first coming of Christ to the earth was the signal for a general counter-offensive on the part of the forces of hell. The Gospels give the impression that a multitude of evil spirits had gotten together in Palestine to oppose the Savior's ministry and to turn men's attention to themselves. There was indeed much at stake. After having unsuccessfully tempted Jesus in the wilderness, Satan, by mobilizing all his allies, tried to set up an obstacle before Him. This diabolical frenzy went on right up to the pages in the book of the Acts (see 5:16; 8:7; and 16:16) and far beyond.

Prophecy makes plain that the last days will also see the infernal powers redoubling their efforts: Satan and his angels will fight one last time in heaven against Michael and his angels; then they will be precipitated together down to the earth. In regard to this, John cried out: "Woe for the earth and for the sea: because the devil is gone down unto you, having great wrath, knowing that he hath but a short time" (Rev. 12:12). Paul says this: "The Spirit saith expressly, that in later times some shall fall away from the faith, giving heed to seducing spirits and doctrines of demons, through the hypocrisy of men that speak lies . . ." (I Tim. 4: 1, 2).

Through the Antichrist and the false prophet, the power of Satan will perform "all power and signs and lying wonders, and with all deceit of unrighteousness . . ." (II Thess. 2:9, 10). See also Rev. 13:2b, and 14 and 15. At the time of her judgment the great Babylon will become "a habitation of demons, and a hold of every unclean spirit" (Rev. 18:2).

As the glorious appearing of Jesus Christ approaches, the emissaries of hell will do their utmost to reunite the armies of the entire world in Palestine, in the very place where the Lord is to triumph: "They are spirits of demons, working signs; which go forth unto the kings of the whole world, to gather them together unto the war of the great day of God, the Almighty . . . and they gathered them together into the place which is called in Hebrew Har-Magedon [or Ar-Magedon]" (Rev. 16:14, 16). But the final victory of the Lord over all His united enemies will be only the greater for that.

One can wonder how it is that the Lord has such an extended patience with the demons and with Satan. It is simply that He is the same with them as He is with us. When the destruction of the Amorites in Canaan was already certain, God still granted them a delay of four hundred years (from Abraham to Joshua), for their iniquity was "not yet full" (Gen. 15:16). The tares, as well as the wheat, are to ripen in view of the harvest (Matt. 13:30). The Antichrist will appear only "in his own season," when the total depravity of the race will set judgment in motion (II Thess. 2:6). Satan and his angels likewise have before them a lapse of time, brief from the point of view of God, though long from that of men, which will permit their iniquity to reveal itself fully and then will provoke the inescapable manifestation of the Divine justice.

It is evident that God, knowing all things, could have immediately crushed His adversaries by force. But His glory would not have shone forth in the same way. Satan accused God of being a tyrant and of merely obtaining from His creatures a service based on fear and self-interest (Job 1:9). To that God answered by the incarnation and the sufferings of His Son, and by the miracle of bringing into the church what had been only rebellious sinners. After such a demonstration of holiness and love, the Lord, in a manner worthy of His Person, will be able to manifest His power by throwing Satan and his demons into the lake of fire.

## 5. THE STRUGGLE OF THE DEMONS AGAINST MEN

Unable to reach the Lord of glory, the evil spirits make men their favorite target. They act toward them in many different ways and with all their strength second the work of the great tempter.

### a. *Demonic influence*

It is certain that all sinners are subjected to demonic influence, since all unregenerate men are sons of the devil (John 8:44; I John 3:8, 10). If they refuse in repentance and faith to let God snatch them away from this tyrant, they put themselves increasingly under his sway. What Paul hopes is that . . . the enemies of the Gospel, in a "return to soberness," will "recover themselves out of the snare of the devil, having been taken captive by him unto his will" (II Tim. 2:25, 26).

Without any doubt, this is the spirit of evil "that now worketh in the sons of disobedience" (Eph. 2:2). To drive out this evil spirit it is not enough to act as did the scribes and Pharisees to whom Jesus addressed Himself in Matthew 12:38, 43-45. Sensing the impurity of their hearts, they sought to chase it out by their own efforts, their religion, and their rites, thus doing their utmost to sweep and garnish their house. But this house remained empty, since Christ had been made unwelcome in it. Unable alone to resist the evil powers, they saw demons seven times more numerous invade their souls and make them more sinful and more miserable than before. Those Jews, at first self-righteous and strict observers of the law, rapidly and in spite of themselves became men full of pride, hypocrites, hardened sinners, and then finally murderers of the Son of God. It is the same for any sinner, who cannot, in spite of his best efforts, keep his house empty: either his heart will be inhabited by the Lord, who desires to make it His temple; or the individual will increasingly become the plaything of the enemy.

b. *Possession*

The Bible shows us by many examples that evil spirits are literally capable of taking complete possession of the sinner who gives himself up to them. The experience of *Judas* indicates the steps that can lead to such a possession. This man was one of the twelve and was certainly chosen by the Lord, as were his comrades, because of his piety and his seriousness. The common purse had been entrusted to him, a mark of confidence (John 13:29). Then, being inclined to cupidity and even to theft, he began to appropriate what had been put into it. That is why he felt so disturbed about the loss of those three hundred deniers spent for the perfume that Mary poured on Jesus (John 12:5, 6). Then the devil insinuated into the heart of Judas the plan of betraying Jesus, for a miserable sum of money (John 13:2). The unhappy disciple resisted all the warnings and all the appeals of the Lord during the Last Supper, and we read about him these terrible words: "After the sop [which revealed him as the betrayer] then entered Satan into him" (John 13:27; Luke 22:3-6). He was thereafter capable of anything: not only did he deliver his Lord to death, but he dared to identify Him by a kiss in the obscurity of the garden (Matt. 26:48, 49). Then, when an overdue repentance drove him to despair, he committed suicide (Matt. 27:3-5). This is the kind of treatment given his victims by the one who is a liar and a murderer from the beginning.

The most tragic word regarding Judas was pronounced by Jesus: "Did not I choose you, the twelve, and one of you *is* a devil!" (John 6:70). This is the frightful culmination of possession: it is not simply that the man *has* a *demon,* but that he *is* a *devil!* The one who believes in Jesus receives the divine nature and becomes like the Lord (II Peter 1:4; I John 3:2). For the impenitent, there is a transformation in the

wrong way, which makes him like his father, the devil. The
sheep and the goats that are to be separated by the judgment
are not of the same species. And the Lord will say of those
on His left: "Depart from me, ye cursed, into the eternal
fire which is prepared for the devil and his angels" (Matt.
25:41). The impenitent goes away then to perdition for
having chosen to give himself over to Satan and to become
entirely one of his.

A propos of possession, it seems that a demon, deprived of a
body, has a wild desire to take possession of some being,
through whom it can find a new means of satisfying its pas-
sions. Such spirits are often called *impure* (Mark 1:23; 3:11;
5:2; 7:25, etc.) A curious passage, Jude 6 and 7, speaks of
"angels that kept not their own principality, but left their
proper habitation" and of "Sodom and Gomorrah, and the
cities about them, having in like manner with these given
themselves over to fornication and gone after strange flesh."
One might wonder if this text is not akin to the passage in
Genesis 6:1-4, already cited, relative to the union of the "sons
of God" and the "daughters of men" (p. 109). Even if we
believe that this refers to a marriage of the descendants of
Seth to the daughters of Cain, we can well suppose that the
demons were in the picture in some way or other. It is very
possible that evil spirits, incapable of any real incarnation,
but avid to possess bodies, directly drove the men at the
time of the flood, and later the men of Sodom, to uncleanness
and to sins against nature.

Let us add further that the adjective "unclean" given to
evil spirits can have a more general meaning and can refer
to their whole nature, which is profoundly sinful.

This frenzy for possession is likewise manifested by the
legion of demons that were cast out of the demoniac of
Gadara. They fervently begged Jesus not to command them
to go into the abyss, but begged Him to permit them to enter

into the swine, a plea which the Lord allowed (Luke 8: 31, 32).

The Scriptures tell us that there is no peace for the wicked (Isa. 57:21). There is still less peace for the demons, proof of which lies in their feverish agitation. "But the unclean spirit, when he is gone out of the man, passeth through waterless places, seeking rest, and findeth it not. Then he saith, I will return into my house whence I came out" (Matt. 12: 43, 44).

All this explains why the calling on the spirits by the spiritists has so often and so easily resulted in true demon possession. We have just seen how the demons lie in wait for the hearts and bodies that will give themselves over to them. There is nothing more dangerous than the state of inertia and expectancy on the part of those who imprudently wish to get in contact with them. May we be forgiven for inserting here a warning in regard to which we do not want to be misunderstood. It is absolutely certain that some meetings where people wait for external manifestations of the Holy Spirit have been troubled by disorders which have not come from God. Have not these unfortunate situations arisen because the neophyte has often been given this advice: "Make yourself passive; let yourself go; let your tongue hang loose; you are to have the experience, cost what it may"? This attitude, which amounts to a carnal abdication without discernment (much different from a completely conscious and spiritual abandonment to the will of God) has in some cases facilitated the invasion of evil spirits. Thus have come about not only disorders, but also true cases of obsession or even of possession, in people who have naively believed that they were doing nothing but seeking the Holy Spirit. We have personally seen several examples of this. This must not keep us from aspiring to the gifts of the Spirit—quite the contrary—as long as this is according to the will of God. His will may be different for each one of us, but it always is char-

acterized by order, peace, and propriety (I Cor. 12:11; 14:
33, 40).

One disturbing question is this: one might wonder whether
there is a limit to demon possession. The Scriptures affirm
that Jesus drove seven demons out of Mary Magdalene (Luke
8:2). The demoniac of Gadara had several demons in him,
actually a legion (Luke 8:30). We have already spoken of
the man with the swept and emptied house, in which eight
spirits came to establish themselves by force (Matt. 12:43-45).
Peter said to Ananias: "Ananias, why hath Satan filled thy
heart to lie to the Holy Spirit . . .?" (Acts 5:3).

The Antichrist will be the extreme example of a man
wholly delivered to Satan. The devil will, in return, grant
him "his power, and his throne, and great authority" (Rev.
13:2). That man will accept at so great a price the offer of
universal domination that Jesus refused when He was
tempted in the wilderness. Thus, filled with diabolical
strength, the Antichrist will be able to work many lying
wonders and to lead astray all those who perish for having
resisted the truth (II Thess. 2:9, 10). Those close to Hitler
have often recounted that he used to give the impression of
being a man possessed. The great ruler whose universal
reign seems imminent will be even more possessed.

Let us repeat that the key to all this serious problem of
possession is given us in these two very simple and concise
admonitions: "Neither give place to the devil!" (Eph. 4:
27). "But be filled with the Spirit" (Eph. 5:18).

c. *Certain illnesses*

All illnesses are not directly the result of sin (for example,
that of the man born blind, recorded in John 9:2, 3) and
cannot in every case be attributed to a Satanic intervention.
But it is still true that the Scriptures several times establish
a connection between some illnesses or physical infirmities
and the activity of demons.

Job's boils were inflicted by Satan with God's permission

(2:6, 7) . To those who reproached Him for healing on the Sabbath Day, Jesus answered: "Ought not this woman . . . whom Satan had bound, lo, these eighteen years, to have been loosed from this bond . . .?" (Luke 13:16) . Peter spoke to the Gentiles gathered in the house of Cornelius of "Jesus of Nazareth . . . who went about . . . healing all that were oppressed of the devil" (Acts 10:38) . Paul called his "thorn in the flesh" a "messenger of Satan to buffet me, that I should not be exalted overmuch" (II Cor. 12:7) .

According to the Gospels, some demon possessions involved particular maladies. A demoniac was dumb and, when delivered, began to speak (Matt. 9:32, 33) . Another was both blind and dumb (Matt. 12:22) . The daughter of the Canaanitish woman was "grievously vexed with a demon," but the nature of her suffering is not told us (Matt. 15:22) . The boy that Jesus healed after the Transfiguration was beside himself and had "a dumb spirit"; in his sudden attacks (resembling what is now known as epilepsy) , he would fall into the fire or the water, roll on the ground, foam at the mouth, shriek, grind his teeth, stiffen out, and fall down completely exhausted. (See the three accounts, in Matt. 17:15, Mark 9: 17-26, and Luke 9:39-42.)

At other times it was a question of a true dementia. The two demoniacs of Matthew 8:28 dwelt in the tombs and were so furious that no one dared go near them. The one that Mark tells about in particular could not be bound, even with a chain. "He had been bound with fetters and chains, and the chains had been rent asunder by him, and the fetters broken in pieces: and no man had strength to tame him. And always, night and day, in the tombs and in the mountains, he was crying out, and cutting himself with stones" (Mark 5:3-5) . Our insane asylums have cases just like this, who have to be put in strait jackets and padded cells. I am obviously not at all in a position to speak scientifically about insanity. But I shall never forget what I once saw in an exposition of drawings made by the insane. Many of them had to do with religious subjects, most of them being unbalanced and terrifying representations. And there is certainly one form of insanity characterized by religious madness. What a subject for a Christian psychiatrist!

d. *The work of seduction*

There is a strange passage in I Kings 22:19-23. King Ahab, hardened by sin, refused the warnings of the prophet Micaiah and preferred the flattering words of the false prophets. Where did these false prophets get their unanimity and their self-confidence? From a direct intervention of evil spirits. Micaiah said: "I saw Jehovah sitting on his throne, and all the host of heaven standing by him . . . And Jehovah said, "Who shall entice Ahab, that he may go up and fall at Ramoth-gilead? And one said on this manner; and another said on that manner. And there came forth a spirit, and stood before Jehovah, and said, I will entice him. And Jehovah said unto him, Wherewith? And he said, I will go forth, and will be a lying spirit in the mouth of all his prophets. And he said, Thou shalt entice him, and shalt prevail also: go forth, and do so!"

The fact that God permits such an evil power to act troubles us at first. But in the case of Ahab, let us recognize that the Lord was solemnly warning the king at the same time. The latter knew very well then what he was choosing. Paul wrote of practically the same thing when he said, in the passage already mentioned in regard to the Antichrist, that his appearing would be "with all power and signs and lying wonders, and with all deceit of unrighteousness for them that perish; because they received not the love of the truth, that they might be saved. And for this cause God sendeth them a working of error, that they should believe a lie: that they all might be judged who believed not the truth, but had pleasure in unrighteousness" (II Thess. 2:9-12) .

The seduction by the evil spirits does not so much drive

men to impurity and to guilty acts. It lets loose a terrible power of error and of lies. According to Paul, men in the last days will give heed to "seducing spirits and doctrines of demons, through the hypocrisy of men, that speak lies, forbidding to marry, and commanding to abstain from meats which God created to be received with thanksgiving . . ." (I Tim. 4:1-3). Man can be neither saved nor set free apart from the truth of God. The demons therefore will make every effort to turn him at any cost from the divine revelation and to confront him with false doctrines, which make salvation impossible. The Lord, in Revelation 2:24, appeals to those in Thyatira who have not accepted this pernicious teaching and who have not known "the deep things of Satan." Paul had already warned us that the worship of idols (and of statues) is really a "communion with demons" and a participation at their table (I Cor. 10:19-22). By what masterpieces of chicanery do evil spirits thus prey on naive souls who have been delivered over to them without defense by their superstition and error!

Another great means of deception is divination by all the resources of occultism. Men desire not only to hear pleasant things, but also at any cost to lift the veil of the future. In speaking of spiritualism we mentioned above how dangerous this pursuit is. Let us also remember the case of the maid of Philippi "having a spirit of divination . . . who brought her masters much gain by soothsaying" (Acts 16:16). This kind of business is still very lucrative today if we can believe the advertisements in our newspapers. It is evident that the demons, without being omniscient, have a knowledge superior to ours. But since they use that knowledge for our destruction, let us beware about consulting them concerning anything at all.

    e. *Direct attacks*

When Satan and his angels cannot succeed in making Christians stumble by subtlety, they have recourse to violence.

"Fear not the things which thou art about to suffer: behold, the devil is about to cast some of you into prison, that ye may be tried . . . Be thou faithful unto death . . ." (Rev. 2:10). At other times, by stirring up trouble, the enemy keeps the servants of God from making known the Gospel. "When the Jews of Thessalonica had knowledge that the word of God was proclaimed of Paul at Berea also, they came thither likewise, stirring up and troubling the multitudes. And then immediately the brethren sent forth Paul to go as far as to the sea . . ." (Acts 17:13, 14). It is doubtless for similar reasons that the apostle wrote to the Thessalonians: "Because we would fain have come unto you, I Paul once and again; and Satan hindered us" (I Thess. 2:18).

## 6. THE JUDGMENT OF THE DEMONS

a. The fall of the angels and that of man had similar effects. Adam and Eve, immediately driven out of paradise, continued living on the earth created for them, though they were from then on under the curse. The fallen angels were immediately excluded from fellowship with the thrice-holy God; but, from their kingdom of darkness, they can still come to present themselves before Him and can operate "in the heavenly places" (Job 1:6; I Kings 22:19-22; Eph. 6:12). God has not spared His angels that have sinned, but He has cast them into the abyss of darkness to be reserved unto judgment (II Peter 2:4). "Angels that kept not their own principality, he hath kept in everlasting bonds under darkness unto the judgment of the great day" (Jude 6).

b. The term "abyss" sometimes designates that place to which the demons have been relegated and from which they cannot come out except by God's permission. They are terrified at being henceforth shut up there with no chance of getting out. The demons called "Legion" begged Jesus not to torment them before the time and pleaded insistently with

Him not to consign them to the abyss (Matt. 8:29 and Luke 8:31).

The book of the Revelation speaks of the pit of the abyss from which diabolical grasshoppers went out which "have over them as king the angel of the abyss: his name in Hebrew is Abaddon, and in the Greek tongue he hath the name Apollyon [destroyer]" (9:1, 2, 11). This angel of the abyss can certainly be none other than Satan himself. So as to clearly mark the infernal origin of the Beast that personifies the Antichrist, the dictum is that it "is about to come up out of the abyss, and to go into perdition" (Rev. 17:8). It is into the abyss too that Satan will be cast and chained for the duration of the thousand years (Rev. 20:1-3).

c. Since the appearance of Christ, described in the beginning of the Gospels, the demons know that the hour of their condemnation is near. Much more than men, they know who the Lord is; they tremble, and in their terror they cannot refrain from proclaiming His name. The man that had the spirit of an unclean demon cried out: "Ah! what have we to do with thee, Jesus thou Nazarene? Art thou come to destroy us? I know thee who thou art, the Holy One of God . . . And demons also came out from many, crying out, and saying, Thou art the Son of God. And rebuking them, he suffered them not to speak, because they knew that he was the Christ" (Luke 4:33, 34, 41). The demoniac of Gadara cried out: "What have we to do with thee, thou Son of God? art thou come hither to torment us before the time?" (Matt. 8:29; see also Acts 16:17).

This understanding that the demons have produces in them no work of either repentance or sanctification. James has this to say on the subject: "Thou believest that God is one; thou doest well: the demons also believe, and shudder" (2:19). Many people, then, who are content merely to believe in the existence of God have no faith except that of the demons. Their beliefs make no change at all in their lives; still, if they would stop a moment to think, they too would tremble at the thought of the inevitable judgment.

Let us note again that the struggle against evil spirits occupies a great place in the ministry of Christ. Just to cite Matthew's record, we see that Christ healed demoniacs and lunatics (4:24); He cast out spirits by His word (8:16); He delivered the two sufferers of Gadara (8:28-32), the dumb man possessed with a demon (9:32), and then another blind and dumb demoniac (12:22), the daughter of the Canaanitish woman (15:22), and the epileptic boy (17:15). As Peter said, He truly "went about doing good, and healing all that were oppressed of the devil; for God was with him" (Acts 10:38). He had come to "destroy the works of the devil" (I John 3:8).

d. The cross accomplished the ruin of the kingdom of darkness. Christ, "having despoiled the principalities and the powers . . . made a show of them openly, triumphing over them in it" (Col. 2:15). Since that time the evil spirits can only go on toward the full execution of that judgment. When they said to Christ: "Art thou come hither to torment us before the time?" the demons showed that they were living as though haunted by the fatal moment.

e. The glorious return of the Lord will bring in the great settling of accounts. Satan and his angels will put up one last fight in heaven, from whence they will be finally expelled by Michael and his heavenly militia (Rev. 12:7-9). After having given free course to their rage during the reign of the Antichrist and the battle of Armageddon (Rev. 12: 12; 16:14), the demons will be driven from the world scene during the millennium: "And it shall come to pass in that day, that Jehovah will punish the host of the high ones on high, and the kings of the earth upon the earth. And they shall be gathered together, as prisoners are gathered in the pit, and shall be shut up in the prison; and after many days shall they be visited . . . Jehovah of hosts will reign in Mount

Zion, and in Jerusalem . . ." (Isa. 24:21-23). According to this text, the demons will then be shut up, with their leader; it is with him also that at the end of the thousand years they will be cast into the lake of fire and brimstone, there to be tormented day and night for ever and ever (Rev. 20:10). According to Christ's own words, they will go "into the eternal fire which is prepared for the devil and his angels" (Matt. 25:41). There, according to Jude 6, they will be kept in everlasting bonds under darkness. Already, on earth, the unclean spirits confess with trembling the Lordship of Christ. In the other world, the word in Philippians 2:11 will see a complete fulfillment: even in hell (here: "under the earth") every knee shall bow and every tongue shall confess that Jesus Christ is Lord, to the glory of God the Father. But this confession, triumphant in heaven, will be for the demons and the reprobates the acknowledgment of their total perdition.

## 7. THE VICTORY OF BELIEVERS OVER THE DEMONS

Our freedom from the dominion of evil spirits is an already accomplished fact: "Giving thanks unto the Father . . . who delivered us out of the power of darkness, and translated us into the kingdom of the Son of his love" (Col. 1:12, 13). But it is a question of much more than a passive deliverance: believers are called on to seize by faith the Lord's victory and resolutely to take the offensive. Jesus constantly repeated one thing to His own: "He called unto him his twelve disciples, and gave them authority over unclean spirits." Then He sent them out with these marching orders: "Cast out demons" (Matt. 10:1, 8). "And he appointed twelve that they might be with him, and that he might send them forth to preach and to have authority to cast out demons . . . He . . . began to send them forth by two and two; and he gave them authority over the unclean spirits . . . And they went out . . . And they cast out many demons . . . These signs [the Lord declared, after His resurrection] shall accompany them that believe:

in my name shall they cast out demons" (Mark 3:14; 6:7, 13;
16:17). Luke, in his turn, gives these very significant words:
"He [Jesus] called the twelve together ,and gave them power
and authority over all demons . . ." (9:1). When the seventy
disciples came back from their first mission, they exclaimed
with joy: "Lord, even the demons are subject unto us in thy
name. And he [Jesus] said unto them, "I beheld Satan fallen
as lightning from heaven. Behold, I have given you authority
to tread upon serpents and scorpions, and over all the power
of the enemy: and nothing shall in any wise hurt you. Nevertheless in this rejoice not, that the spirits are subject unto
you; but rejoice that your names are written in heaven"
(Luke 10:17-20).

Still, it remains that the attacking of evil spirits is a redoubtable undertaking. The disciples met with defeat in
the case of the epileptic boy, and they asked Jesus for an explanation of their powerlessness. He answered them: "Because of your little faith . . . This kind goeth not out save
by prayer and fasting" (Matt. 17:14-21). Some Jews attempted exorcism, saying, "I adjure you by Jesus whom Paul
preacheth!" The evil spirit answered them: "Jesus I know,
and Paul I know; but who are ye? And the man in whom the
evil spirit was leaped on them, and mastered both of them,
and prevailed against them, so that they fled out of that house
naked and wounded" (Acts 19:13-17). In order to grapple
with infernal powers, one must indeed belong to Christ, the
great Conqueror, and be His purified instrument as Paul was.
Barring that, it would be very dangerous to do it.

The first Christians, moreover, did not hesitate to take
hold of the power that the Lord had provided for them. We
read in the Acts: "By the hands of the apostles were many
signs and wonders wrought among the people . . . And there
also came together the multitude . . . bringing sick folk, and
them that were vexed with unclean spirits: and they were
healed every one" (5:12, 16). In Samaria, "from many of

those that had unclean spirits, they came out, crying with a loud voice . . . and there was much joy in that city" (8:7, 8). Scarcely arrived in Europe, Paul cast out the spirit, the Pythoness, whose propaganda he refused to accept, since it would have compromised the Gospel message (16:16-18). Finally, at Ephesus, the application of cloths which Paul had touched sufficed to cast out the evil spirits (19:12).

Let us raise a question at this point which applies to us personally: Was the gift of casting out spirits part of the unusual signs that marked the beginning of the new dispensation (such as certain ones of Christ's miracles, various earthquakes, resurrections, and the wind and the tongues of fire at Pentecost, etc.?) Or is this gift to continue throughout the Church age? Let us note first that it is never mentioned in the epistles. Paul does speak of the gift of the discerning of spirits, but says nothing of a gift to cast them out (I Cor. 12:10—unless one wants to include this in the more general term: "the gift of working miracles"). John said: "Try the spirits," but he said nothing about driving them out either (I John 4:1). This silence in all the closing part of the New Testament (written especially for the Church) is surely meant to make us prudent in considering this delicate domain. But we believe, nonetheless, that all the texts cited speak rather strongly of the prerogative of Christians, if they are possessed of enough faith and if they are called to this ministry, to resolutely bring to God cases of demon possession. In the generation preceding ours, the two Blumhardts demonstrated, not only that cases of demon possession exist today, but also that such persons could literally be cured by faith, fasting, and prayer.

So let us, even in the face of all the powers of darkness, know how to maintain an attitude of entire assurance toward God and of perfect submission to Him. It is He who governs all His creatures, and He cannot fail to faithfully fulfill His promises. It is true that Paul, buffeted in his body by an angel from Satan, was not delivered from that testing; but he was miraculously sustained in the testing, so that the victory of the Lord was fully manifested in him (II Cor. 12:7-10).

One word more: according to Paul, it is believers who will judge the angels (that is to say, who will judge demons primarily), (I Cor. 6:3). Why then should we fear those who will have to appear before us, or why should we make compromises with them?

Finally, Jesus enjoins us to humility in these words: "In this rejoice not, that the spirits are subject unto you; but rejoice that your names are written in heaven!" (Luke 10: 20).

PART FOUR

# THE RESURRECTION

*Chapter IX*

# THE RESURRECTION OF
# JESUS CHRIST

### 1. ITS IMPORTANCE

THE RESURRECTION OF JESUS CHRIST is the cornerstone of all the Biblical teaching regarding the future life. If Christ arose and showed Himself alive to His own after His death, there really is something after this life. The great argument of unbelievers is that "no one has ever come back from the grave" and that therefore there is no hereafter. "When we're dead," they say, "we're done for. Let's eat and drink, for tomorrow we die!" But the events surrounding the resurrection reduce all such reasonings to nothing and bring us the irrefutable demonstration of eternal life.

So when Paul summed up the essentials of the Christian faith, the cross and the resurrection of the Saviour were all he needed: "I delivered unto you first of all that which also I received: that Christ died for our sins according to the scriptures; and that he was buried; and that he hath been raised on the third day according to the scriptures . . . So we preach, and so ye believed" (I Cor. 15:3, 4, 11). We "believe on him that raised Jesus our Lord from the dead, who was delivered up for our trespasses, and was raised for our justification" (Rom. 4:24, 25; see also II Cor. 5:15).

As for Peter, he went so far as to say that it is by the resurrection of Jesus Christ that God saves us (I Peter 3:21).

Let us see why this resurrection is both so certain and so fundamental.

## 2. ANNOUNCEMENT IN THE OLD TESTAMENT

According to Paul, Christ was raised "according to the scriptures" (I Cor. 15:4). Walking with His disciples after the resurrection, Jesus said to them as He opened up their minds to an understanding of the Scriptures: "All things must needs be fulfilled, which are written in the *law* of Moses, and the *prophets,* and the *psalms,* concerning me . . . Thus it is written, that the Christ should suffer, and rise again from the dead the third day" (Luke 24:44-46).

The *Law,* that is, the Jewish Pentateuch, contains two very striking pictures of the resurrection of Jesus:

### a. *Isaac on Mount Moriah*

God told Abraham that the promised covenant and consequent salvation would be effected by means of his son Isaac (Gen. 17:19); on the other hand, He was asking for that son as a sacrifice (Gen. 22:2). When Abraham left his servants at the foot of the mountain, he said to them: "I and the lad will go yonder: and we will worship, and [*we will*] come again to you" (vs. 5). He must have believed then that, in some way or other, God was going to give Isaac back to him. Hebrews 11:19 says: "Accounting that God is able to raise up [Isaac] even from the dead; from whence he did also in a figure receive him back." Abraham had been commanded to go to one of the mountains in the land of Moriah. Solomon's temple was also to be built "on mount Moriah" (II Chron. 3:1). Since there are a number of hills there, one might wonder if Calvary was not the same location as that where the sacrifice of Isaac had taken place. At any rate, the Father gave His Son as a total sacrifice on the cross. But He received Him back by a true resurrection.

### b. *Aaron's rod*

According to the epistle of Hebrews, Aaron was a type of Jesus, our High Priest. But certain Levites and leaders of the people, led by Korah, Dathan, and Abiram, exhibited jealousy of his priesthood and revolted against the divine choice (Num. 16:1-3, 8-11). To confirm this choice, the Lord had a rod brought into the sanctuary for each tribe and one brought for Aaron; in the morning, Aaron's rod, a simple, dry, lifeless stick, had budded and had borne almonds (Num. 17:1-8). The choice of Jesus as Messiah and High Priest was also violently contested by the leaders of the Jews; but God gloriously confirmed it when He put life back into Jesus' body, which had been placed, dead, in the tomb. Christ was "declared the Son of God with power . . . by the resurrection from the dead" (Rom. 1:4).

*The prophets* consistently announced "the sufferings of Christ, and the glories that should follow them" (I Peter 1: 10, 11). After depicting the agony and death of the Messiah, Isaiah 53 adds: "When thou shalt make his soul an offering for sin, he shall see his seed, he shall *prolong his days,* and the pleasure of Jehovah shall prosper in his hand. He shall see of the travail of his soul, and shall be satisfied . . . Therefore will I divide him a portion with the great, and he shall divide the spoil with the strong; because he poured out his soul unto death . . ." (Isa. 53:10-12). The prophet envisioned very clearly, then, all the perspectives that the resurrection would open up before the Crucified One.

*Jonah,* according to Jesus' own words, is also a type of the resurrection: "An evil and adulterous generation seeketh after a sign; and there shall no sign be given to it but the sign of Jonah the prophet; for as Jonah was three days and three nights in the belly of the whale, so shall the Son of man be three days and three nights in the heart of the earth" (Matt. 12:39-40).

*The Psalms* teach the same thing. David wrote: "My heart is glad, and my glory rejoiceth: my flesh also shall dwell in safety. For thou wilt not leave my soul to Sheol; neither wilt thou suffer thy holy one to see corruption" (Ps. 16:9,

10). Peter commented on this passage on the Day of Pentecost; he mentioned that since David had stayed in his grave, he could not have been talking about himself. But, because David was a prophet and because he remembered that God had promised by an oath to put one of his descendants on His throne, it is the resurrection of Christ which he foresaw. This is what he was referring to when he said that the grave would mean neither abandonment nor corruption of the flesh (Acts 2:29-31). Paul recognized in Psalm 2, verse 7, an allusion to the fact that the Father had begotten the Son, to make Him the first-fruits from the dead: ". . . the promise made unto the fathers, that God hath fulfilled the same unto our children, in that he raised up Jesus, as also it is written in the second Psalm, Thou art my Son, this day have I begotten thee" (Acts 13:32, 33; see also verses 34-37). Let us cite again Psalm 110:1, which, according to Acts 2:32-36, announces the glorification of the risen Lord: "The Lord said unto my Lord, Sit thou on my right hand, till I make thine enemies the footstool of thy feet."

So the Old Testament affirms that the resurrection of Christ, far from being something invented by deluded disciples, has always been in God's plan. For us who believe in the authority of the Holy Scriptures, this testimony is of the utmost importance. Is it necessary to say that it entirely abolishes the lamentable suggestion of certain unbelieving scholars that the idea of the resurrection of Jesus came to the disciples from the pagan myths about death and resurrection, such as in the case of Adonis, lover of the goddess Ashtoreth (Ishtar), or from the equally impure Eleusinian mysteries?

### 3. Announcement by Jesus Himself

Fully conscious of the purpose of His coming to earth, Christ constantly announced both His death and the resurrection which was to follow three days later. (See, for example, Matthew 16:21; 17:22, 23; 20:19, etc.) On the morning of the resurrection, the angels reminded the women of the words of the Lord (Luke 24:6-8).

To the Jews who demanded a sign that would accredit Him, Jesus on two occasions replied that they would see the greatest of all signs, that is, His resurrection: He compared His own case with that of Jonah (Matt. 12:38-40).

At another time "the Jews . . . answered and said unto him, What sign showest thou unto us, seeing that thou doest these things? Jesus answered and said unto them, Destroy this temple, and in three days I will raise it up. The Jews therefore said, Forty and six years was this temple in building, and wilt thou raise it up in three days ? But he spake of the temple of his body. When therefore he was raised from the dead, his disciples remembered that he spake this; and they believed the scripture, and the word which Jesus had said" (John 2:18-22).

After the Transfiguration, which manifested the glory of Christ, Moses and Elijah talked with Him "of his decease which he was about to accomplish at Jerusalem" (Luke 9: 31). After coming down from the mountain, Jesus charged His disciples not to tell anyone what they had seen "save when the Son of man should have risen again from the dead. And they kept the saying, questioning among themselves what the rising again from the dead should mean" (Mark 9:9, 10). Therefore the disciples could not have concocted such a doctrine themselves.

Finally, Jesus constantly mentioned the activity that would characterize Him after the cross: His return, His judgments, His kingdom, and His glory (Matt. 16:27; 24:30; 25:31, etc.). Thus He did not fail to make it crystal clear that He would rise again. And if this great event did not take place, how is it that we can still believe in Him?

4. THE RESURRECTION PRECEDED BY A DEATH DULY AND PUB-
   LICLY ATTESTED TO

The argument of many unbelievers is that Jesus, taken off the cross, was found to have merely fainted away. Revived by rest and the coolness of the tomb, He was then enabled to disappear of His own accord. Now the death of the Lord, on the contrary, was attested to by many witnesses and had multiplied proofs.

a. The centurion and the soldiers were seized with fright and cried out: "Truly this was the Son of God" (Matt. 27:54).

b. The women, with the two Marys, were there, looking on (Matt. 27:55; Mark 15:47).

c. All the others whom Jesus knew were also present (Luke 23:49).

d. The crowd who had been present at that spectacle went back smiting their breasts (Luke 23:48).

e. To put an end to it, the soldiers broke the legs of the two thieves; but, seeing that Jesus was dead already, they merely pierced His side (John 19:32-34).

f. At once there came out "blood and water," that is, blood already decomposed (John 19:34).

g. In answer to Joseph's request, Pilate, astonished that death had come so quickly, had the fact confirmed to him by the centurian (Mark 15:44, 45).

h. Joseph of Arimathea, a distinguished councillor, took Jesus down from the cross, wrapped Him in a shroud, and put Him in his own sepulchre (Mark 15:43-46).

i. He was aided by Nicodemus, another respected personnage (John 19:39).

j. Both bound His body in tight cloths "as the custom of the Jews is to bury" (John 19:40).

k. To embalm Him, they took about a hundred pounds of myrrh and of aloes (John 19:39, 40); in such a small place, that enormous quantity of spices would have been enough to have asphyxiated Jesus, if He had not been dead already.

l. A great stone was rolled before the door of the tomb (Matt. 27:60).

m. All this was closely observed by the women (Matt. 27:61; Luke 23:55).

n. The high priests and the Pharisees, fully persuaded of Jesus' death, feared that the disciples would steal away His body to make people believe that there had been a resurrection (Matt. 27:65, 66).

o. Pilate allowed them to put a guard before the tomb (Matt. 27:62-64).

p. For even greater surety, the stone was sealed (vs. 66).

q. Special miracles of impressive solemnity drew attention to the death of Jesus, things which could not go unnoticed: the rent veil of the temple, the earthquake, and the appearance of several saints raised from the dead (Matt. 27:51-53).

r. The four evangelists and the apostles give an absolutely unanimous testimony throughout the New Testament to the great event of the death of Jesus.

Thus this fact is irrefutable. Let us see if the same thing can be said of the resurrection.

5. THE WITNESSES OF THE RESURRECTION OF CHRIST

Peter declared: "Him God raised up the third day, and gave him to be made manifest, not to all the people, but unto witnesses that were chosen before of God, even to us, who ate and drank with him after he rose from the dead" (Acts 10:40, 41).

Who were those witnesses, and what proofs did they provide?

a. The women, gathered together, saw the empty tomb (Mark 16:1-8).

b. Mary Magdalene was the first to meet the risen Jesus and to speak with Him (Mark 16:9, 10; John 20:11-18).

c. Peter ran to the tomb and was the first to enter it (Luke 24:12; John 20:6). A little later, Jesus appeared directly to him (Luke 24:34).

d. John, who was with Peter, entered in also. But he was convinced at once, for the text adds: "and he saw, and believed" (John 20:8).

e. The guards, after trembling with fear, went to tell the high priests (Matt. 28:4-11).

f. The high priests, with the elders, offered the soldiers a large sum of money if they would spread abroad a false rumor, so as to impress the governor (Matt. 28:12-15). If the elders had not been convinced of the truth of the soldiers' story, they would neither have made the sacrifice nor have run that risk.

g. The two disciples on the Emmaus road (Luke 24:13-33).

h. The eleven, and those that were gathered with them (Mark 16:14; Luke 24:36).

i. The disciples, together with Thomas, eight days later (John 20:20-29).

j. The eleven, in Galilee (Matt. 28:16).

k. More than five hundred brethren at once, of whom Paul said "the greater part remain until now" (I Cor. 15:6). So it was possible to verify their testimony for a long period of time. It is probable that that encounter took place also in Galilee, where Jesus and the angels had expressly arranged a meeting with the disciples and the brethren (Matt. 28:7, 10). Considering the terrible persecution which was raging at Jerusalem and the state of the disciples before Pentecost, one could scarcely have imagined such a large gathering—and a public one too—in the capital. It is thought by some that the appearance to the five hundred brethren coincided with the meeting with the eleven which we have just mentioned (Matt. 28:16).

l. The seven disciples on the shores of the Lake of Tiberias (John 21:1-23).

m. James (I Cor. 15:7).

n. The apostles, mentioned several times, who saw the risen Lord during the forty days and who gathered around Him up until His departure from the Mount of Olives (I Cor. 15:7; Acts 1:3-12).

o. Saul of Tarsus, on the Damascus road (I Cor. 15:8).

We must admit that this crowd of several hundred "witnesses that were chosen before of God" is impressive and that it is impossible to refute what they have to tell us. Their testimony is all the more significant in that the disciples felt all the reluctance in the world believing it, it being only in spite of themselves that they finally had to submit to the evidence. This we see in numerous passages. Matthew 28:17: before Jesus came up (vs. 18), some doubted. Mark 16:8: the women "fled from the tomb; for trembling and astonishment had come upon them; and they said nothing to any one; for they were afraid." Mark 16:10, 11: Mary Magdalene "went and told them that had been with him, as they mourned and wept. And they, when they heard that he was alive, and had been seen of her, disbelieved."

Mark 16:13, 14: the disciples on the Emmaus road "went away and told it unto the rest; neither believed they them. And afterward he was manifested unto the eleven themselves as they sat at meat; and he upbraided them with their unbelief and hardness of heart, because they believed not them that had seen him after he was risen."

Luke 24:3, 4: the women "found not the body of the Lord Jesus . . . they were perplexed thereabout . . . they were affrighted and bowed down their faces to the earth." Luke 24:11: when, at last, the women spoke, influenced, it seems, by Mary Magdalene, the disciples took their words "as idle talk; and they disbelieved them."

Luke 24:22-25: the disciples on the Emmaus road confirmed the testimony of the women and of those who had seen the empty tomb without, however, believing it themselves. Then Jesus said to them: "O foolish men, and slow of heart to believe in all that the prophets have spoken! . . ." And it was only after their return to Jerusalem that, for the first time, they heard the disciples say "The Lord is risen indeed!" (vs. 34).

Luke 24:36-41: When Jesus at last stood in their midst, "they were terrified and affrighted, and supposed that they beheld a spirit." Since "they still disbelieved for joy and wondered," Jesus partook of something to eat before them.

John 20:8, 9: Troubled, Peter and John entered into the sepulchre; then John "saw and believed. For as yet they knew not the scripture, that he must rise again from the dead."

John 20:11-18: Mary Magdalene, in her panic, was not at all prepared to admit the resurrection. She was weeping, certain that His enemies had taken away her Lord. Her eyes filled with tears, she first took Jesus to be the gardener, until suddenly she recognized Him by the tenderness of His voice.

John 20:19: The disciples, the evening before the resurrection, had shut their doors "for fear of the Jews." So at that time they did not yet believe.

John 20:24-29: Thomas flatly declared: "Except I shall see in his hands the print of the nails . . . and put my hand into his side, I will not believe!" And Jesus had to say to him: "Be not faithless, but believing."

Such a list of texts as the above completely destroys the objection that the disciples, gripped with the desire of finding Jesus alive again at any cost, had mistaken hallucinations for reality. It has been claimed that upon speaking at dusk with an unknown traveler, or upon seeing at dawn by the distant river bank a willow with branches swaying in the wind, they imagined that they saw Him whom they could not bring themselves to give up. Now the texts have just indicated to us the exact opposite. The disciples were so little expecting the resurrection and they still had so little confidence in the promises of Jesus that they could only be convinced with great difficulty; it was not until they had had an abundance of proofs that they at last came to an all the more unshakable and unanimous certainty.

The striking thing is not simply the initial incredulity of the disciples, but their fright and their deep dismay before the fact that so stunned them. Thus the angels, and Jesus Himself, had constantly to reassure and to calm them.

The angel said to the women: "Fear not ye . . . Be not amazed" (Matt. 28:5; Mark 16:6).

As for Jesus, He emphasized this even more strongly: "Fear not . . . Why are ye troubled? and wherefore do questionings arise in your heart? . . . Woman, why weepest thou? . . . Peace be unto you . . . Peace be unto you" (Matt. 28:10; Luke 24:38; John 20:15, 19, 21).

The psychological attitude of the witnesses of the resurrection, therefore, is not that of people desiring, anticipating, and finally forging together out of many little pieces some imaginary event.

Is it necessary, moreover, to call attention to the fact that the "witnesses that were chosen before of God" were outstanding for their seriousness and their stability? Those solid fishermen of Galilee were certainly not carried away by their emotions; the apostles and Saul of Tarsus showed throughout their whole lives their good sense and their sincerity; the women had proved their self-denial and their courage; even the guards and the priests spoke in spite of themselves and against their own interests. Any fact at all, if attested to in an ordinary court by such remarkable individuals, and so many of them, would be accepted as true without the slightest hesitation.

As concerns the resurrection, there is still more to be said.

6. OTHER FACTS ACCOMPANYING AND CONFIRMING THE
RESURRECTION OF CHRIST

a. *The stone rolled away.* This stone was very big, and the women had been anxiously wondering who would roll it away

for them.  Then the entrance of the tomb stood entirely open
(Mark 16:3, 4) .

b. *The testimony of the angels.* All the accounts are explicit: angels spoke to the disciples, in or in front of the sepulchre, to calm their terror and to affirm to them the Lord's
resurrection.  Those angels showed themselves, either one or
two at a time; and there is nothing contradictory in the accounts.  According to Matthew, one of them rolled away the
stone and rendered the guard powerless (28:2-4) .  According to Luke, the angels pronounced these beautiful words:
"Why seek ye the living among the dead?" (24:5) .  To how
many "Christians" could not the same question be put!

c. *An earthquake* accompanied the rolling away of the
stone (Matt. 28:2) , so that the event could not go unnoticed.

d. *The empty tomb* is perhaps the most conclusive piece of
evidence.  How could that empty tomb be explained, after
the taking of so many precautions, when the Jews, fully informed, had had so much interest in denying the resurrection?
Why had they not been able to produce the body of Jesus, an
accomplishment which would have immediately brought all
discussion to an end?  How could the disciples have snatched
away the body, and what could they have done with it?  In
that case their testimony to the resurrection would have been
deliberate trickery.  Would they have been willing to die by
the thousands for having insisted on something that they
thought was a forgery?  We believe beyond the shadow of a
doubt that the first Christians, as well-informed Jews, were
absolutely convinced that the tomb was empty.

e. The *linen cloths* were on the ground, while folded by
itself was the *napkin* that had been around Jesus' head
(Luke 24:12; John 20:5-7) .  The details were noted by eye-
witnesses, this not being the way people invent stories.  It is
clear that the body was not taken away in haste, which is
what the situation would have been had the disciples tried to
steal it while the guards slept.  In that case, they would not

have had time to unroll the linen cloths, and they would not have taken care to fold by itself the napkin that had been around the head.

f. *Jesus' voice* and the way in which He pronounced Mary Magdalene's name caused Him to be recognized (John 20:16). The voice is, in fact, one of the surest means of recognizing anyone without hesitation.

g. *The familiar gesture* of the Lord's in breaking the bread and giving thanks suddenly opened the eyes of the disciples on the Emmaus road (Luke 24:30, 31).

h. To prove that He was not simply an apparition, Jesus had the disciples *touch His body* and the prints of His wounds: "See my hands and feet, that it is I myself; handle me, and see; for a spirit hath not flesh and bones, as ye behold me having" (Luke 24:39). To Thomas, who was still doubting, He said: "Reach hither thy finger, and see my hands; and reach hither thy hand, and put it into my side: and be not faithless, but believing. Thomas answered and said unto him, My Lord and my God! Jesus saith unto him, because thou hast seen me, thou hast believed: blessed are they that have not seen, and yet have believed" (John 20:27-29).

i. As a final measure to convince His disciples, Jesus had a broiled fish and a honeycomb brought to Him, and *He ate* before them (Luke 24:41-49). Impressed by this event, Peter was to recount it in the house of Cornelius (Acts 10:41).

j. After His resurrection, the Saviour accomplished the conspicuous *miracle* of the wonderful drought of fishes, which made John say at once: "It is the Lord!" (John 21:6-8, 11). It is even pointed out to us that there were in the net exactly one hundred and fifty-three big fish.

k. Always manifesting tender care, Jesus prepared for His hungry disciples "a fire of coals there, and fish laid thereon, and bread . . . Jesus saith unto them, *Come and break your fast* . . . Jesus . . . taketh the bread, and giveth them, and the fish likewise" (John 21:5, 9-19).

1. The *interview* during which Jesus restored Peter could leave no doubt as to the identity of the Risen One (John 21:15-24). The aged apostle alluded to it again in his second epistle (1:14).

m. *For forty days,* Jesus appeared alive to His disciples, giving them numerous proofs, showing Himself to them and speaking of the things concerning the kingdom of God (Acts 1:3). Cannot it be affirmed that the forty days of intimate communion with the Risen One were the crowning event of the three years of training they had received from Him before the cross? What uncertainty could still linger in their hearts after that? Therefore we see no defection among those privileged first witnesses.

n. *The miracle of the Ascension* deepened still more, if there was any such need, the work of convincing that had already been begun. The disciples, gathered together, with their own eyes saw Jesus rise up alive into glory; and at that time they heard again the testimony of the angels (Luke 24:50-52; Acts 1:9-11). Thus they had the unmistakable proof that the Saviour had risen and that, as He had said, He was from thenceforth to be seated, in His glorified body, at God's right hand.

o. Finally, for the believer, there could have been *no Pentecost* without the resurrection, for Pentecost is the crowning glory of the resurrection. Peter exclaimed: "This Jesus did God raise up, whereof we all are witnesses. Being therefore by the right hand of God exalted, and having received of the Father the promise of the Holy Spirit, he hath poured forth this, which ye see and hear . . . Let all the house of Israel know assuredly, that God hath made him both Lord and Christ, this Jesus whom ye crucified" (Acts 2:32-36). We too know that Christ lives, because He has communicated His life to us, He indwells us, and He is the life of His body, of which He has made us members.

The big argument for those who doubt is this one: "Come

and see!" The angels used it when they showed to the women the empty tomb (Matt. 28:6). Jesus said to the disciples: "See . . . it is I myself; handle me, and see . . ." (Luke 24:39); and He repeated the same thing with even more emphasis to Thomas (John 20:27). Then it is told us of John: "and he saw, and believed" (John 20:8). What are we ourselves going to do?

### 7. HOW IS THE BODY OF THE RISEN LORD PICTURED FOR US?

This question is very important for two reasons:

a. Did Jesus, in His appearances, have a real body; or did He come back only "spiritually"?

b. If our glorified bodies will some day be like the body of the risen Lord (Phil. 3:20, 21), what will they be like?

1.) When Jesus came out of the tomb, He had a real body which could be touched: "They were terrified and affrighted, and supposed that they beheld a spirit. And he said . . . See my hands and my feet, that it is I myself: handle me, and see; for a spirit hath no flesh and bones, as ye behold me having" (Luke 24:37-41).

2). There was something different and something new about that body, and at first the disciples were hesitant about recognizing it: "Some doubted [or, had doubts]. And Jesus came to them and spake unto them" (Matt. 28:17, 18). "And after these things he was manifested in another form unto two of them, as they walked, on their way into the country . . . Jesus himself drew near, and went with them. But their eyes were holden that they should not know him" (Mark 16:12, 13; Luke 24:15, 16). (See also Luke 24:36, 37, which we have just cited.) Mary Magdalene "turned herself back, and beholdeth Jesus standing, and knew not that it was Jesus"; at first she actually took him to be the gardener (John 20:14, 15). "Jesus stood on the beach: yet the disciples knew not that it was Jesus" (John 21:4).

The texts do not stipulate what it was that was changed

about Him. But it is easy to understand that the resurrection could have given His body a different appearance.

3). Still, there was at the same time and without any doubt something of the former body, which after a moment's hesitation the disciples were certain that they recognized. Jesus could say to them: *"It is I myself;* handle me, and see" (Luke 24:39). The disciples on the Emmaus road, whose hearts were already burning as they heard Him again, recognized positively the familiar gesture with which He broke the bread and gave thanks (Luke 24:30-35).

Mary Magdalene was sorrowing, not being able to recognize Him—and probably not even looking very closely at Jesus. But when He pronounced that one word: "Mary," she knew instantly that it was He, turned around, and said to Him: "Master!" Something in the expression and in the tone of His voice had come to her as certain proof.

4). Jesus still bore the marks of His suffering. He showed to the disciples "his hands and his feet" (Luke 24:40). But Thomas had cried out: "Except I shall see in his hands the print of the nails, and put my finger into the print of the nails, and put my hand into his side, I will not believe." That is just what Jesus permitted him to do, saying to him: "Reach hither thy finger, and see my hands; and reach hither thy hand, and put it into my side: and be not faithless, but believing" (John 20:25, 27). Such proof as that swept away all the doubts of the obstinate disciple.

5). Did the risen Christ really need to eat, as He did, before His disciples? (Luke 24:41-43). This passage does not say that He was hungry, but that He wished to prove in a tangible way the reality of His body. He ate to convince His disciples. It would be hard for us to think, in view of other texts relating to the *spiritual,* resurrection body (I Cor. 15:44) that material food is still necessary for the Lord or for His own in the other world.

6). If the body of Jesus was real, it had, all the same, some new properties, to us inexplicable. Just when the Emmaus disciples recognized Him, He disappeared before them (Luke 24:31). On two occasions He presented Himself in the midst of His disciples, although the doors were shut for fear of the Jews (John 20:19 and 26). The day of the Ascension, before the very eyes of the apostles, He rose up into heaven, thus defying the law of gravity. The God who made the worlds could obviously, if it so pleased Him, give His Son a new body, different from ours; and recent discoveries about matter and energy give glimpses of unheard-of possibilities of future transformations in energy itself.

8. AFTER THE ASCENSION, DID JESUS KEEP HIS RESURRECTION BODY?

Certainly, according to the testimony of the Scriptures.

When Ezekiel saw in heaven the Lord's throne, he discerned there "a likeness as the appearance of a man," all surrounded by a brilliant light, a picture of the glory of the Lord (Ezek. 1:26-28).

Daniel wrote: "Behold, there came with the clouds of heaven one like unto a son of man, and he came even to the ancient of days [God the Father] . . . And there was given him dominion, and glory, and a kingdom" (Dan. 7:13).

John, on Patmos, saw the risen Christ: "I saw . . . one like unto a son of man." Then the apostle gives us a detailed description of the glorified body of the Lord, mentioning His head, His hair, His eyes, His feet, His voice, His hand, His mouth, and His face (Rev. 1:13-16). He declares that soon "every eye shall see him" (vs. 7).

Jesus Himself kept the title *Son of man* when He spoke of His glorious return: "The Son of man shall come in the glory of his Father with his angels . . . Ye shall see the Son of man sitting at the right hand of Power, and coming on the clouds of heaven . . . When the Son of man shall come in his glory, and all the angels with them . . . before him shall be gathered all the nations" (Matt. 16:27; 26:64; 25:31, 32).

What joy to know that we shall be welcomed in heaven, not only by the august divine Majesty, but by one of us, the risen Son of man! Jesus, indeed, not only purposed to become incarnate, but also consented to keeping throughout all eternity the marks of our glorified humanity.

## 9. WHO RAISED JESUS FROM THE DEAD?

Jesus is "the resurrection and the life" (John 11:25). He "has life in himself" (John 5:26). He is "a living soul" (I Cor. 15:45). He declared: "I lay down my life, that I may take it again. No one taketh it away from me, but I lay it down of myself; I have power to lay it down, and I have power to take it again; this commandment received I from my Father" (John 10:17, 18). Then He added, speaking of His own body: "Destroy this temple, and in three days I will raise it up" (John 2:19). These texts seem to imply that *it is Jesus,* the source of life, *who raised Himself up.*

Other passages attribute the resurrection to *the Father:* "Whom God raised up, having loosed the pangs of death . . . This Jesus did God raise up" (Acts 2:24, 43, etc) "Christ was raised from the dead through the glory of the Father" (Rom. 6:4). "Paul, an apostle . . . through Jesus Christ, and God the Father, who raised him from the dead" (Gal. 1:1). God's might was "wrought in Christ. when he raised him from the dead" (Eph. 1:20).

Finally, the Scriptures say that it is by *the Spirit* that the resurrection took place: "If the Spirit of him that raised up Jesus from the dead dwelleth in you, he that raised up Christ Jesus from the dead shall give life also to your mortal bodies through his Spirit that dwelleth in you" (Rom. 8:11). "It is the spirit that giveth life" (John 6:63).

So the Bible attributes the resurrection to all three Persons of the Trinity. These are inseparable and do not act except as the three act together.

The creation of the world is attributed to the Father, to the Son, and to the Spirit (Gen. 1:1, 2; Ps. 104:29, 30; Heb. 1:2, 10).

The work of redemption is likewise attributed equally to the three divine Persons:

*God* so loved the world that He gave His only begotten Son (John 3:16).

In none other name (than that of *Jesus*) is there salvation (Acts 4:12).

It is the *Spirit* that gives life . . . If a man is not born of water and of the Spirit, he cannot enter into the kingdom of God (John 6:63; 3:5).

It is not surprising then that it took also the collaboration of all the Persons of the Trinity to effect the great miracle of the resurrection.

## 10. RESULTS OF THE RESURRECTION FOR CHRIST HIMSELF

a. *He was declared to be the Son of God with power* by His resurrection from the dead (Rom. 1:4). True, the divine Sonship of Jesus Christ had been constantly affirmed before that time by the Scriptures (Heb. 1:8-13), by God the Father (Matt. 17:5), and by the Savior Himself (John 5:17, 18; 10:30). But such declarations would have been entirely in vain if Jesus had remained in the tomb. Had He not risen, He would have demonstrated that Scripture had erred; and He would Himself have been a mere man, sinful and powerless—in short, an imposter. But by taking Him out of the grave, God demonstrated that His word is true and that He was fully accepting the Person and work of His Son. As Peter said, it was not possible that Jesus should be held in the bonds of death (Acts 2:24). According to the prophecy of Psalm 2:7, the Father solemnly asserted that the resur-

rection would occur: "Thou art my Son, this day have I begotten thee" (Acts 13:33).

b. *All power was given to the risen Lord.* Jesus declared
to His disciples: "All authority hath been given unto me in
heaven and on earth . . . And lo, I am with you always, even
unto the end of the world" (Matt. 28:18, 20). Henceforth
Jesus is at the right hand of God, crowned with glory and
honor; soon the Lord "will judge the world in righteousness
by the man whom he hath ordained; whereof he hath given
assurance unto all men, in that he hath raised him from the
dead" (Acts 17:31).

c. *"Christ, being raised from the dead, dieth no more;* death
no more hath dominion over him" (Rom. 6:9). ". . . Now no
more to return to corruption" (Acts 13:34). "He, because he
abideth for ever, hath his priesthood unchangeable. Wherefore also he is able to save to the uttermost them that draw
near unto God through him, seeing he ever liveth to make
intercession for them" (Heb. 7:24, 25).

From the very terms, all the present existence and work
of Jesus Christ would not exist without the resurrection.

d. *The Lord, thanks to the resurrection, is more active and
more present than ever before.* The Acts of the Apostles are,
in a sense, misnamed. The book could be entitled "The Acts
of the Living Christ, Produced by the Spirit through the
Disciples."

It was, in fact, the Lord working with His disciples (Mark
16:20).

He gave His commands to His witnesses and sent them out
(Acts 1:2, 8).

He received the spirit of Stephen, the first martyr (Acts
7:55-60).

He converted and called Saul of Tarsus (Acts 9:3-16).

He encouraged His apostle at Corinth (Acts 18:9, 10).

Then He sent him to Rome (Acts 23:11).

These "Acts of the Lord" will not be finished until His re-

turn, since He lives in the heart of each of His disciples:
"Christ liveth in me" (Gal. 2:20) ; "Christ in you, the hope
of glory" (Col. 1:27).

All these affirmations—all these texts—would be absurd if
Jesus had not risen from the dead.

## 11. RESULTS OF THE RESURRECTION OF CHRIST FOR BELIEVERS

So as not to be repeating ourselves in the next chapter, we
shall mention here only three of those results.

a. *The resurrection of Christ makes possible our salvation
and our resurrection.*

Jesus "was delivered up for our trespasses, and was raised
for our justification" (Rom. 4:25). The resurrection proved
that God accepted the expiatory work of the cross. Apart
from it we would have no Savior to justify us.

"If, while we were enemies, we were reconciled to God
through the death of his Son, much more, being reconciled,
shall we be saved by his life" (Rom. 5:10). The cross takes
away our sins and reconciles us to God; the resurrection ac-
complishes the actual work in us and causes us to live before
God.

The risen Jesus lives for ever, and His priesthood is not
transmissible, for it is not interrupted by death. "Wherefore
also he is able to save to the uttermost them that draw near
unto God through him, seeing he ever liveth to make intercession for them" (Heb. 7:23-25).

Since He is alive, we also live with Him; and soon we shall
be raised like Him: "Yet a little while, and the world beholdeth me no more; but ye behold me: because I live, ye
shall live also" (John 14:19). "He that raised up the Lord
Jesus shall raise up us also with Jesus, and shall present us
with you" (II Cor. 4:14).

Hence the strong affirmations of the apostles can be com-
prehended. Peter declares that we are saved by the resurrection of Jesus Christ (I Peter 3:21). And Paul repeats em-

phatically that if Christ had not been raised, our faith would be vain and we would be of all men the most pitiable (I Cor. 15:14, 17-19).

b. *Christ, the last Adam, creates a new humanity.*

In Romans 5:12-31, Paul compares Adam to Jesus Christ. The first man by one disobedience dragged the whole race into condemnation; Christ by a single act of righteousness— His death on the cross—brought justification to all men. In I Corinthians 15, the apostle goes even further, in emphasizing the effect of the resurrection of Jesus Christ on the whole race: "Since by man came death, by man came also the resurrection of the dead. For as in Adam all die, so also in Christ shall all be made alive" (vss. 21, 22).

*Adam,* the first man, became a living soul.

*Christ,* the last Adam, became a life-giving spirit (one who communicates life).

*Adam* is earthly, "animal"; and his sons are earthly, in his image.

*Christ,* the second Man, is from heaven; those whom He begets in the new humanity will likewise be heavenly, in His image (vss. 45-49).

c. *Christ is the firstfruits of those who are dead* (I Cor. 15:20 and Acts 26:23).

Both before and since Jesus Christ there have been resurrections: but all those people without exception had to go back into the tomb. Only Christ, "being raised from the dead, dieth no more" . . . "now no more to return to corruption" (Rom. 6:9; Acts 13:34); only He has entered as fully victorious into the future life. All the believers who have died, even the most saintly of them, continue for the time being under the dominion of death, as far as their bodies are concerned. Their souls are certainly saved and in the Lord's presence; but their bodies are still in the tomb, and they are awaiting "the redemption" of them (Rom. 8:

23). In the end of time, that will all change. ". . . So also in Christ shall all be made alive. But each in his own order: Christ the firstfruits; then they that are Christ's at his coming" (I Cor. 15:22, 23).

Finally, let us note that if Christ is the firstfruits of those who are dead, that fact is a solemn guarantee of the resurrection of those dead. After the firstfruits are gathered, the harvest cannot be long delayed.

## 12. EFFECTS OF THE RESURRECTION OF CHRIST ON THE FIRST DISCIPLES

We have seen the sorrow, terror, and unbelief with which the disciples first accepted the resurrection. But when that irrefutable fact had once been impressed on them, their whole attitude became inexplicably changed. The women were filled with an immense joy. As soon as they recognized the risen Lord, they fell down before Him; the disciples did the same thing (Matt. 28: 9, 17). The disciples on the Emmaus road felt their hearts burning within them; then at that same hour they returned to the city to bear their testimony (Luke 24:32, 33). Thomas exclaimed: "My Lord and my God!" (John 20:28). After worshipping Christ as He went back up to heaven, the brethren returned to Jerusalem with great joy; they were continually in the temple, praising and blessing God (Luke 24:52, 53). Then they went everywhere to carry the good news. For the faithful Church, Jesus was no longer the Carpenter or the humble Prophet of Nazareth; He was the One whose perfect divinity had vanquished death for us all.

It might be said that the disciples became in a special way *the witnesses of the resurrection*. From the very first, the day of the resurrection, those who saw the empty tomb and the living Christ were charged with proclaiming the news:

| | |
|---|---|
| Matthew 28:7, 8: | "Go quickly, and tell his disciples, He is risen from the dead" . . . They ran to take the news. |
| Mark 16:7: | "Go tell his disciples and Peter . . ." |
| Mark 16:10: | "She went and told them . . ." |
| Mark 16:13: | "They went away and told it unto the rest." |
| Mark 16:15: | "Go ye into all the world, and preach the gospel." |
| Luke 24:9: | They "told all these things to the eleven." |
| Luke 24:35: | "They rehearsed the things that happened . . . and how he was known of them." |
| John 20:17: | "Go unto my brethren, and say to them, I ascend unto my Father." |

When the Church came into being and grew, the apostles and disciples presented themselves as "witnesses of the resurrection":

Acts 1:22: To replace Judas, Peter asked if someone else could not be associated with the disciples as "witness . . . of his resurrection."

Acts 2:32: "This Jesus did God raise up, whereof we all are witnesses." (See also 3:15.)

Acts 4:33: "With great power gave the apostles their witness of the resurrection of the Lord Jesus."

Thus it is easy to see the central place that this message, along with that of the cross, occupied in the preaching recorded in the book of the Acts. See for example the sermons of Peter (Acts 2:24-36; 3:15; 5:31; 10:40, 41), and of Paul (Acts 13:32-37; 17:31; 26:6-8, 23). This emphasis is so strong that Festus summed up like this the dispute that separated the Jews from the apostle of the Gentiles: They "had certain questions against him of their own religion, and *of one Jesus, who was dead, whom Paul affirmed to be alive* (Acts 25:19). Paul too made it clear that it was because of the hope of the resurrection that he was called in question, accused by the Jews, and bound with chains (Acts 23:6; 26:6-8; 28:20). And this same apostle wrote to the Romans: "It is Christ Jesus that died, yea rather, that was raised from the dead, who is at the right hand of God, who also maketh intercession for us" (8:34).

In our life and testimony, are we attributing this much importance to the resurrection?

### 13.  DENIAL OF THE RESURRECTION AND ITS CONSEQUENCES

He that has "the power of death," the devil, must have roared when he saw his prey escaping from him. Since then, the arch Liar has sought relentlessly to deny the two great facts which have ruined his dominion: the cross and the resurrection. At the time of the apostles, as in our day, many men rose up to claim that the story of the resurrection was only a legend. These deniers are to be found not only among atheists, but even among preachers. In a famous book, one of the best-known theologians of the present day speaks of taking out of the New Testament the myths, among which the resurrection of Christ figures prominently (Bultmann, *Jesus Christ in Mythology*).

They claim that Jesus was raised only "spiritually," that His body stayed in the grave—since for them the miracle of a physical resurrection is, by definition, impossible. They maintain that Jesus continued to live on in the spirit of His disciples, who were impregnated with His memory, His example, and His teachings—and that the disciples were so obsessed by the idea of that spiritual presence that they invented the stories contained in the Gospels.

Now let us put this very clearly: a "spiritual" resurrection of Jesus is an absurdity. Certainly the soul of the Savior was in the abode of the dead, but it did not ever cease to exist (Acts 2:27). It is Jesus' body that was brought back to life—and without that bodily resurrection the whole evangelical testimony would be nonexistent.

"Now if Christ is preached that he hath been raised from the dead, how say some among you that there is no resurrection of the dead? But if there is no resurrection of the dead, neither hath Christ been raised . . . then is our preaching vain, your faith also is vain" (I Cor. 15:12-14). In this celebrated passage, Paul rises up against the negation of the resurrection and indicates its fatal consequences:

a. The resurrection of Christ and that of the dead are closely linked (vs. 12).

b. If the one were to fall through, the other would also cease to exist (vss. 13, 16).

c. In such a case, the preaching and the writings of the apostles would be nothing but fraud on the part of false witnesses (vss. 14, 15).

d. Our faith would be vain, and the Gospel would be divested of its content (vss. 14, 17). Could we believe in a Savior who was still in the grave, thus a sinner and powerless?

e. The work of Christ would be nonexistent: we would be yet in our sins, and the dead in Christ would have perished (vss. 17, 18).

f. We believers would be of all men the most pitiable (vs. 19). Having been deceived in this life, we would have put our hope in a delusion—and we would have no salvation in the other world.

g. The faith in the resurrection which the early Church went so far as to express in baptism for the dead would be only a mockery (vs. 29; see p 91).

h. The sufferings and the struggles of the servants of God (because of his faith, Paul even fought with beasts at Ephesus) would be totally useless (vss. 30-32). And where would be the justice of God?

i. If the dead were really not to be raised, the materialists would be quite right in saying: "Let us eat and drink, for tomorrow we die" (vs. 32). Life would have no more significance; only that which is material would count. But we have already seen that, far from being able to satisfy us, everything material leaves us alone at last with our despair. When for unbelievers the "tomorrow we die" becomes "today," that will be the fatal meeting with God and eternal perdition.

j. Those who deny the resurrection of our Lord—and ours, as a consequence—are evil companions who corrupt good morals (vs. 33). To become involved with such people means to jeopardize one's faith—and eventually even one's conduct. If we have been influenced by any such compromise, let us come back to our senses and not continue on in sin. Those who deny the resurrection do not know God: they are without Christ, without hope, and without God in the world (Eph. 2:12). Let us rather pray for them and seek to communicate to them our faith, the faith of those who know by experience that

*Christ is risen indeed!*

## Chapter X

# THE RESURRECTION OF BELIEVERS

### 1. DESTINED TO LIFE, NOT TO DEATH

DEATH, AS WE WERE SAYING, was not in God's original plan; man has come to know death as the wages of his sin. But the Lord is never discomfited; and His purposes never fail to be accomplished. By the resurrection of the soul and of the body, He takes the upper hand again and places us in a much higher position than that of Eden. God is going to realize His goal, which is the reestablishment of all things (Acts 3:21); and He will do more than that.

"As I live, saith the Lord Jehovah, I have no pleasure in the death of the wicked; but that the wicked turn from his way and live. Turn ye, turn ye from your evil ways; for why will ye die, O house of Israel?" (Ezek. 33:11).

### 2. THE RESURRECTION ACCORDING TO THE OLD TESTAMENT

It has often been said that the Old Testament has little to say about the future life. That is true, in a sense, for the revelation is progressive and the greatest light on this subject is brought us by Jesus Christ and His apostles.

For the Jews, the immediate presence of the Lord was so real that it seemed to eclipse the vision of the future life. The Old Testament does not formulate a dogma of immortality in any definite way; but it puts the believer in communion with the living God, who will lead him to immortality (as expressed by S. Salmond, *The Christian Doctrine of Immortality*, pp. 231, 296). It may be said of those of the old covenant that they had glimpses principally of the sojourn

190

of the dead—as a place beneath the earth—but not yet as the place known as eternal hell; and at the same time of the Messianic reign—as the reign on earth—but not yet as the reign in heaven.

Still, when one makes a close study of the Old Testament, he is astonished at all that it does declare—and in an increasingly exact way—about the resurrection.

a. *The resurrections of the Old Testament*

Three examples of resurrection occur in the midst of the history of Israel to affirm that if God wishes, death does not have to be final:

I Kings 17:21: Elijah raised the son of the widow of Zarephath;

II Kings 4:34: Elisha did the same for the son of the Shunammite woman;

II Kings 13:21: A dead man that was being buried was raised to life when he simply came in contact with the bones of Elisha.

b. *The raptures*

Enoch (Gen. 5:24) and Elijah (II Kings 2:11) were taken up into heaven without having died (Heb. 11:5).

These various examples of resurrections and of raptures announce prophetically what will happen some day to believers: the dead in Christ will come out of their graves—whereas the living (believers) will be caught up with them into heaven without having died (I Thess. 4:16, 17).

c. *The types of the resurrection*

We have already mentioned three, namely:

*Isaac* (Gen. 22:5).

*Aaron's rod* (Num. 17:8).

*Jonah* (Matt. 12:39, 40. See p. 165).

We find another in *the vision of the dead bones* of Ezekiel 37. The prophet saw a valley full of bones, which represented the house of Israel, dispersed without life over the face of the whole earth. God asked him, "Can these bones live?" and Ezekiel answered: "Oh, Lord Jehovah, thou knowest." (That is to say, such a possibility would go beyond the understanding and the power of man.) Then the Lord caused His Spirit to blow at two different times on those bones. They went together again, the flesh and skin grew back on them, the Spirit entered into them, and they stood up on their feet, like a very great army. And God concluded that vision by a marvelous promise to Israel: "I will cause you to come up out of your graves . . . O my people. I will put my Spirit in you, and ye shall live" (vss. 13, 14). Beyond the prophecy of a national restoration of Israel, we have here an astonishing vision on the subject of the resurrection, for the Old Testament. Soon the Spirit of God will blow on all the bones, not only the dispersed ones, but also those reduced to powder all over the earth. He will revive all the dead; and the result will indeed be a great army, a very great army.

d. *Other promises and allusions to the resurrection*

This is the comment that Jesus made on the incident of the burning bush (Exod. 3:6) : "But that the dead are raised, even Moses showed, in the place concerning the Bush, when he calleth the Lord the God of Abraham, the God of Isaac, and the God of Jacob. Now he is not the God of the dead, but of the living: for all live unto him" (Luke 20:37, 38). "Have ye not read that which was spoken unto you by God, saying, I am the God of Abraham, and the God of Isaac, and the God of Jacob?" (Matt. 22:31, 32). If the dead were not "living," as far as God is concerned, and destined to resurrection, He would not have said "I *am*," but "I *was* the God of Abraham."

Job uttered a sublime cry: "I know that my Redeemer liveth, and at last he will stand up upon the earth: And after my skin, even this body, is destroyed, then without my flesh, shall I see God, whom I, even I, shall see on my side, and mine eyes shall behold, and not as a stranger. My heart is consumed within me" (Job 19:25-27).

Isaiah, announcing the resurrection of the Messiah, said again: "And he will destroy in this mountain the face of the covering that covereth all peoples . . . He hath swallowed up death for ever; and the Lord, Jehovah, will wipe away tears from off all faces" (25:7, 8). "Thy dead shall live; my dead bodies shall arise. Awake and sing, ye that dwell in the dust . . . the earth shall cast forth the dead" (26:19). "And many of them that sleep in the dust of the earth shall awake, some to everlasting life, and some to shame and everlasting contempt . . . But go thou thy way till the end be; for thou shalt rest, and shalt stand in thy lot, at the end of the days" (Dan. 12:2, 13).

Finally, let us cite Hosea 13:14: "I will ransom them from the power of Sheol: I will redeem them from death: O death, where are thy plagues? O Sheol, where is thy destruction?"

With such revelations in the Old Testament, the Jews at the time of Christ believed in the resurrection—all but the Sadducees, the liberals of the day (Matt. 22:23). Herod did not know what to make of the miracles of Jesus. "It was said by some that John [the Baptist] was risen from the dead . . . and by others that one of the old prophets was risen again" (Luke 9:7, 8).

Paul said to Felix: "So serve I the God of our fathers, believing all things which are according to the law, and which are written in the prophets; having hope toward God, which these also themselves look for, that there shall be a resurrection both of the just and unjust" (Acts 24:14, 15; see also Acts 23:6-8).

## 3. THE RESURRECTIONS IN THE GOSPELS AND THE ACTS

Besides the three resurrections taken from the Old Testament, we find six more in the New:

a. the son of the widow of Nain (Luke 7:13-16)

b. Jairus' daughter (Luke 8:55)

c. Lazarus (John 11:44)

d. the saints raised at the time of Jesus' death (Matt. 27:52, 53)

e. Dorcas (Acts 9:40)

f. Eutychus (Acts 20:9, 10)

Let us make several observations about them:

1). The resurrections were a part of the miracles intended to accredit the ministry of the One who is "the resurrection" and to accredit that of His apostles (John 5:36; Matt. 10:8).

2). They were relatively numerous and quite sufficient to prove both the possibility and the reality of a life after death. They prepared the way for the more detailed revelations which were to be given.

3). As we have noted, they were all temporary. Every one of those persons had to die a second time (a not very interesting experience and one which the Scriptures do not describe in any case). Christ is—and will continue to be, until His return—the only true Risen One, the firstfruits from among the dead.

4). None of those raised in either Old Testament or New Testament times recounted a thing, as far as we know, about the experience of going through death into the abode of the dead. Our curiosity could well make us want to question them about it, but God has not permitted this. In the whole realm of the future life, the Scriptures, in their sober restraint, have to satisfy us.

5). However extraordinary the experience of resurrection must have been for the dead and for their families, what God is reserving for us is infinitely better. The eleventh chapter of Hebrews tells us that "women received their dead by a resurrection; and others were tortured, not accepting their deliverance, that they might obtain a better resurrection (vs. 35).

To put off one's death a few years, to come back to this

world of sorrows after having already taken leave of it—that would not be the most desirable of experiences. For Paul, to depart and to be with Christ—that was what would have been far better (Phil. 1:23). Let us rejoice with him over the fact that, whatever happens, God has provided for us the better resurrection.

4. NATURE'S TEACHING OF THE GREAT LESSON OF THE RESUR-
RECTION

The same God made the material world and the spiritual world. Thus it is not surprising that identical laws often govern these two spheres. After having called in the testimony of the Scriptures—that which we have just considered—Paul resorted to nature for proofs and illustrations of that which he was presenting (I Cor. 15:4, 35-41).

a. *Death produces life*

"But some one will say, How are the dead raised? and with what manner of body do they come? Thou foolish one, that which thou thyself sowest is not quickened except it die" (I Cor. 15:35, 36). "Except a grain of wheat fall into the earth and die, it abideth by itself alone; but if it die, it beareth much fruit" (John 12:24). Let us keep in mind two specific examples of this great universal law:

1). *The grain of wheat.* At the Convention at Morges, we heard the eminent scholar, Professor Henri Devaux, of Bordeaux, member of the French Academy of Science, give two studies on this subject. In an authoritative way, our friend demonstrated to us the perfect scientific exactitude of this verse: John 12:24. The grain of wheat literally dies to produce the little new plant, which will itself bear fruit.

2). *The potato.* Who has not seen potatoes harvested? Sometimes the tubercle put into the ground in the spring is still there: it is brown, hard, and seemingly intact. In such a case it has, so to speak, produced nothing. By way of contrast, the potato that has given an abundant harvest has become practically nonexistent: it has divested itself of its substance, having entirely transmitted its life to the new plant; there is nothing left of it but a little unrecognizable rottenness.

So death produces life. If that law exists in the natural world, why should it seem absurd or terrifying in the spiritual world?

b. *There is an immense difference between the seed and the plant, or body, which it produces.*

"That which thou sowest, thou sowest not the body that shall be, but a bare grain, it may chance of wheat, or of some other kind; but God giveth it a body even as it pleased him, and to each seed a body of its own" (I Cor. 15:37, 38). The mustard seed "is less than all seeds; but when it is grown, it is greater than the herbs, and becometh a tree, so that the birds of the heaven come and lodge in the branches thereof" (Matt. 13:31, 32).

Reflection on the seed brings us a great lesson:

1). *There is an enormous disproportion between the seed— often imperceptible—and the new plant.* From an acorn comes the mighty oak—likewise there will be an undreamed- of difference between the body put into the tomb and the resurrection body.

2). *The seed conserves the life under the appearance of death.* A dry, hard grain, just a particle, a kernel which seems to be dead—all these seeds still contain life in a dormant state. There is just one way to distinguish them from really dead seeds: that is, to put all of them into the ground to see which ones are capable of germinating.

If this is true, why should one be astonished if God con- siders our bodies like seeds, which, put into the ground, still contain an enormous capacity for a future life?

3). *The seed keeps its germinating power for a very long time.* For many years, sometimes, it seems, for centuries, the seed can stay alive. After the felling of a huge forest, we find the terrain quickly covered with thousands of flowers, the seeds of which could not have been carried, in such great quantities, from the outside: they had simply been in the soil for an indefinite period of time, awaiting the first favorable opportunity to germinate. Seeds have even been known to resist a temperature of −423.4° Fahrenheit.

The same God who works these miracles will also be able to give back life to sleeping bodies, even after thousands of years.

4). *Although the difference is great between the seed and the new plant, still a given seed always produces a like plant.* What has been sown is harvested, not something else. A carrot seed does not yield lettuce, and beans do not yield peas. That is why what Paul says cannot surprise us: "Whatsoever a man soweth, that shall he also reap . . . he that soweth unto the Spirit shall of the Spirit reap eternal life" (Gal. 6:7, 8). The life that we lead down here will continue, and it will infallibly produce the same results in the other world. Some, having lived for God, will be raised for a glorious eternity; others, having lived for themselves, will be raised for judgment.

5). *The way that the seed is transformed into the new plant is a mystery to us.* In a little seed are contained all the elements which constitute the individual and the species: form, dimension, color, and distinctive characteristics. That, to any unprejudiced mind, is a veritable miracle, that is to say, an inexplicable phenomenon.

No more can we explain how the remains put into the ground can become the resurrection body. Only God knows how all the elements of the physical body, scattered in the dust, will become reassembled; but that could be of no difficulty to Him.

The early church Fathers and some Catholic doctors teach that the very particles of our present bodies will be reassembled to form the resurrection bodies. For that reason they are strongly opposed to cremation. True, the body of Jesus Christ Himself was raised up and transformed before it had had time to become decomposed. But what, for example, has become of the bodies of Adam and of the patriarchs? What about people burned by incendiary bombs, if fire could hinder the reconstitution of the body? Then, if one ventures out on this ground, he might wonder exactly what body will be raised: the one at the time of death and decrepitude—or the body the person had in his youth? They say that our bodies wear out and that all their particles are completely renewed every seven years, to pass into other bodies. Which of these particles will make up the resurrection of a given individual? Just the raising of these questions suffices to show that God alone can solve them. He who has created so many things still incomprehensible to us will, in His own way, be able to work out what He has promised: to bring forth new bodies which will be the glorious continuation of our present bodies.

Since we have alluded to cremation, let us add this: In antiquity, cremation was so tied in with pagan rites that it was odious to the Israelites. The Canaanites had the habit of burning their children alive in honor of the god Moloch (Deut. 12:31). In our day, some pagan religions have retained cremation; and in the not very distant past, Hindu women used to throw themselves on their husbands' funeral pyres. For these reasons many Christians have certain scruples about cremation. Burial seems to them the more natural way of carrying out that which is implied in Genesis 3:19: "Till thou return unto the ground, for out of it wast thou taken." Let us respect these scruples, realizing at the same time that this question has nothing to do with our salvation.

c. *The animal world also brings us the lesson of the resurrection.* After having spoken of seeds and plants, Paul mentions the flesh of men, of four-footed beasts, of birds, and of fish (I Cor. 15:39). There are also different phases of the lives of the above: fertilization, gestation or incubation, birth, and then life, untroubled and full-blown.

We can compare man's present state to that of gestation: life has been given us, in principle; but it is limited and has need of daily growth. Soon the resurrection will set us free, when we shall know for ever the full-blown and perfected life of heaven.

We can also learn a great deal from the insects, especially the caterpillar, that becomes a butterfly. Its development has three phases: the *caterpillar,* often nondescript in appearance, which crawls and which lives on leaves; the *chrysalis,* into which the creature is placed as in a casket, immobile and inanimate; and finally the *butterfly,* with brilliant wings, which flies in the sunshine and which is sustained by the sweetness of the flowers. If we had not learned by experience, who could make us believe that these three in reality form a single entity, at different stages of its development! So man's earthly existence is often dull and sad; he is put into the grave, where all seems ended; but then he is raised, glorious, into the presence of God.

The larvae of the dragonfly live in water; but the perfected insect, changing elements, takes off into the air. Is it any more to be wondered at to see man departing from earth for heaven?

d. The whole universe is occupied by bodies of infinite diversity. There are plants, man, and different kinds of animals: four-footed beasts, birds, fish, etc. (vss. 37-39). Scholars today have identified seven hundred ninety thousand different species! The same variety occurs again in inanimate bodies, terrestrial and celestial. The sun, the moon, and the billions of stars also show the inexhaustible richness of the creation. And the God who has done all this is entirely capable, as though it were child's play, of making different bodies for us, after having provided us with one kind.

e. Putting aside Paul's text, we could find other resurrection parables in nature, for example those in the *cycle of the seasons*. Springtime, the youth of the year—youth, the springtime of life! Summer, maturity, laden with fruit. Autumn, harvest and stripping. Winter, apparent death, snow-covered as with an icy shroud. Then a new cycle begins. As though by a wave of a magic wand, the buds burst out, everything turns green, the birds sing, the flowers emit their perfume, and there is general rejoicing. Man—and humanity itself—goes through an analagous cycle: youth, maturity, retardation, death—but death is only apparent and provisional. The resurrection and the eternal springtime will soon follow along.

This great lesson from nature is both marvelous and clear. Even children understand it—whereas adults stop their ears so as not to hear it.

To the one that asked "How are the dead raised, and with what manner of body do they come?" Paul answered without mincing words: "Thou foolish one!" Then he reminded him of those very simple things which we have just seen. Shall we be among the intelligent ones who yield to the laws of the spiritual and the natural world—or among the foolish ones who admit only what pleases them and who deny the evidence?

## 5. WHAT WILL THE RESURRECTION BODY BE LIKE?

"But some one will say, How are the dead raised? and with what manner of body do they come?" (I Cor. 15:35) .

The Scriptures answer this question in a way fully to satisfy us.

First of all, they assert the fact that the resurrection will certainly be a physical one, just as it has been a spiritual one from the moment of the new birth. The death of the body has come in because of sin, not as God's original will. If redemption is to be complete, the body also must be regenerated. It does not bring us a deliverance "from the body," but the deliverance—the adoption—of the body itself (Rom. 8:23). Let us go on now to the description of the resurrection body.

a. *The body, sown in corruption, is raised in incorruption* (I Cor. 15:42).

Our mortal bodies are of a corruptible quality. What a struggle it is to keep them from dangerous infections, from the germs that are constantly attacking them! Then as soon as the spirit no longer animates them, as soon as life ceases, these bodies become decomposed with a terrible rapidity. All flesh is as grass: it fades and disappears. Beauty, strength, and youth—all of these are engulfed in the tomb.

But "the dead shall be raised incorruptible . . . for this corruptible must put on incorruption" (I Cor. 15:52, 53).

There will soon be no more sickness, no more suppurating wounds, no corruption. There will be security and incorruption.

b. *Sown in dishonor, the body is raised in glory* (I Cor. 15:43).

The Bible does not teach us to despise the body. There is not anything vile about it per se. With all its organs, it is a marvelous work of the Creator, who has made all things well (Gen. 1:31). The believer's body, besides, is the temple of the Holy Spirit (I Cor. 6:19). Paul warns us against a certain asceticism and despising of the body, which "are not of any value against the indulgence of the flesh" (Col. 2:20-23). Why then does the same apostle say that the body is sown in dishonor? Because the body, good in itself, has become the instrument of sin and of our rebellious will. It is with it that we satisfy our lusts—that we speak and act as we ought not to. It is therefore important that this body be held firmly in tow to keep it from departing from the right way. "I buffet my body and bring it into bondage: lest by any means, after that I have preached to others, I myself should be rejected"

(I Cor. 9:27). "If by the Spirit ye put to death the deeds of the body, ye shall live" (Rom. 8:13).

Some day this body will be raised in glory. It will no longer have either spot or wrinkle; and it will be able to carry out the will of God perfectly, being presented as a living sacrifice, holy, acceptable to God.

Not only has sin stained our bodies, but also it has made them ugly. Adam and Eve, fresh from the Creator's hand, must have been marvelously beautiful. Today, we may as well admit, ugliness is more common among men than beauty—in spite of all the flattery that a mirror may give to a person individually. The glorious body will doubtless be perfect and splendid. Down here, physical beauty, so often used for evil purposes, is a veritable trap; up there, it will do nothing but glorify God and contribute to our happiness.

c. *Sown in weakness, the body is raised in power* (I Cor. 15:43).

Destined to die, our bodies are essentially infirm. One can say that, from the moment of birth, the "outward man is decaying" (II Cor. 4:16). Vitality decreases, illness comes, and then old age follows, with its wrinkles and decrepitude. This explains why an octogenarian could say: "I am a young man vexed by the body of an old man!" Some people have never enjoyed a full measure of health: they are afflicted with some infirmity, an accident has crippled them for life, or they are deprived of one of the essential senses. And what can we say of those who, constantly tortured by physical suffering, never, humanly speaking, really enjoy life? Indeed, even for those who have perfect health, the present body is only a prison. Its strength is measured, and its senses are less acute than those of many animals. It is so "weak" in itself that it has to be constantly nourished, and its duration is extremely limited.

This body will be raised full of strength, having no longer either infirmity or lack of power. We can also believe that the bodies of all the elect will be perfectly developed. Those who died very young or infirm or decrepit will receive perfect bodies, like the body of the Lord Himself.

d. *Sown a "natural body," it will be raised a spiritual body"* (I Cor. 15:44).

The terms Paul uses astonish us and demand an explanation. The expression "natural body" is in reality in the Greek "psychic body," that is, not "animal body," but rather "animated body." (The word *soul* is "psyche" in Greek, and it is "anima" in Latin.) In I Corinthians 2:14 Paul also speaks of the "natural man" (psychical, in this case: unregenerate) in opposition to the spiritual man, one led by the Spirit.

Now the "natural body" will become a "spiritual body." Is there not a contradiction between these two words, that which is corporal not being, by definition, spiritual? Let us remember first of all that God is capable of creating an infinite variety of bodies, as it pleases Him. In the example that we have just seen, the body of the caterpillar could be called "natural"—and would it be going too far to speak metaphorically of the butterfly as representing the "spiritual body" that mounts up to heaven in the air? When the Church is caught up, the new, spiritual bodies of those that are raised again will be carried away in the air by the breath of the Spirit of God to meet the Lord (I Thess. 4:16-18). When we are thus raised, the divine Spirit will reign not only over our spirits and our hearts, but also over our bodies, liberating them from physical and earthly constraints.

Moreover, the notions that we have about the constitution of matter have changed a great deal. X-rays and radio waves penetrate bodies and walls and cross spaces; still, for all that, they are material emanations. Atomic discoveries are leading scholars to declare that matter is made of force in movement, perhaps of concentrated electricity. It will be easy for God to group in a different way the energy which is in our present bodies, to make out of them the "spiritual bodies" of which Paul speaks.

Let us quote, on this question, a modern astronomer: "Physicists have established [or believe they have established, R. P.] that matter can be entirely reduced to imponderable electrical particles, which in turn are mere particles of energy. However, what is that energy? How does one account for it? Mystery . . . Thus, in a way, modern physics can be said to have turned matter into something spiritual, or at least into something volatile and evanescent. As for Time and Space, which we used to hold on to as if they were substantial ropes capable of preserving us from dizziness, they too now fall away and fade into a kind of metaphysical mist. Thus one clearly sees how great is the error of those who have been bent on contrasting science and mysticism. Indeed mysticism, which is to say the feel and grasp of an unknowable, inconceivable, inexpressible something, is the very point where modern science leads, its inescapable conclusion" (Charles Nordmann, *L'Au-dela*, Hachette, Paris, 1927, pp. 251, 2). Does not Paul's language, after that, seem singularly ahead of human concepts? On the other hand, a comparison can help us picture the transition from a natural body to a spiritual body:

Water has many different aspects; it can be

| ice | water | vapor |
|---|---|---|
| solid | liquid | gaseous |
| tangible | visible | invisible |
| firm | yielding | impalpable |
| white | transparent | colorless |

And still, it is always substantially the same! What intelligent man would deny that the Creator has power to give another form to the elements which constitute our present physical beings?

In the first body, the emphasis is placed on the soul: "a

natural body . . . the first man, Adam, became a living [psychical] soul." In the new body, the emphasis is placed on the spirit: "a spiritual body . . . the last Adam [Jesus] became a life-giving spirit" (I Cor. 15:45).

"Howbeit that is not first which is spiritual, but that which is natural; then that which is spiritual" (vs. 46). This verse lays down one of the laws that God has consistently applied in the execution of His plan in respect to man. He has always purposed to give to creatures an alternative, so that they might make use of their free will and of their liberty of choice. But the Lord reserves to Himself the right to intervene, in order to restore what has been spoiled and to bring the rough draft to perfection.

| *There was* | *There will be* |
|---|---|
| the heaven and the earth | the new heavens and the new earth |
| the earthly paradise | the heavenly paradise |
| the first Adam | the last Adam, Jesus Christ |
| Hagar, the first covenant | Sarah, the new covenant (Gal. 4:24, 25) |
| Ishmael, the son of unbelief | Isaac, the son of faith |
| Esau, the secular man | Jacob, the man broken by God |
| Israel | The Church |
| Aaron, the "high priest" | Jesus Christ, the true High Priest |
| the physical birth | the new birth |
| the natural body | the spiritual body |

Is there need of re-emphasizing the progress in each case between the first of these terms and the second, and the planned character of all that God Himself is accomplishing in the realm of the Spirit?

In speaking of the role of the soul in the first body and in the new one, Erich Sauer, after calling to mind that the atoms of our present bodies are replaced every seven years, adds: The soul continually is building from the material which surrounds it a "new" body, so that the body is renewed, even though it continues to maintain its identity. Like a magnet, the soul draws and effects the conjunction of the millions of the atoms of the body. In death, it loses that magnetic power; but in the resurrection it receives it again, and indeed to a far greater degree. A comparison can also be drawn from coal. In its ordinary form, it is nothing but common carbon; but crystallized, it becomes a sparkling diamond (*The Triumph of the Crucified,* pp. 108, 109).

Before leaving this point, let us note that in our opinion the Creed is wrong as it is sometimes recited, in the expression "the resurrection of the flesh." (The French word in the Creed is "chair," *flesh,* H. I. N.). This expression is not in the Bible, which speaks of the resurrection of the body; but specifically it is the resurrection of a spiritual body, not of a fleshly one. This fact will obviously have enormous consequences, particularly these:

> believers will be delivered from the seductions of the flesh, and unbelievers will be deprived of the enjoyments of the flesh.

e. *The new body will be like the one that the risen Lord had.* The first man, Adam, taken from the earth, is earthy; the second Man (Jesus) is from heaven. "As is the earthy, such are they also that are earthy: and as is the heavenly, such are they also that are heavenly. And as we have borne the image of the earthy, we shall also bear the image of the heavenly" (I Cor. 15:47-49).

"For our citizenship is in heaven; whence also we wait for a Saviour, the Lord Jesus Christ: who shall fashion anew the body of our humiliation, that it may be conformed to the body of his glory, according to the working whereby he is able even to subject all things unto himself" (Phil. 3:20, 21).

In the preceding chapter we saw the changed and glorified

body with which Jesus went back into heaven (p. 176). What joy to know that we shall have bodies like His! For Paul was right in speaking of our present bodies as those "of our humiliation."

To a beautiful character and a noble mind, with all of its lucidity and all its vast accumulation of knowledge, what humiliation for the body to become feeble, pain-racked, and then disintegrated! But God will carry out His promise. He has predestinated us "to be conformed to the image of His Son, that he might be the firstborn among many brethren" (Rom. 8:29). "We shall be like him, for we shall see him even as he is" (I John 3:2). These words do not mean simply that we shall be clothed in the spiritual perfection of the Lord. In the first place, God created man in His own image. Jesus in the incarnation became like us in all things (Heb. 2:17). He desires to make us conformed now to Him in the risen spirit and body.

f. *The new body will be clothed upon with immortality.* "This mortal must put on immortality" (I Cor. 15:53, 54). The resurrection will be final, and in heaven "death shall be no more" (Rev. 21:4). This truth has a great corollary: "They that are accounted worthy to attain to that world, and the resurrection from the dead, neither marry, nor are given in marriage: for neither can they die any more: for they are equal unto the angels; and are sons of God, being sons of the resurrection" (Luke 20:35, 36). This does not mean that we shall not meet again with joy those whom we have loved on earth. But it is evident that men, once become immortal, will have no more need of begetting children to perpetuate the race.

g. *We are still waiting for the resurrection of our bodies.* "For the earnest expectation of the creation waiteth for the revealing of the sons of God . . . even we ourselves groan within ourselves, waiting for our adoption, to wit, the redemption of our body. For in hope were we saved" (Rom. 8:19-24).

At the time of the apostles, certain men turned away from the truth, claiming that the resurrection had already taken place, thus overthrowing the faith of some (II Tim. 2:18). For the enemy, any argument is good. When he does not succeed in destroying faith in the resurrection (I Cor. 15: 12), he discredits it, by reducing it to an absurdity. In our day the Jehovah's Witnesses and the Angels of the Lord claim that since the return of Christ in 1914, they have already been resurrected. Being part of the 144,000, they have entered, they say, into the millennium, not to die any more. Needless to state, as the years go by, these people die just like everybody else, including the famous "Angel of the Lord," Mr. Freytag—which fact does not prevent the cult from making many disciples.

This word: "We wait for the redemption of our body" is to keep us from another danger, not so great, but just as real. It consists of this: Some say that Jesus on the cross perfectly completed the redemption of our bodies, as He did that of our souls. According to Matthew 8:16, 17, it is said that He delivers us now from all our physical infirmities: "When even was come, they brought unto him [Jesus] many possessed with demons: and he cast out the spirits with a word, and healed all that were sick: that it might be fulfilled which was spoken through Isaiah the prophet, saying, Himself took our infirmities, and bare our diseases." (It should be noted that this passage from Matthew does not refer to the work of Jesus on the cross, but to His healing ministry among the crowds in Palestine.) They claim further: Since Jesus has redeemed our bodies, the believer cannot and is not to be ill any more. God wills nothing, they say, short of our healing; and it is an insult to Him for us to pray, "Lord, heal me if it is according to Thy will"! But in order to be logical about this view, one would have to go on further to claim that no one should become old or die, since his body has already been redeemed.

May God keep us from speaking against divine healing. We ought humbly to acknowledge that we have not often enough consulted the divine Physician and that we have too often put our confidence in men—also that, through unbelief, we have been guilty of abandoning to their unhappy lot those who have to suffer. Let us rather put into practice the exhortation of James to pray for the sick (5:14, 15); and when God really grants it, let us be able to recognize the gift of healing that Paul speaks about (I Cor. 12:9). But let us not go beyond what the Scriptures promise. Until the resurrection we do not yet have the glorious bodies described in I Corinthians 15. We are forced to submit to growing old, as the outer man is being destroyed; and, if the Lord tarries, we shall surely have to die some day from some sickness. (See II Kings 13:14.) Paul, Timothy, and Trophimus all suffered in their bodies (II Cor. 12:7-10; I Tim. 5:23; II Tim. 4:20); and God, seemingly, did not intervene on their behalf, as some would like to have it. Paul called Luke "the beloved physician" (Col. 4:14). So let us be strong in faith, but also submissive and balanced. Let us not by our unbelief hinder God from acting in our bodies. But let us accept His will—always "good, acceptable, and perfect"; and knowing that we are saved only by hope, let us await with joy the adoption, the redemption, of our bodies!

Regarding this aspect of salvation, let us quote again the remarkable writer, Erich Sauer:

"All that we have we await; all that we await we already have."

| | |
|---|---|
| We have eternal life (John 3:36) | and we are to lay hold of it (I Tim. 6:12) |
| We have redemption (Eph. 1:7) | and we wait for it (Rom. 8:23) |
| We are sons of God (Rom. 8:14) | and we await the adoption—of our bodies (Rom. 8:23) |

| | |
|---|---|
| We are already in the kingdom (Col. 1:13) | and we enter hereafter into the kingdom (Acts 14:22) |
| We receive this kingdom now (Heb. 12:28) | and we shall inherit it (I Cor. 6:9, 10) |
| We have been glorified (Rom. 8:30) | and we shall be glorified (Rom. 8:17). |

We already have everything, but our enjoyment of it is as yet only partial. Until the redemption of the body, our coming of age (Rom. 8:23), the invested capital is reserved in heaven (I Peter 1:4; II Tim. 1:12; Col. 1:5). Until that time we are making use of the interest. But the fact that we are now collecting the interest is the proof that the capital is ours. Thus our present possession is a guarantee of the future, a firstfruits of the full harvest (Rom. 8:23), an earnest, a pledge of the coming sum total (Eph. 1:14; II Cor. 1:22; 5:5). (*The Triumph of the Crucified*, p. 97).

h. *When we receive the resurrection body, we know it is not a question of being unclothed, but of being clothed upon.* In the passage from II Corinthians 4:16 to 5:4, Paul speaks of our "outward man"—the body—which is perishing, while our inner man is being renewed from day to day. Then he compares the body to a tent, destined for destruction. This is a striking picture; our flesh is not much more durable than a canvas: it is light and is exposed to injuries and misfortunes; and it can last, at the most, for only a few seasons. On the other hand, "we have a building from God, a house not made with hands, eternal in the heavens. For verily in this we groan, longing to be clothed upon with our habitation which is from heaven." This "habitation" is at the same time the heavenly city, whose builder and maker is God (Heb. 11:10) and the new body, which we are going to put on—no longer a tent, but a permanent dwelling place. "For indeed we that are in this tabernacle do groan, being burdened; not for that we would be unclothed, but that we would be clothed upon, that what is mortal may be swallowed up of life" (II Cor. 5:4). We have already said in connection with the death of the righteous that to leave this world is not really to die, since by the regeneration of the soul and the resurrection of the body "what is mortal is swallowed up of life." An unbeliever, seeking to comfort a dying Christian, said to him, "My poor friend, how sorry I am that you have to leave the land of the living!" But the dying man, radiant, replied: "You are wrong. I am leaving the land of the dying to go to the country of the living!"

6. WHEN WILL THE RESURRECTION OF BELIEVERS TAKE PLACE?

We must make a distinction here. The believer's spiritual life begins at the time of the new birth. At that instant he passes out of death to receive eternal life (John 5:24). But when will the resurrection of the body take place? On this question the Scriptures are clear.

a. *At the last day*

Jesus solemnly declares four times that at the last day He will raise up whoever believes in Him (John 6:39, 40, 44, and 54).

b. *At the second coming of Christ*

"In Christ shall all be made alive. But each in his own order: Christ the firstfruits; then they that are Christ's *at his coming*" (I Cor. 15:22, 23).

c. *At the rapture of the Church*

Paul affirms this in two well-known passages: I Corinthians 15:51-53 and I Thessalonians 4:13-18. In our book, *The Return of Jesus Christ,* pp. 109-135, we have made a detailed study of the rapture of the Church. We are reminding our readers of it so that here we can limit ourselves to that which has to do directly with the resurrection.

Here is the way Paul depicts this great event:

1). At the moment set by God, known only to Him,
2). in the twinkling of an eye,

3). Jesus will come from heaven;

4). He will bring with Him all the "dead in Christ" and will give to them their resurrection bodies (I Thess. 4:14, 16).

5). At that moment He will "change" the bodies of the believers living on the earth, who therefore will not have to depart by the way of the grave. Paul is explicit: "Behold, I tell you a mystery: We all shall not sleep, but we shall all be changed . . . the dead shall be raised incorruptible, and we shall be changed" (I Cor. 15:51, 52).

6). All believers, those changed and those raised from their graves, will together be lifted up into the air, to be forever with Him (I Thess. 4:17).

In the book just cited (pp. 118-131), we have explained why we believe in the rapture of the Church before the three and a half years of tribulation. It seems evident to us, moreover, that I Thessalonians 4:14-17 and Revelation 20:4-6 represent two phases of the blessed resurrection:

| *According to I Thess. 4:14-17* | *According to Rev. 20:4-6* |
| --- | --- |
| the Lord descends from heaven | the scene is on the earth (Rev. 19:19; 20:1, 8) |
| the dead in Christ are raised | first there is a judgment, vs. 4 |
| the living are changed | the judges are, seemingly, the glorified saints of whom Paul speaks in I Cor. 6:2, seated on thrones |
| all together are taken up in the clouds at the meeting of the Lord in the air | there is mentioned here only the resurrection of those who, during the tribulation period, will have refused to worship the Antichrist and who will have been martyred |

Jesus is the *firstfruits* of those who are dead.

The Church lifted up represents the *harvest*.

The martyrs raised after the tribulation are like the *gleaners* of the harvest.

If it seems surprising that the first resurrection is to take place as two different phases separated by the tribulation time, we might say this: In John 5:24, 25 Jesus speaks of the spiritual resurrection even now granted to all sinners who have put their trust in the Son of God: "He that . . . believeth . . . hath passed out of death into life. Verily, verily, I say unto you, The hour cometh, and now is, when the dead shall hear the voice of the Son of God; and they that hear shall live." Now that "hour" of grace in which re-generation is possible has already lasted more than nineteen centuries. Then Jesus goes on to speak of the resurrection of the body: "The hour cometh, in which all that are in the tombs shall hear his voice, and shall come forth; they that have done good, unto the resurrection of life; and they that have done evil, unto the resurrection of judgment" (vss. 28, 29). If we understand correctly, that particular "hour" will last quite a long time, since it will continue from the rapture of the Church until the resurrection of the tribulation martyrs and the end of the thousand years. (See also what John says about the "last hour," in which period we have been ever since Jesus came into the world, I John 2: 18.)

d. *At the time of the "first resurrection"* (Rev. 20:5, 6)

The resurrection of believers is called "first" as over against that of the wicked, which will take place a thousand years later. The two verses cited above are the only ones which give it that name. But, as we understand it, the "first resurrection" is clearly as much for the raptured Church as for the martyrs brought back to life after the tribulation, three and a half years later. In fact, all believers, the con-querors by faith, are to reign with Christ, first for a thousand years down here, and then forever in heaven (Rev. 2:27; 3:21; 20:4b, 6; 22:5); all will escape the second death, being inscribed in the book of life (Rev. 2:11; 20:6, 14, 15); all are priests of God and of Christ (Rev. 1:6; 20:6; I Peter 2:5, 9).

What a marvelous perspective, and how we wish that that triumphal day were already here!

### 7. BY WHOM SHALL WE BE RAISED?

We have seen that the resurrection of Jesus Christ was brought about by the joint action of the three Persons of the Trinity. The same will be true for our own resurrection.

"*God* both raised the Lord, and will raise up us through his power" (I Cor. 6:14). See also II Cor. 4:14. "Even so them also that are fallen asleep in Jesus will God bring with him" (I Thess. 4:14). "He that raised up Christ Jesus from the dead shall give life also to your mortal bodies through his Spirit that dwelleth in you" (Rom. 8:11).

*Jesus Christ* said: "I am the resurrection and the life: he that believeth on me, though he die, yet shall he live" (John 11:25). "Every one that beholdeth the Son, and believeth on him . . . I will raise him up at the last day" (John 6:40). This declaration is made again in verses 39, 44, and 54. "As the Father hath life in himself, even so gave he to the Son also to have life in himself . . . the hour cometh, in which all that are in the tombs shall hear his [Jesus'] voice, and shall come forth" (John 5:26, 28). "The Lord Jesus Christ . . . shall fashion anew the body of our humiliation, that it may be conformed to the body of his glory, according to the working whereby he is able even to subject all things unto himself" (Phil. 3:21).

*The Holy Spirit* is He that giveth life (John 6:63). As it is by Him that our souls are regenerated through the new birth (John 3:5-8), it is also by Him that God will give life to our bodies: "If the Spirit of him that raised up Jesus from the dead dwelleth in you, he that raised up Christ Jesus from the dead shall give life also to your mortal bodies through his Spirit that dwelleth in you" (Rom. 8:11).

Ezekiel, after having prophesied the regeneration by the Spirit (36:26, 27), also predicted the resurrection of the dry bones by the Spirit: "Thus saith the Lord Jehovah unto these bones: Behold, I will cause breath to enter into you, and ye shall live . . . Come from the four winds, O breath, and breathe upon these slain, that they may live! . . . The breath came into them, and they lived" (Ezek. 37:5, 9, 10).

It is not surprising that the Scriptures speak thus of the action of the Spirit. Since He gave life to the first body of a man made out of the dust (Gen. 2:7), we can count all the more on His soon giving life to our "spiritual bodies" (I Cor. 15:44).

All the works of God are perfect. They all benefit from the united power of the Father, the Son, and the Holy Ghost. With what assurance can we put ourselves in the hands of Him who doeth all things well!

8. WHO WILL HAVE PART IN THE GLORIOUS RESURRECTION?

It is clear that everyone will not be raised in the way we have just described. We shall shortly see that there will be a second resurrection, that of the ungodly. To have part in the first resurrection one needs:

a. *To have done good:* those will be raised unto life (John 5:29). They that "by patience in well-doing seek for glory and honor and incorruption" will abundantly receive eternal life (Rom. 2:7).

b. *To belong to Jesus Christ:* "This is the will of him that sent me, that of all that which he hath given me I should lose nothing, but should raise it up at the last day . . . No man can come to me, except the Father that sent me draw him: and I will raise him up in the last day" (John 6:39-44).

"In Christ shall all be made alive . . . they that are Christ's, at his coming" (I Cor. 15:22, 23).

c. *To believe in Jesus and in His sacrifice.* "Every one that beholdeth the Son, and believeth on him . . . I will raise him up at the last day . . . He that eateth my flesh and drinketh my blood hath eternal life; and I will raise him up at the last day" (John 6:40-54). "I am the resurrection and the life: he that believeth on me, though he die, yet shall he live" (John 11:25).

d. *To be willing to lose his life down here* so as to find it again up there (Matt. 10:39). "If we died with him, we shall also live with him" (II Tim. 2:11).

e. *To be among the just* (Acts 24:15). We know what this term means. Since all men are sinners, there is not one "just" among them (Rom. 3:10); still, he who believes in Jesus Christ is *justified*—declared freely and fully just (Rom. 3:24; 4:5).

f. *To have received the Holy Spirit,* who unites us to Christ and who soon will give life to our mortal bodies (Rom. 8:9, 11).

g. *To be among the dead "in Christ" or among the living in Him* (I Thess. 4:16). It is evident that one must first have become, by faith, a new creature "in Christ" (II Cor. 5:17) if he is to have part in the soon-coming glorious resurrection.

Do we meet these conditions? "Blessed and holy is he that hath part in the first resurrection: over these the second death hath no power; but they shall be priests of God and of Christ, and shall reign with him a thousand years" (Rev. 20:6).

The fact that all men will not participate in the first resurrection explains why the Scriptures call it "the resurrection from among the dead." This expression occurs forty-nine times in the Bible, in each case having to do with Christ and the believers. They are raised *from among* the dead, leaving the ungodly in their graves until the resurrection of the dead (that is, of all the dead) in view of the last judgment. God "raised up Christ from [among] the dead" (Rom. 8:11; 1:4). When the disciples first heard Jesus say that the Son of Man should be raised "from the dead" (that is, "from the midst of the dead"), they did not understand Him (Mark 9:9, 10). Up until then they had doubtless pictured only a general resurrection of all the dead, and they would have taken it that Jesus meant being raised "with the dead." As for Paul, he was not satisfied simply with the perspective of resurrection. He strove to attain, if possible, "unto the resurrection from among the dead," the only blessed and glorious one (Phil. 3:11. It says literally "to attain unto the out-resurrection, that which is from among the dead".)

## 9. IN WHAT MEASURE DO WE ALREADY PARTICIPATE IN THE RESURRECTION OF CHRIST?

We have studied the resurrection of the dead and our own future resurrection. There remains for us to touch on an extremely important point: we are enjoined to participate even now in the death and the resurrection of Jesus Christ, and this very participation is the primary condition of our victory over the grave.

"We were buried therefore with him through baptism into death: that like as Christ was raised from the dead through the glory of the Father, so we also might walk in newness of life. For *if* we have become united with him in the likeness of his death, we shall be also in the likeness of his resurrection . . . But if we died with Christ, we believe that we shall also live with him . . . Even so reckon ye also yourselves to be dead unto sin, but alive unto God in Christ Jesus" (Rom. 6:4, 5, 8, 11).

"Faithful is the saying: For if we died with him, we shall also live with him" (II Tim. 2:11).

Having consented to die with Christ, by the consecration of our whole being and by the abandonment of our will, we are already, in principle, raised with Him by faith. "When we were dead through our trespasses [God] made us alive together with Christ . . . [He] raised us up with him, and made us to sit with him in the heavenly places, in Christ Jesus" (Eph. 2:4-6). Our souls are regenerated, and we are already sealed by the Spirit unto the day of redemption (Eph. 4:30). "Having been buried with him in baptism, wherein ye were also raised with him through faith in the working of God, who raised him from the dead. And you, being dead through your trespasses and the uncircumcision of your flesh, you, I say, did he make alive together with him, having forgiven us all our trespasses" (Col. 2:12, 13).

Henceforth, the living Christ Himself indwells us. We can say with Paul: "For I through the law died unto the law, that I might live unto God. I have been crucified with Christ: and it is no longer I that live, but Christ liveth in me" (Gal. 2:19, 20).

This marvelous experience is within reach of every one of us, but it is still linked to the same condition: ". . . always bearing about in the body the dying of Jesus, that the life also of Jesus may be manifested in our body. For we who live are always delivered unto death for Jesus' sake, that the life also of Jesus may be manifested in our mortal flesh. So then death worketh in us, but life in you" (II Cor. 4:10-12). Paul regarded everything as loss, as refuse, that he might gain Christ, so as to know Him "and the power of his resurrection, and the fellowship of his sufferings, becoming conformed unto his death," if by any means he might "attain unto the resurrection from the dead" (Phil. 3:8-11).

Having paid that price, the believer lives henceforth as one truly raised, already belonging to the world on high, awaiting the glorious return of Jesus Christ. "If then ye were raised together with Christ, seek the things that are above, where Christ is, seated on the right hand of God . . . For ye died, and your life is hid with Christ in God. When Christ, who is our life, shall be manifested, then shall ye also with him be manifested in glory" (Col. 3:1-4).

10. CONCLUSION

After having meditated on so many texts, we better understand the prime importance of the resurrection: it is one of the pillars of the Christian faith. If we hoped in Christ in this life only, we would be of all men the most pitiable (I Cor. 14:19). But, thanks be to God, we are, on the contrary, the very happiest!

We would then endeavor to be "accounted worthy to attain to that world, and the resurrection from the dead" (Luke 20:35). May God help us to renounce all things in order to know Christ and the power of His resurrection and the fellowship of His sufferings, becoming conformed unto His death, to attain, if we can, the resurrection from among the dead! (Phil. 3:8-11).

When Paul finished preaching the resurrection at Athens, "some mocked; but others said, We will hear thee concerning this yet again . . . But certain men . . . believed." The same apostle cried out before King Agrippa: "Why is it judged incredible with you, if God doth raise the dead?" (Acts 17:32-34; 26:8). We know that we shall everywhere meet those same reactions on the part of people who deny the evidence and who despise their own best interests. But, fortified by God, we intend, like the first disciples, to be everywhere witnesses to the resurrection.

Then, together with all those who believe, we shall soon raise the song of triumph over the last enemy:

"Death is swallowed up in victory.

O death, where is thy victory?

O death, where is thy sting? . . .

Thanks be to God, who giveth us the victory through our Lord Jesus Christ!" (I Cor. 15:54-57).

## Chapter XI

# THE JUDGMENT SEAT OF CHRIST
# AND THE REWARD OF THE
# BELIEVER

1. BELIEVERS' ESCAPE FROM THE SINNERS' JUDGMENT AND PERDITION

WHAT TAKES PLACE at the moment when resurrected believers meet their Lord? It is infinitely terrible for sinners to appear before the great Judge. But for the redeemed there is no longer any fear of God's anger or of perdition, either one. Christ came, above all, not to judge, but to save. "He that believeth on him is not judged . . . He that heareth my word, and believeth him that sent me, hath eternal life, and cometh not into judgment, but hath passed out of death into life" (John 3:17, 18; 5:24).

Believers have been forgiven, justified, washed, pardoned, and purified of all sin by the Savior's blood (Rom. 3:24; I Cor. 6:11; I John 1:7, 9). "There is therefore now no condemnation to them that are in Christ Jesus" (Rom. 8:1). "While we were yet sinners, Christ died for us. Much more then, being now justified by his blood, shall we be saved from the wrath of God through him" (Rom. 5:8, 9). Since we have been converted to God, we wait for His Son from heaven, "who delivereth us from the wrath to come . . . God appointed us not unto wrath, but unto the obtaining of salvation through our Lord Jesus Christ" (I Thess. 1:10; 5:9). Jesus "is able to save to the uttermost them that draw near unto God through him"; and the Lord, having pardoned us, will remember our sins against us no more (Heb. 7:25; 8:12).

So it is with an immense joy and the assurance of eternal salvation that sincere believers picture their meeting with the Lord: "Herein is love made perfect with us, that we may have boldness in the day of judgment . . . There is no fear in love: but perfect love casteth out fear, because fear hath punishment . . . Abide in him; that, if he shall be manifested, we may have boldness, and not be ashamed before him at his coming" (I John 4:17, 18; 2:28).

## 2. THE JUDGMENT SEAT OF CHRIST

However, though by pure grace we escape the judgment of sinners, the Scriptures as clearly affirm that Jesus Christ will examine our works and our service to see whether we deserve a reward.

The Lord Himself declares: "Behold, I come quickly; and my reward is with me, to render to each man according as his work is" (Rev. 22:12). For the ungodly, the "reward" is eternal death and perdition; for believers, it is eternal life. "For we know him that said [to the ungodly], Vengeance belongeth unto me, I will recompense. And again [to believers] the Lord shall judge his people" (Heb. 10:30, 31).

All the children of God, without exception, will have to present themselves before Him: "Why dost thou judge thy brother? or thou again, why dost thou set at nought thy brother? for we shall all stand before the judgment seat of God . . . So then each one of us shall give account of himself to God" (Rom. 14:10-12). "Wherefore also we make it our aim . . . to be well pleasing unto him . . . For we must all be made manifest before the judgment seat of Christ; that each one may receive the things done in the body, according to what he hath done, whether it be good or bad" (II Cor. 5:9, 10).

The parables in the Gospels repeatedly teach us that

some day the Master will require His servants to give an
account: "Therefore is the kingdom of heaven likened unto
a certain king, who would make a reckoning with his servants . . . The lord of those servants cometh, and maketh a
reckoning with them" (Matt. 18:23; 25:19) . The rich man
said to his unfaithful steward: "Render the account of thy
stewardship" (Luke 16:2) . Whether we have been faithful
or unfaithful, God will soon take back what He has entrusted to us and will ask us what we have done with it.
It will be impossible to conceal a thing, for "all things are
naked and laid open before the eyes of him with whom we
have to do" (Heb. 4:13) .

Paul declares: "With me it is a very small thing that I
should be judged of you or of man's judgment . . . He that
judgeth me is the Lord. Wherefore judge nothing before
the time, until the Lord come, who will both bring to light
the hidden things of darkness, and make manifest the coun-
sels of the hearts" (I Cor. 4:3-5) .

It is to Jesus that God has given all judgment, since He
is the Son of man (John 5:22, 27) . Thus John depicts our
Lord with eyes like a flame of fire, able to search the reins
and hearts (Rev. 2:18, 23) . Paul purposed to keep a good
conscience to the end; and, in spite of his imperfections, he
did not fear this Judge, who was also his Savior. He wrote
with calm assurance: 'Henceforth there is laid up for me
the crown of righteousness, which the Lord, the righteous
judge, shall give to me at that day" (II Tim. 4:8) .

3. WITH WHAT DOES THE JUDGMENT SEAT OF CHRIST HAVE
   TO DO?

The life and the service of each believer will be examined
in all their aspects, for the Lord is not unjust to forget and
to let a single good act go without its promised reward (Heb.
6:10) . On the other hand, He is too holy to let one single

imperfection remain in those whom He admits into His presence.

a. *Works*

We are saved by grace, apart from works; but having been regenerated in Christ, we are to practice the good works which He Himself has prepared in advance for us (Eph. 2:8-10). It is entirely natural for the Lord to examine every one of our actions: "Whatsoever good thing each one doeth, the same shall he receive again from the Lord, whether he be bond or free" (Eph. 6:8). "Jehovah is a God of knowledge, and by him actions are weighed" (I Sam. 2:3). Paul speaks of the "revelation of the righteous judgment of God: who will render to every man according to his works: to them that by patience in well-doing seek for glory and honor and incorruption, eternal life . . . God shall judge the secrets of men, according to my gospel, by Jesus Christ" (Rom. 2:5-7, 16). "Let us not be weary in well-doing: for in due season we shall reap, if we faint not. So then, as we have opportunity, let us work that which is good toward all men, and especially toward them that are of the household of faith" (Gal. 6:9, 10).

The classic passage on this point is I Corinthians 3:10-15. Our works have no value if they are not built on Christ, our only foundation (vss. 10, 11, 14). But on that foundation the believer can build with quite varied materials: precious and durable, or base and perishable. The works compared to wood, hay, and stubble are the actions, even the religious ones, which are motivated by selfishness, pride, envy, and self will. One can pray, give alms, or preach the Gospel in a self-seeking way. (See, for example, Matthew 6:1, 2, 5; 7: 22; Philippians 1:17, etc.). Those works will not survive the judgment fires. Others, however, are like gold, silver, and precious stones. They are inspired by love, sincere zeal, and the pursuit of the will and glory of God; they undergo victoriously the judgment test (I Cor. 3:12, 14).

Are our works of that sort? It was in regard to acts of that quality that John wrote: "Blessed are the dead who die in the Lord from henceforth: yea, saith the Spirit, that they may rest from their labors; for their works follow with them" (Rev. 14:13).

b. *Work*

God, who acts without ceasing, has granted to us the privilege of being able to work with Him. Our endeavor is the measure of our zeal and of our gratitude and will not go unnoticed: "Each shall receive his own reward according to his own labor. For we are God's fellow-workers . . . Wherefore, my beloved brethren, be ye stedfast, unmovable, always abounding in the work of the Lord, forasmuch as ye know that your labor is not vain in the Lord" (I Cor. 3:8, 9; 15: 58). "God is not unrighteous to forget your work and the love which ye showed toward his name in that ye ministered unto the saints, and still do minister" (Heb. 6:10).

"The husbandman that laboreth must be the first to partake of the fruits" (II Tim. 2:6).

The master, in the parable, gives his goods into the keeping of his stewards, counting on their unremitting work: "Straightway he that received the five talents went and traded with them, and made other five talents." And the man who hid his talent in the earth, so as not to do anything, heard himself spoken of as a "wicked and slothful servant" and was cast out (Matt. 25:14-30). Thus he lost, not only his reward, but also every chance he might have had to be saved.

As for Paul, that model for the believers, he could declare right to the apostles' faces that he "labored more abundantly than they all" (I Cor. 15:10).

Shall we also have some work to present to the Lord?

c. *The strivings of an athlete*

Paul compares the Christian life to the efforts of an athlete who goes into training and who then runs to carry away the prize: "Know ye not that they that run in a race run all, but one receiveth the price? Even so run, that ye may attain. And every man that striveth in the games exerciseth self-control in all things. Now they do it to receive a corruptible crown; but we an incorruptible" (I Cor. 9:24, 25).

"Forgetting the things which are behind, and stretching forward to the things which are before, I press on toward the goal unto the prize of the high calling of God in Christ Jesus" (Phil. 3:13, 14).

The judgment seat of Christ will show whether we have been just triflers or serious and enduring runners of the race.

d. *Testimony*

All believers are called to testify and to serve, in a general sense. But it goes without saying that those to whom God has entrusted a special ministry have a unique responsibility: "Be not many of you teachers, my brethren, knowing that we shall receive heavier judgment" (James 3:1). "Obey them that have the rule over you, and submit to them: for they watch in behalf of your souls, as they that shall give account" (Heb. 13:17). "I have made thee a watchman . . . When I say unto the wicked, Thou shalt surely die; and thou givest him not warning, nor speakest to warn the wicked from his wicked way, to save his life; the same wicked man shall die in his iniquity; but his blood will I require at thy hand" (Ezek. 3:17, 18). Thus Paul was happy to be able to say to the elders of Ephesus: "I testify unto you this day, that I am pure from the blood of all men. For I shrank not from declaring unto you the whole counsel of God" (Acts 20:26, 27). Daniel also speaks of the reward of those who have turned many to righteousness (12:3).

The value of a ministry is measured by its fruits, whether visible or known only to God, as well as by the souls won. Paul said to the Philippians: "Ye are seen as lights in the world . . . that I may have whereof to glory in the day of

Christ, that I did not run in vain neither labor in vain" (Phil. 2:15, 16).

e. *The exercise of gifts received*

To each of the members of the body of Christ the Lord gives a work to be performed through the gift of the Spirit (I Cor. 12:7, 11, 27). This gift is to be developed and used to the service of others for the common good (I Peter 4:10). God bestows on us other gifts: intelligence, artistic or musical talents, health, beauty, etc. The parable of the talents, which are entrusted to each one according to his ability, teaches us that what is important is to develop those talents in the light of the great accounting, and not to hide them in the earth (Matt. 25:15-18).

Anyone seeing the poverty of our religious groups, their superficiality of consecration, and the lack of serious workers, realizes that many so-called Christians are concealing their talents so that they will not have to use them. One trembles in recalling the day when the Master will come to claim what is His due. Other Christians, perhaps not in the same category, still need to give heed to this word of Paul to Timothy: "I put thee in remembrance that thou stir up the gift of God which is in thee through the laying on of my hands. For God gave us not a spirit of fearfulness; but of power and love and discipline" (II Tim. 1:6, 7). How sad it would be to have to appear at the judgment seat of Christ with an atrophied gift, one having borne little fruit, when the Lord has expected much fruit of us, indeed, constantly more fruit!

f. *The use of our material goods*

Men are strange creatures: either they make an idol out of money, or else they claim that it is too material to have anything to do with spiritual life—this being asserted so they can go on enjoying it at their ease. God has certainly given us "richly all things to enjoy" (I Tim. 6:17). But He also wills that His children dedicate their goods to Him and use them according to His will. Our use of temporal goods will be condemned or rewarded at the last day.

"That thine alms may be in secret: and thy Father who seeth in secret shall recompense thee" (Matt. 6:4). "Love your enemies, and do them good and lend, never despairing; and your reward shall be great, and ye shall be sons of the Most High . . . Sell that which ye have, and give alms; make for yourselves purses which wax not old, a treasure in the heavens that faileth not, where no thief draweth near, neither moth destroyeth. For where your treasure is there will your heart be also . . . And when thou makest a feast, bid the poor, the maimed, the lame, the blind: and thou shalt be blessed; because they have not wherewith to recompense thee: for thou shalt be recompensed in the resurrection of the just" (Luke 6:35; 12:33, 34; 14:13, 14).

"Charge them that are rich in this present world . . . that they do good, that they be rich in good works, that they be ready to distribute, willing to communicate; laying up in store for themselves a good foundation against the time to come, that they may lay hold on the life which is life indeed" (I Tim. 6:17-19). In the parable of the unfaithful steward (Luke 16:1-13), Jesus again makes clear His teaching on this point. The steward, using his master's goods, was able to win over some friends, who later would take him in when he became destitute. He was praised, certainly, not for his unfaithfulness, but for the prudence with which he worked out a sure future for himself. Jesus declared that the children of light do not know how to act so prudently, and He adds: "Make to yourselves friends by means of the mammon of unrighteousness; that, when it shall fail, they may receive you into the eternal tabernacles . . . If therefore ye have not been faithful in the unrighteous mammon, who will commit to your trust the true riches? And if ye have not been faithful in that which is another's, who will give you that which is your own?" (vss. 9, 11, 12). "The unrighteous mammon" does not mean riches which have been wrongly acquired, but those which have been unequally divided up. Is it right, in fact, that one is born rich and another poor, one intelligent and another foolish, one handsome and another repulsive-looking? Our riches, moreover, are not our own, but God's; we are only stewards of them and shall soon have to give an account, handing them back, right down to the last penny. Then, if we have been faithful, God will give us the true riches, those that are to be our own; that is, the eternal riches that will be granted to us forever.

Let us note another great principle on the subject of liberality: "But this I say, He that soweth sparingly shall reap also sparingly; and he that soweth bountifully shall reap also bountifully . . . God loveth a cheerful giver" (II Cor. 9: 6, 7). If the reward for giving is the ability to give still more (vss. 8-11), and if God takes note of even the widow's mite, we can all use our material goods in a spiritual way so as to please their true Owner.

g. *Suffering*

The life of the faithful Christian is always accompanied by suffering: in the footsteps of his Savior, he has a share in the cross in order to participate later in the glory. "Blessed are ye when men shall reproach you, and persecute you . . . Rejoice, and be exceeding glad: for great is your reward in heaven" (Matt. 5:11, 12). "But insomuch as ye are partakers of Christ's sufferings, rejoice; that at the revelation of his glory also ye may rejoice with exceeding joy" (I Peter 4: 13). "Ye . . . took joyfully the spoiling of your possessions, knowing that ye have for yourselves a better possession and an abiding one" (Heb. 10:34). "For our light affliction, which is for the moment, worketh for us more and more exceedingly an eternal weight of glory" (II Cor. 4:17, 18).

It is not easy for anyone to rejoice in sufferings. But we can do it with God's help, if we are truly convinced that "the sufferings of this present time are not worthy to be

compared with the glory which shall be revealed to usward"
(Rom. 8:18).

h. *The strong faith and the living hope of the believer*
"Cast not away . . . your boldness, which hath great recompense of reward" (Heb. 10:35). "I have fought the good
fight, I have finished the course, I have kept the faith: henceforth there is laid up for me the crown of righteousness . . .
and not to me only, but also to all them that have loved his
appearing" (II Tim. 4:7, 8).

Loving the Lord's appearing doubtless means, first of all,
loving the Lord Himself, and then "looking for and earnestly
desiring" His glorious return (II Peter 3:12), preparing
oneself every day for that return, and seeking to prepare one's
fellow-men for it.

4. CRITERION BY WHICH THE APPRAISALS AT THE JUDGMENT
   SEAT OF CHRIST WILL BE MADE

We have seen that the whole life of the believer will be
examined from the point of view of his service. We shall
appear before the Lord as servants, witnesses, ambassadors,
sentinels, stewards, administrators. Now just what is required of all these?

"Let a man so account of us, as of ministers of Christ, and
stewards of the mysteries of God. Here, moreover, it is required in stewards, that *a man be found faithful*" (I Cor.
4:1, 2).

That word "faithful" appears over and over in the refer-
ences to the settling of accounts: "Who then is the faithful
and wise servant, whom his lord hath set over his household . . .? Well done, good and faithful servant: thou hast
been faithful over a few things. I will set thee over many
things" (Matt. 24:45; 25:21). "He that is faithful in a very
little . . . If therefore ye have not been faithful in the unrighteous mammon . . . And if ye have not been faithful in

that which is another's . . ." (Luke 16:10, 11, 12). "Be thou faithful unto death, and I will give thee the crown of life" (Rev. 2:10).

God is not asking that we always achieve success or that we possess marked abilities. (Each one receives "according to his several ability," Matt. 25:15.) But He wills that we be faithful—first in the little things—and then in the more important ones which He entrusts us with afterward. Let us take care not to be cast out with the unfaithful servants! (Luke 12:46).

As for the Lord, even when we fail, He abides faithful and cannot deny Himself. Thus He declares to His own: "I will give them their recompense in truth, and I will make an everlasting covenant with them" (Isaiah 61:8).

## 5. WHAT WILL BE THE MEASURE OF THE RECOMPENSE?

It will be in proportion to the service of each one.

Salvation is the same for all, according to the parable recorded in Matthew 20:1-16. All the laborers received one shilling, whether they had been employed for the whole day, for a few hours, or simply for the last hour. There is only one eternal life and one heaven, given to the thief on the cross just the same as to Paul, "who labored more abundantly than they all."

The reward, on the other hand, is in relation to individual service: "Each shall receive his own reward according to his own labor" (I Cor. 3:8). As the unfaithful servants were beaten with more or with fewer stripes (Luke 12:47, 48), even so the faithful servants received a greater or a a lesser reward: one was put over ten cities, whereas the other was given only five. The one who had gained ten pounds was given an eleventh, according to the principle that "unto every one that hath shall be given"—thanks to his faithful and persevering efforts (Luke 19:17-26). Some, for whom the Father has prepared it, will even be placed at the right hand and at the left hand of the Lord (Matt. 20:23).

## 6. WHAT WILL BE THE DIFFERENT REWARDS?

### a. *The crowns*

The athlete is crowned when he has competed according to the rules. The Lord promises:

*the crown of life,* to those who have endured temptation unto death (James 1:12; Rev. 2:10);

*the crown of righteousness,* to those who have loved His appearing (II Tim. 4:8);

*the incorruptible crown of glory,* to those who have tended the flock as faithful shepherds (I Peter 5:4).

Down here, laurels fade and glory is soon gone. But up there our crowns will never lose their brilliance, and we shall not have run for a corruptible reward (I Cor. 9:25).

The crown promised to overcomers is to be earned and kept through perseverance in the struggle: "Hold fast that which thou hast, that no one take thy crown" (Rev. 3:11).

One might say, furthermore, that all true believers are to be—and will be—conquerors (Rom. 8:37; II Cor. 2:14). The vanquished, those who do not endure to the end, will show by that very thing that they do not belong to Christ.

### b. *The reign*

The Lord reserves the reign to those who have been faithful to the end: Christ declared to those who had served Him in the person of His brethren: "Inherit the kingdom" (Matt. 25:34).

The good servants were given authority over either ten or five cities (Luke 19:17, 19). Jesus will apportion the kingdom with regard to those who continued with Him in His temptation, and He will cause them to sit on twelve thrones.

"He that overcometh, and he that keepeth my works unto the end, to him will I give authority over the nations . . . He that overcometh, I will give to him to sit down with me in my throne . . ." (Rev. 2:26; 3:21).

"If we endure, we shall also reign with him" (II Tim. 2:12).

c. *The inheritance*

"Servants, obey . . . whatsoever ye do, work heartily, as unto the Lord, and not unto men, knowing that from the Lord ye shall receive the recompense of the inheritance: ye serve the Lord Christ . . ." (Col. 3:22-24). The inheritance is promised to all the sanctified (Acts 20:32), and the seal of the Spirit on all our hearts is the certain pledge of it (Eph. 1:14). Having become children of God, we are heirs, and joint-heirs with Christ, the only begotten Son, to whom alone all things rightfully belong (Rom. 8:17; Heb. 2:2). This is such unheard-of-grace that God has to illumine the eyes of our understanding that we may know "what [is] the riches of the glory of his inheritance in the saints" (Eph. 1:18). Infinite blessings indeed are included in this inheritance:

The meek shall inherit the earth (Matt. 5:5).

Everyone that has left all else to follow the Lord will inherit eternal life (Matt. 19:29).

The angels are minstering spirits for the sake of them that shall inherit salvation (Heb. 1:14).

Through faith and patience we shall inherit the promises (Heb. 6:12).

Women, as well as their husbands, inherit the grace of life and the blessing (I Peter 3:7, 9). God has chosen the poor of this world "to be rich in faith, and heirs of the kingdom which he promised to them that love him" (James 2:5).

This inheritance is obtained through the death of Christ. If a person is to inherit anything on earth, there must first occur the death of the testator; likewise, there had to be the death of Christ with the shedding of His blood to assure us of the eternal inheritance (Heb. 9:15-18). In order to receive it, we then have to be born again and adopted into the family of God. "So that thou art no longer a bondservant, but a son; and if a son, then an heir through God" (Gal. 4:7). For the time being, we are like inheritors that are minors, for whom a guardian holds and administers the estate. But at "the day appointed of the Father," we shall take possession of all that is laid up for us (vss. 1, 2). Let us note, in conclusion, that a victorious faith is indispensable if one is thus to lay hold of the possession: "It is of faith, that it may be according to grace," so that the promise made to Abraham finds its fulfillment in us (Rom. 4:13-16). After having revealed the splendors of heaven, the Lord adds: "He that overcometh shall inherit these things; and I will be his God, and he shall be my son" (Rev. 21:7).

The person who understands this cries out: "The lines are fallen unto me in pleasant places; yea, I have a goodly heritage!" (Ps. 16:6) "Giving thanks unto the Father, who made us meet to be partakers of the inheritance of the saints in light!" (Col. 1:12) "Blessed be . . . God . . . who begat us again . . . unto an inheritance incorruptible, and undefiled, and that fadeth not away, reserved in heaven for you!" (I Peter 1:3, 4).

d. *The harvest*

"Whatsoever a man soweth, that shall he also reap." Every present action will have its eternal repercussion, either in blessing or cursing. "For he that soweth unto his own flesh shall of the flesh reap corruption; but he that soweth unto the Spirit shall of the Spirit reap eternal life. And let us not be weary in well-doing: for in due season we shall reap, if we faint not" (Gal. 6:7-9).

Jesus said that the harvest will take place at the end of the world (Matt. 13:39). Then the Lord will repay us for the good deeds that we have done. But the harvest will also be that of souls won by our testimony, whom we shall see gathered into the heavenly home. Paul wrote to his spiritual children in Thessalonica and in Corinth: "What is our hope, or

joy, or crown of glorying? Are not even ye, before our Lord
Jesus at his coming?" (I Thess. 2:19). "We are your glory-
ing, even as ye also are ours, in the day of our Lord Jesus"
(II Cor. 1:14).

The Christian's testimony is often accompanied by suffering and shame. But "they that sow in tears shall reap in joy.
He that goeth forth and weepeth, bearing seed for sowing,
shall doubtless come again with joy, bringing his sheaves
with him" (Ps. 126:5, 6). What joy for us—parents and
pastors and friends—to be able to meet God accompanied by
those whom we have brought to saving faith by His grace!
And, all the more significant, the Lord often uses the very
humblest as soul-winners! How precious it will also be for
us to be able to say: "Behold, I and the children whom God
hath given me!"

On the other hand, how sad it will be for those who have
not won anyone else to the Lord and who will thus have to
appear alone in His presence! We see, moreover, that the
harvest will be much more abundant than we can imagine:
"Cast thy bread upon the waters; for thou shalt find it after
many days . . . In the morning sow thy seed, and in the evening withhold not thy hand" (Eccl. 11:1, 6). The Word of
God never returns unto Him void, and the seed planted in
a person's heart can become productive entirely unbeknown
to us. Once again, what matters is this: that we be faithful,
even if we do not see all the results. The promise is explicit:
if we sow sparingly, we shall reap sparingly; but if we sow
bountifully, we shall reap bountifully (II Cor. 9:6).

e. *Praise*

For the sincere believer, how sweet it will be to hear the
Lord say: "Well done, good and faithful servant; thou hast
been faithful over a few things; I will set thee over many
things; enter thou into the joy of thy lord" (Matt. 25:21).
"Then shall each man have his praise from God" (I Cor.
4:5). The trial of our faith will result in "praise and glory

and honor at the revelation of Jesus Christ" (I Peter 1:7).

This approval by the Master and this recognition of His servants' work will be manifested in a way far beyond anything we could have dreamed of. Blessed are those servants whom the lord when he cometh shall find watching! "Verily I say unto you, that he shall gird himself, and make them sit down to meat, and shall come and serve them" (Luke 12:37).

Jesus Christ, when He was down here with His disciples, was in their midst as One that served, thus giving them an example. But is it not past comprehension that in the glory of heaven He will descend from His throne to serve us!

f. *The service accrued*

The reward for faithful service is a more extensive and more important service. On earth we can be faithful in only small things, and our service is marred by many imperfections. But in heaven we shall have the joy of doing infinitely better. "Who then is the faithful and wise steward, whom his lord shall set over his household, to give them their portion of food in due season [which is a very limited responsibility]. Blessed is that servant, whom his lord when he cometh shall find so doing! Of a truth I say unto you, that he will set him over all that he hath" (Luke 12:42-44). "Thou hast been faithful over a few things, I will set thee over many things . . . For unto everyone that hath shall be given, and he shall have abundance" (Mat. 25:21, 29). We shall speak further of our service in heaven and shall see the unlimited possibilities it opens up to us.

To those who serve Him in suffering and humility the Lord promises a glorious reward: "Our light affliction, which is for the moment, worketh for us more and more exceedingly an eternal weight of glory" (II Cor. 4:17, 18). You are saddened by various trials "that the proof of your faith . . . may be found unto praise and glory and honor at the revelation of Jesus Christ . . . And when the chief Shepherd shall be manifested, ye shall receive the crown of glory . . ." (I Peter

1:7; 5:4). "Glory and honor and peace to every man that worketh good" (Rom. 2:10).

"And they that are wise shall shine as the brightness of the firmament; and they that turn many to righteousness as the stars for ever and ever" (Dan. 12:3). "Then shall the righteous shine forth as the sun in the kingdom of their Father" (Matt. 13:43).

## 7. WHEN WILL THE REWARDS BE GIVEN OUT?

The reward is not at the death of the believer; it will not take place until the Lord's return.

"After a long time the lord of those servants cometh, and maketh a reckoning with them" (Matt. 25:19).

"Thou shalt be recompensed in the resurrection of the just" (Luke 14:14).

"Each man's work shall be made manifest: for *the day* shall declare it . . . and the fire itself shall prove each man's work of what sort it is" (I Cor. 3:12, 13. "The day" is obviously the great day of the Lord.)

"Until the Lord come . . . then shall each man have his praise from God" (I Cor. 4:5).

" . . . That I may have whereof to glorify in the day of Christ, that I did not run in vain . . ." (Phil. 2:16).

"For what is our hope, or joy, or crown of glorying? Are not even ye, before our Lord Jesus at his coming?" (I Thess. 2:19).

"Herein is love made perfect with us, that we may have boldness in the day of judgment" (I John 4:17).

"Behold, I come quickly; and my reward is with me, to render to each man according as his work is" (Rev. 22:12. See Isa. 62:11).

The Lord's return is imminent, and this word will soon be accomplished:

"The time of the dead to be judged [has come], and the time to give their reward to thy servants the prophets, and to the saints, and to them that fear thy name, the small and the great" (Rev. 11:18).

## 8. THE LOSS OF THE REWARD

Several of the texts cited have already implied that it is possible for anyone to lose his reward.

The well-known passage in I Corinthians 3:10-15 says that "if any man's work shall be burned, he shall suffer loss." Naturally, this has nothing to do with a purgatory where the believer is supposed to complete the expiation of his imperfections:

a. The fire under consideration does not burn people, but works.

b. It neither improves the state of the believer, nor makes him suffer; but it tests and eliminates that in his past life which is not worthy of a reward.

c. It is "the day" that will lead to this judgment of works (vs. 13); that is, the day of the Lord, the day of His glorious return—although according to the Roman Church, purgatory is supposed to begin right away after death.

d. Finally, this test is instantaneous: it is applied to the believer fixed on the one foundation, Jesus Christ; and he will receive his reward, if he is to have one, and go at once to the wedding feast with the heavenly Bridegroom.

Imagine the consternation of the one who in an instant will see the disappearance of all his works, since they had been inspired by self-seeking, and who will lose everything except his life. Does he not resemble Lot, the carnal believer, settled down in Sodom in the midst of the world and its compromises? In the day when judgment fell, Lot did indeed escape the fire; but he lost his goods, his wife, and even his honor (Gen. 19). How many times he must have regretted not having followed the selfless and pure example of Abraham, to whom God at the same time made the promise of a great reward (Gen. 15:1)!

The New Testament constantly warns the Christian about this subject. "They that run in a race run all, but one receiveth the prize . . . I buffet my body, and bring it into bondage, lest by any means, after that I have preached to others, I myself should be rejected" (I Cor. 9:24, 27). The word "rejected" (in the Greek, *adokimos*) can be translated "reproved." (The Amplified New Testament also gives it this sense in II Corinthians 13:7, where *approved* is contrasted with *unapproved*.) Paul does not say that, after having preached to others, he may lose his salvation. What he fears is not being "approved" and thus losing his reward.

The apostle adds: "If . . . a man contend in the games, he is not crowned, except he have contended lawfully" (II Tim. 2:5). "I laid before them the gospel which I preach . . . lest . . . I should be running, or had run, in vain" (Gal. 2:2). "That I may have whereof to glory in the day of Christ, that I did not run in vain neither labor in vain" (Phil. 2:16).

"Look to yourselves, that ye lose not the things which we have wrought" (II John 8). "Abide in him; that, if he shall be manifested, we may have boldness, and not be ashamed before him at his coming" (I John 2:28).

Those who do "good works" to be admired by men will receive no reward from God. They already have their reward down here, in the satisfaction of their pride. But none of that will go with them into the other world (Matt. 6:1, 2, 5).

It would be extremely dangerous to reason like this: "The reward is not of any great importance provided I am saved and justified, even so as by fire"! Such a train of thought would denote a complete lack of reverence and of love toward God and would simply carry with it the loss of salvation. That, unfortunately, is the very way many people will lose everything, in spite of apparently brilliant exploits: after having prophesied, cast out demons, and done many miracles in the name of Christ, they will be rejected (Matt. 7:22, 23). Whereas sincere believers will receive the inheritance as a reward, the others will be deprived of it. Ishmael, the son of the bondwoman, could not receive the inheritance from Abraham along with Isaac, the son of the free woman—the one truly born by faith (Gal. 4:22, 31). Carnal, unregenerate men have no share in the inheritance of the children of God, those born again by faith. "Neither fornicators, nor idolators, nor adulterers, nor effeminate, nor abusers of themselves with men, nor thieves, nor covetous, nor drunkards, nor revilers, nor extortioners, shall inherit the kingdom of God . . . neither doth corruption inherit incorruption" (I Cor. 6:9, 10: 15:50. See also Ephesians 5:5.)

May we take these things to heart so as not to lose either our souls or the fruit of our labor!

9. CONSIDERATION OF VARIOUS QUESTIONS RELATING TO THE REWARD

In conclusion, let us consider a few more questions which are raised by the subject of rewards.

a. Is it not just such a doctrine that makes religion "the opiate of the people"? You say to the working men and to the poor: "Submit yourselves; suffer in silence while your boss stuffs his pockets with cash. And some day you will have your 'pie in the sky' "! But this fallacious reasoning combines two things which have nothing to do with each other: 1.) The social relationship between employers and employees is established in the Bible on the basis of the strictest justice. Unjust employers, like the unjust workers, will be severely punished (Eph. 6:5-9; James 5:1-6, etc.) 2.) The reward encourages well doing. How could it be immoral or anti-social? The person who understands the will of God in regard to rewards will conduct himself in an exemplary way in all his dealings with his fellow man. He will thus contribute to the good of all as well as to his own happiness.

b. "You are nothing but egotists," other objectors insist, "if you need a reward for doing good. As for us, we do good just for the sake of doing good, out of pure love!" We reply that the reward puts no premium on egotism, since, in order to serve Christ, one must actually renounce himself and lose his life, in devotion to others. On the other hand, it is an indisputable fact that the great projects of disinterested charity in the world have been carried on largely by true Christians: hospitals, orphanages, the Red Cross, work among prisoners, aid to fallen women, etc. As for the "pure love" existing apart from faith and the fear of God, we must admit that there is not much of it to be seen in a world like this!

c. Is it correct to speak of *meriting* a reward, when salvation is by grace? We must have an understanding of terms here. In one sense, we *merit* nothing but perdition—and God does not owe us a thing. He saved us by pure goodness; and then, to encourage us, He promises also to reward our service. But even that service is by grace, and what we accomplish is only our strict obligation. "What hast thou that thou didst not receive?" (I Cor. 4:7). Does the Master "thank the servant because he did the things that were commanded? Even so ye also, when ye shall have done all the things that are commanded you, say, We are unprofitable servants; we have done that which it was our duty to do" (Luke 17:7-10). That should be enough to keep us humble and to make us appreciate as we ought the infinite grace of God. If He acts as He does toward us, it is because He disposes of His own in sovereign grace and as He wills. And who can criticize Him for that or look unfavorably on His goodness? (Matt. 20:15).

d. Although the reward is primarily for the other world, does it not often begin even in this one? Yes, it certainly does. In the Old Testament the promises and the rewards were essentially earthly ones. (See for example Deuteronomy 28:1-14.) In the New Testament the principal emphasis is on the life that is eternal. But that does not hinder many blessings from being granted to the believer beginning right now. "There is no man that hath left house, or brethren . . .

or children, or lands, for my sake . . . but he shall receive a hundredfold now in this time, houses, and brethren . . . and children, and lands, with persecutions; and in the world to come eternal life" (Mark 10:29, 30). "Honor thy father and mother . . . that it may be well with thee, and thou mayest live long on the earth" (Eph. 6:2, 3). Of course, the earthly reward can be only a token of the glorious heavenly reward.

e. Some timid and modest people will perhaps sigh wistfully, "All this is very fine, but it is not for me. I am not one of those who, like Paul, can expect a great reward." This is faulty reasoning. As we have said, the principal requirement is that a steward be found faithful, and that, first of all, in small things. There are so many promises addressed to all the children of God, even to the humblest. Note even this: "He that receiveth a prophet in the name of a prophet shall receive a prophet's reward; and he that receiveth a righteous man in the name of a righteous man shall receive a righteous man's reward. And whosoever shall give to drink unto one of these little ones a cup of cold water only, in the name of a disciple, verily I say unto you he shall in no wise lose his reward" (Matt. 10:41, 42). Thus, not only will the prophets and the righteous be rewarded, but also those who have received them. And anyone at all has had a thousand opportunities to give a cup of cold water, a gesture, which, though costing nothing, is of value because of the love and the smile that accompany it. According to Hebrews 6:10, God is not unrighteous to forget one's work, his love, and his service rendered to the saints. The Lord who delighted in the gift of the widow's mite, something unnoticed or despised by men, will be able, in the most humble and modest of folk, to find reasons for bestowing magnificent rewards.

f. Let us be certain that God will fulfill His promise. He could have done without saving us in the first place, and He could have refrained from giving any rewards at all. But since, in His grace, He has decided as He has, He will be no man's debtor and will recompense the smallest act of faithfulness. He said this Himself: "I will give them their recompense in truth" (Isa. 61:8). Jesus added: "Thy Father who seeth in secret shall recompense thee" (Matt. 6:4, 6). "So that men shall say . . . Verily there is a God that judgeth in the earth" (Ps. 58:12).

g. Let us understand clearly that not only is God the reward giver, but He is Himself our supreme reward. Note the word of the Lord to Abraham: "I am thy shield and thy exceeding great reward" (Gen. 15:1). Jesus declared: He that overcometh . . . I will give him the morning star." Then He added: "I am . . . the bright, the morning star" (Rev. 2: 26, 28; 22:16). Indeed this is what counts for us. Life eternal is to know the Father and the Son (John 17:3). Likewise, our reward is to please God, to bring joy to Him, to see our love and our service approved by Him—in short, to find ourselves drawn ever closer to Him.

## 10. CONCLUSION

Do we give to the question of rewards all the attention that it merits? Let us not treat it lightly, since the Word of God attributes such importance to it.

If we love the Lord, we shall not be able to endure the idea of doing nothing for Him. Such failure on our part would, moreover, be fatal for us, for the Scriptures give us this explicit word: *They shall not appear before Jehovah empty* (Deut. 16:16).

On the other hand, the prospect of the reward will completely change the direction of our lives and the object of our affections: "Make for yourselves purses which wax not old, a treasure in the heavens that faileth not, where no thief draweth near, neither moth destroyeth.

*"For where your treasure is, there will your heart be also"* (Luke 12:33, 34).

If we regard the reward with contempt, it probably means simply this: our treasure is still on earth!

The certainty of the recompense helps us, besides, to rejoice in the most severe trials and to win the victory: "When men shall . . . persecute you . . . *rejoice and be exceeding glad: for great is your reward in heaven*" (Matt. 5:11, 12).

Moses is given as an example for us: lifted up to the very steps of the throne, he preferred the reproach and affliction of the people of God to the treasures and honors of Egypt, *"for he looked unto the recompense of reward"* (Heb. 11:26).

May we be ready to follow the Lord in every place and to the end, our feet planted solidly on the ground, but our eyes fixed on the reward. Then the word addressed to Ruth shall be ours also: "Jehovah recompense thy work, and *a full reward be given thee of Jehovah,* the God of Israel, under whose wings thou art come to take refuge" (Ruth 2:12).

What more could we want?

A *full* reward—
      not a partial one
            and not a perishing one.
Are we sure we shall receive it?

## Chapter XII

# THE MARRIAGE FEAST OF
# THE LAMB

### 1. GOD'S DESIRE TO HAVE FELLOWSHIP WITH MAN

GOD IS LOVE, and one can conclude that He has created man so as to have in His presence those whom He can love. According to the Scriptures, "It is not good that . . . man should be alone." And if the Lord has made us in His own image, we may rightly believe that He does not wish to remain alone either.

After the fall of man, the Old Testament constantly shows us Jehovah as the Husband of Israel, who is seeking to draw His people into intimate communion with Himself: "I bare you on eagles' wings, and brought you unto myself . . . Ye shall be mine own possession from among all peoples . . ." (Exod. 19:4, 5). *"For thy Maker is thy husband"* (Isa. 54:5). The writings of the prophets contain wonderful words of love which God addresses along these lines to Israel. (See, for example, Isaiah 54:6-10; Ezekiel 16:6-14, etc.) Zephaniah goes so far as to say: "Jehovah, thy God . . . will rejoice over thee with joy; he will rest in his love; he will joy over thee with singing" (3:17).

This love, an exclusive one, wants to be reciprocated.

"Thou shalt love Jehovah thy God with all thy heart, and with all thy soul, and with all thy might . . . Thou shalt be perfect with Jehovah thy God . . . Jehovah thy God is a devouring fire, a jealous God" (Deut. 6:5; 18:13; 4:24).

Unfortunately Israel has been unfaithful. The nation

"committed adultery with stones and with stocks" [i.e., with idols]. For this very cause . . . I had put her away and given her a bill of divorcement" (Jer. 3:6-9). But in the end of time, He promises to take her again to Himself. "At that day, saith Jehovah . . . thou shalt call me Ishi [my husband], and shalt call me no more Baali [my master] . . . And I will betroth thee unto me for ever" (Hosea 2:16-20). "Thou shalt be called Hephzibah [i.e., My delight is in her], and thy land Beulah [Married]; for Jehovah delighteth in thee, and thy land shall be married . . . and as the bridegroom rejoiceth over the bride, so shall thy God rejoice over thee" (Isa. 62.4, 5). Besides, it will no longer be just the Lord seeking His own; His own will turn at last to Him: "O virgin of Israel, turn again . . . for Jehovah hath created a new thing in the earth: A woman shall encompass a man" (Jer. 31:21, 22).

## 2. JESUS CHRIST, THE HEAVENLY BRIDEGROOM

The bridegroom announced by the prophets can be none other than God incarnate, Jesus Christ. Away back in the Psalms, we have a "love song" to the glory of the One for whom the Church waits: "Thou art fairer than the children of men . . . Thy throne, O God, is for ever and ever . . . God, thy God, hath anointed thee with the oil of gladness . . . At thy right hand doth stand the queen in gold of Ophir" (Ps. 45:2, 6, 7, 9). The divine fiancé is also presented in the Song of Solomon. He is the king, the beloved who is "chiefest among ten thousand," the altogether lovely One.

In the New Testament, John the Baptist spoke of the great joy he had in hearing the voice of the bridegroom, of him "that hath the bride" (John 3:29). Jesus gave Himself that name several times in the parables: Matthew 9:15; 22:2; 25:1. And Paul wrote: "I am jealous over you with a godly jealousy: for I espoused you to one husband, that I might present you as a pure virgin to Christ" (II Cor. 11:2).

All the divine attributes are brought together in the Person

of Jesus. He is the Creator, the Lord and Master, the Lamb
slain, the Judge. But how blessed it is for the Church to
think of Him as the divine Bridegroom!

### 3. THE CHURCH, THE BRIDE OF CHRIST

The Bride, of whom John the Baptist spoke, is obviously
the Church, the body of all the redeemed of Jesus Christ.
Paul has just told us that he had espoused the Corinthians to
one Husband, that he might present them as a pure virgin to
Christ. The apostle develops the figure of marriage to il-
lustrate the relationship of the Lord to His own, that of husband and wife. Christ is the head of the Church, which is in
subjection to Him: He loves it unto death, nourishes it, and
cherishes it (Eph. 5:23-32).

The Revelation speaks of the wife of the Lamb (19:7). In
describing the heavenly Jerusalem, John wrote: "Come
hither, I will show thee the bride, the wife of the Lamb"
(21:9). The prayer which concludes the Bible calls with
fervor for the return of the Bridegroom: "And the Spirit and
the bride say, Come! . . . Amen! come, Lord Jesus!" (Rev.
22:17, 20).

One remarkable thing is that the Bride so clearly designated by the New Testament already appears several times in
the types and prophecies of the Old Testament.

According to Paul, Adam was the figure of "him that was
to come," i.e. of Christ (Rom. 5:14). Among earthly creatures he found no companion worthy of him. God plunged
him into a deep sleep, pierced his side, and took from it *Eve*
(Gen. 2:18-24); likewise, it is from the pierced side of Christ
who died for us that God has taken the Church, now sharing
His nature, having been regenerated by His sacrifice.

*Sara,* the free wife of Abraham, represents the heavenly
Jerusalem, whereas Hagar, the bondwoman, is the type of
"the Jerusalem that now is," still in bondage to the law (Gal.
4:22-27).

Some see in Genesis 24 this appealing parable: Abraham sent his servant Eliezer into a strange country to find a wife of his kindred for Isaac, the heir of the divine promises. Eliezer met the one whose heart God had prepared; and he spoke to her, not of himself, but of the bridegroom who was waiting for her; he gave her magnificent presents, the pledge of the wealth and the happiness which would so soon be hers. Then he led Rebecca out of her country, to the far-off land where the wedding feast would be celebrated. God also is sending His Spirit into the world today, among men created in His own image, to seek out and prepare the Church, the Bride of His Son. The Spirit wins the heart of the Bride by speaking to her, not of Himself, but of the divine Bridegroom; He decks her with His gifts and pledges to her glory and heavenly bliss. She begins to love that One whom she has not yet seen; and when she is ready, He will take her away to meet the Lord, for the celebration in heaven of the marriage of the Lamb.

4. THE COMPANIONS OF THE BRIDE AND THE FRIENDS OF THE BRIDEGROOM

Does the Bride refer to all who go in to the marriage feast with Jesus Christ, or are there guests with her who are in a different relationship to the Lord?

Psalm 45 expresses it like this: "She shall be led unto the king . . . The virgins her companions that follow her shall be brought unto thee . . . They shall enter into the king's palace" (vss. 14-16).

The wise virgins of the parable are not the Bride, but with her they enter in to the marriage feast (Matt. 25:10).

John the Baptist distinguishes between the Bridegroom, the Bride, and the friend of the Bridegroom, which he himself is (John 3:29). In speaking of His forerunner, Jesus said that the smallest in the kingdom of heaven is greater than he (Matt. 11:11). He therefore grants a privileged place to those who enter into the new covenant.

What is one to infer from this? It is clear that the Church, strictly speaking, was not created until Pentecost. For the formation of the body of Christ there had to be the cross, the resurrection, the glorification of the Lord, and the outpouring of the Holy Spirit (John 11:52; Eph. 1:20-23; 2:13-16; 3:5-10). To speak of the Church in connection with the community of Israel in the Old Testament is to give a non-biblical meaning to the terms, since in a literal sense, the believers under the Old Covenant could not yet be a part of the body of Christ.

Still, the Scriptures are very restrained as to the respective position in heaven of the believers of the Old and those of the New Covenant. It is certain that the devout Jews of old share in the salvation brought by Jesus Christ: they looked forward to the sacrifice of the Messiah, and God forgave them because of Him who was to come (John 8:56; Rom. 3:25, 26; 4:1-8). They will have part in the reign, the glorious resurrection, the rewards, and the inheritance of the believers (Dan. 7:27, 12:2, 3, 13). They will sit down at the table in the kingdom of God with the patriarchs, the prophets, and the redeemed of the whole earth (Luke 13:28, 29). According to the Revelation the heavenly Jerusalem, the Bride of the Lamb, has on its gates the names of the twelve tribes of Israel and on its foundation those of the twelve apostles of the Lamb. It also seems that the four and twenty elders seated on thrones in the presence of God represent twelve patriarchs of the Old Covenant and twelve apostles of the New (Rev. 21:12, 14; 4:4). Thus the important thing about heaven will be our admission to the banqueting hall, to the very presence of God. As for the rest, we shall be given more light up there.

## 5. THE PREPARATION FOR THE MARRIAGE

It is impossible to measure the distance which separates

the Lord of glory from the Bride whom He has determined to choose from among sinners. That distance can be spanned only by the grace of that One who is made unto us wisdom and righteousness and sanctification and redemption. Yet the Lord also requires that His Bride do everything she possibly can to prepare herself for such a glorious union.

a. *The Bride puts on her wedding garment.*

"The marriage of the Lamb is come, and his wife hath made herself ready. And it was given unto her that she should array herself in fine linen, bright and pure: for the fine linen is the righteous acts of the saints" (Rev. 19:7, 8).

The Scriptures often speak of the garments necessary for an appearance before God: "Thou . . . knowest not that thou art . . . naked: I counsel thee to buy of me . . . white garments, that thou mayest clothe thyself, and that the shame of thy nakedness be not made manifest" (Rev. 3:17, 18). In the parable of the marriage feast, "the king . . . saw there a man who had not on a wedding garment: and he saith unto him, Friend, how camest thou in hither not having a wedding garment? And he was speechless." Then the king had him cast out (Matt. 22:11, 12). We understand that, according to oriental custom, the wedding garment was provided by the prince for each guest. The man therefore had no excuse if he refused to wear it, no doubt imagining that the clothing he had (his own righteousness) would be quite acceptable for the wedding occasion.

The best robe was given to the prodigal son to cover his rags (Luke 15:22). Isaiah exclaims: "My soul shall be joyful in my God; for he hath clothed me with the garments of salvation, he hath covered me with the robe of righteousness" (Isa. 61:10). In a sense, this new garb is, therefore, pure grace; so we understand the phrase just alluded to in the Revelation (19:8): "it was *given* unto her that she should array herself in fine linen."

But what is the Bride's responsibility, since it is said at

the same time that she "should array herself"? The fine linen
does not simply represent the righteousness of Christ imputed
to the believer. It is also "the righteous acts of the saints"
(Rev. 19:8). We shall have to appear before God clothed in
whatever righteous acts remain after the fire test spoken of
in I Corinthians 3:12-15. This means that we cannot count
on preparing ourselves for the marriage feast of the Lamb
in the twinkling of an eye, once we find ourselves in heaven.
It is here and now that we are to produce works worthy of
our heavenly Bridegroom.

And when we shall have done all that is in our power to
do, let us remember that we are still only "unprofitable servants," having done nothing but our duty (Luke 17:10);
moreover, let us take care to put under the blood of Christ
our still imperfect works. Let us imitate those who, as we
read in the Revelation, have "washed their robes and made
them white in the blood of the Lamb . . . that they may have
the right to the tree of life and may enter in by the gates into
the city" (Rev. 7:14; 22:14). With them, we shall be declared blessed.

Making use of another figure, the psalmist exclaims: "The
king's daughter within the palace is all glorious: her clothing
is inwrought with gold. She shall be led unto the king in
broidered work" (Ps. 45:13, 14). Nothing is too fine for the
bride's gown; but what gold or embroidered work will be
more precious in the eyes of the Bridegroom than our works
of righteousness and of love?

b. *Without sanctification no man shall see the Lord*

This word, in Hebrews 12:14, is applicable to the Church
as well as to the individual believer. Christ purposes to "present the church to himself a glorious church, not having spot
or wrinkle or any such thing, but . . . holy and without
blemish" after having Himself sanctified her (Eph. 5:26, 27).
"Wherefore, beloved, seeing that ye look for these things,
give diligence that ye may be found in peace, without spot

and blameless in his sight" (II Peter 3:14). "And now, my little children, abide in him; that, if he shall be manifested, we may have boldness, and not be ashamed before him at his coming" (I John 2:28).

Let us work then on our sanctification with fear and trembling, at the same time remembering that as we believe and obey, Jesus is sanctifying us wholly—body, soul, and spirit—for the day when He will celebrate His union with us (Phil. 2:12, 13; I Thess. 5:23, 24).

## 6. THE MARRIAGE OF THE LAMB

So far our fellowship with Christ, however precious and real it may be, exists only by faith, not by sight (II Cor. 5:7). It is in "hope" that believers consider Christ as their betrothed: "Whom not having seen ye love; on whom, though now ye see him not, yet believing, ye rejoice greatly with joy unspeakable and full of glory: receiving the end of your faith, even the salvation of your souls" (Rom. 8:24; I Peter 1:8, 9). A betrothed couple looks forward with anticipation to the wedding day. Christ loves the church with an infinite love and longs for the moment of His perfect union with her; the Church loves Him because He first loved her, and she cries with the Spirit: "Come!" (I John 4:19; Rev. 22:17).

Finally will arrive the longed-for day of our "gathering together unto Him" (II Thess. 2:1). The Bride will be adorned and made worthy of the Bridegroom, who will take her and make her sit down with Him on the throne (Rev. 3:21).

A true marriage is a union for life—that of which we are speaking is a union for eternity (I Thess. 4:17).

The betrothed are wholly each other's; we shall be Christ's, and He will give Himself to us without the slightest reserve: "The two shall become one flesh. This mystery is great; but I speak in regard of Christ and of the church" (Eph. 5:31, 32). Then shall this word be truly fulfilled: "All are yours; and ye are Christ's; and Christ is God's" (I Cor. 3:23).

The wife is in subjection to her husband; finally the Church will be in entire subjection to her heavenly Head, with joy and gratitude.

A couple builds their home on love; Christ has long divinely loved the Church; in the future she will be able to reciprocate His heavenly and perfect affection.

## 7. JOY BURSTING FORTH IN HEAVEN

There is no more joyous occasion than a wedding. If there is joy in heaven over one sinner that repents, a prodigal son who has come back home (Luke 15:7, 25), what jubilation will characterize the marriage of the only begotten Son and the cohort of the redeemed who have attained perfection!

The queen and her companions are ready: "With gladness and rejoicing shall they be led: they shall enter into the king's palace" (Ps. 45:15). God is able "to guard you from stumbling, and to set you before the presence of his glory without blemish in exceeding joy" (Jude 24). Jesus says to His own: "Ye . . . now have sorrow: but I will see you again, and your heart shall rejoice, and your joy no one taketh away from you" (John 16:22). "Hallelujah! . . . Let us rejoice and be exceeding glad, and let us give the glory unto him: for the marriage of the Lamb is come" (Rev. 19:6, 7). Then will be heard music and rejoicing (Luke 15:24, 25). Then shall our hearts fully know joy unspeakable and full of glory! (I Peter 1:8).

## 8. THE MARRIAGE SUPPER

Every marriage has its feast. The guests rejoice with the happy pair, and they all have fellowship together around a sumptuously laden table. This figure is very often used in the Bible in connection with the marriage of the Lamb. ". . . Jehovah of hosts [will] make unto all peoples a feast of fat things, a feast of wines on the lees, of fat things full of marrow, of wines on the lees, well refined. And . . . in this mountain . . . he hath swallowed up death for ever" (Isa. 25:6, 7). "A certain king . . . made a marriage feast for his son, and sent forth his servants . . . saying, Tell them that are bidden, Behold, I have made ready my dinner; my oxen and my fatlings are killed, and all things are ready: come to the marriage feast . . . The wedding was filled with guests . . . The king came in to behold the guests" (Matt. 22:2-4, 10, 11).

Jesus speaks elsewhere of the happy servants whom the Master, when he comes, shall find watching: He shall gird himself and make them sit down to meat and shall come and serve them (Luke 12:37). To this marvelous banquet there will come to sit down the patriarchs, the prophets, and the redeemed from all the four corners of the earth (Luke 13:28, 29). "Blessed are they that are bidden to the marriage supper of the Lamb!" (Rev. 19:9).

## 9. When will the marriage of the Lamb take place?

The texts that we have just cited say clearly: Immediately after the Rapture, the Church is to undergo the judgment of her works; she "prepares" herself, adorning her person with fine linen, shining and pure. The marriage will then be celebrated in heaven. During that time there will be enacted on earth the Great Tribulation, the reign of Antichrist, and the judgment of his impure wife, Babylon the Great. Christ will then descend from heaven with His sanctified Bride and will establish in glory His reign of righteousness and peace (Rev. 19:1-20:6).

In the succession of the last prophetic visions in the book of Isaiah there can be seen a remarkable prototype of the events given above. The prophet at the same time has a glimpse of what the Messiah will do for Israel, the earthly Jerusalem, and for the heavenly Jerusalem: "Jehovah delighteth in thee, and thy land shall be married . . . As the bridegroom rejoiceth over the bride, so shall thy God rejoice over thee" (Isa. 62:5, 6).

The divine Bridegroom, united with His beloved, will come back to carry out the judgment of Armageddon, when He will tread down the people in the winepress of His fierce wrath (Isa. 63:1-6 and Rev. 19:13, 15).

After that, the Lord will respond to the cry of the prophet: "Oh that thou wouldest rend the heavens, that thou wouldest come down!" (Isa 64:1). He will make manifest His triumph and will create the new heavens and the new earth (Isa. 65 and 66).

### 10. WHERE WILL THE MARRIAGE BE CELEBRATED?

In heaven, of course. The queen and her companions will be introduced in the midst of rejoicing: "They shall enter into the king's palace" (Ps. 45:14-16). "The king hath brought me into his chambers" (Song of Solomon 1:4). The Gospels speak of the place where the marriage feast will be held, clearly a room in the king's palace. In the beginning of Revelation 19, John transports us into heaven; then after the celebration, heaven opens and Christ descends with the armies of heaven for the Battle of Armageddon (vs. 11).

No comment is needed on this. The eternal union of Christ and His Church can be consummated only in the glory of the divine abode. Jesus has gone on ahead in order to prepare a place for us; soon He will return to take us to be with Him for ever (John 14:3).

### 11. THE PRESENTATION OF THE BRIDE

Sometimes an engagement is a secret understanding; the fiancée may be unappreciated or even despised, especially if her origin was a lowly one. But the wedding day puts her in full view and assures her that from then on she will share in the consideration and position which her husband has.

The Church, betrothed to Christ, has for a long time been scoffed at, assailed by various testings, and even subjected to insults. But lifting her up to His throne, as a king makes known to his subjects their new queen, the Lord presents her in all solemnity.

a. *First Jesus Christ makes this glorious Church to appear before Him,* without spot or wrinkle, or any such thing, but holy and without blemish (Eph. 5:27). He draws her out of her obscurity, imperfection, and remoteness, in order to place her at His side, in full splendor.

b. *The Lord presents His Bride to heaven.* The principalities and powers in the heavenly places are to know through the church the manifold wisdom of God (Eph. 3:10). When else will this word be fully accomplished but when the Lord can present His perfected Bride to all the myriads that people the court of the great King?

c. *Finally, the Church is presented to the earth.*

She is to appear, triumphant and radiant, right there where, along with her Lord, she had been misunderstood and despised. Speaking of His enemies, Jesus Christ says to her, "Behold, I will make them to come and worship before thy feet, and to know that I have loved thee" (Rev. 3:9).

Just when the false church, Babylon, has been unmasked and judged down here, Christ will descend from heaven with His glorified Bride, the heavenly Jerusalem (Rev. 17 and 18 and 19:11, 14). After the Battle of Armageddon, He will appear with "the armies which are in heaven . . . clothed in fine linen, white and pure." This, we believe, refers to the redeemed, whose righteous works have just been manifested (vs. 8). When the Lord sets His feet on the Mount of Olives, Zechariah says of Him: "And Jehovah my God shall come, and all the holy ones . . ." (14:4, 5). These "holy ones" are the members of the Church, who have a share in the visible triumph of their Lord and Master. With Him, they too are to judge the world (and also, later, to judge angels. Rev. 20:4; I Cor. 6:2, 3).

At that moment the words of Paul will be fulfilled: "When Christ, who is our life, shall be manifested, then shall ye also with him be manifested in glory" (Col. 3:4). "He shall come to be glorified in his saints, and to be marvelled at in all them that believed" (II Thess. 1:10). Let us keep in mind this stupendous thought, and let us learn how to live in the light of it: It is in us that the Lord will be glorified and admired!

## 12. THE PARTICIPANTS IN THE MARRIAGE OF THE LAMB

*All are invited.*

The parables of the Gospel stress this point: although it is a question of a royal wedding—and a divine one, at that—all without exception are invited: the first guests are the Jews and the devout; next come the heathen and those who stand at the crossroads by the highways and hedges; then are brought in the wicked and the good, the poor, the maimed, the blind, and the lame. The master even gives the order that they be "compelled to come in," so much does he long to have his house filled (Matt. 22:2-10; Luke 14:16-23). Those who take their places at the banquet come from the east and from the west, from the north and from the south, for the whole earth is to have its part in the salvation of our God (Luke 13:29).

*Those who are excluded from the wedding.*

Though all are invited, there are still many who voluntarily absent themselves from the feast. In the same parables we read this: the guests *"would not* come . . ." Paying no attention to the invitation, they went off—one to his fields and another to his trading; still others seized the servants, treated them shamefully, and killed them" (Matt. 22:3-6). *"All,* with one consent, began to make excuse . . ." (Luke 14:18). This is why the Master had the murderers destroyed and why he declared as concerning the indifferent:: "None of those men that were bidden shall taste of my supper."

But there is another way to exclude oneself from the feast. We have already seen that one man came to the table without having put on a wedding garment. He stood speechless before the king, who consequently had him bound hand and foot and cast into outer darkness (Matt. 22:11-13). This wretch had tried to get into heaven without fulfilling the conditions laid down by the Lord. Before the holy God, every sinner is like a ragged derelict. To presume to appear in His presence, he must be clothed "with the garments of salvation" (Isa. 61:10). Like the prodigal son, he must accept "the best robe," which the Father in grace wants to bestow on him (Luke 15:22). Poor, miserable, and naked as he is, he must "buy" from God—freely—white garments, so that the shame of his nakedness may not be made manifest (Rev. 3:18). To use a different figure, he must wash his robes and make them white in the blood of the Lamb (Rev. 7:14).

Many are called, but few are chosen is what Christ said at the end of the parable of the wedding feast (Matt. 22:14). Whose fault is that? May we repeat one last time: those left out of the marriage are those who, by their own foolishness, have not wished to have a part in it.

Blessed are those, on the contrary, who, called to the wedding feast of the Lamb, have decided humbly and joyously to accept such an invitation!

PART FIVE

ETERNAL PERDITION

## Chapter XIII

# THE RESURRECTION OF THE WICKED DEAD

### 1. THE SCRIPTURAL TEACHING ABOUT THE TWO RESURRECTIONS

IN THE PRECEDING SECTION we discussed only the glorious resurrection reserved for the believers. Reluctantly, we must now take up that which awaits unrepentant sinners: "Many of them that sleep in the dust of the earth shall awake, some to everlasting life, and some to shame and everlasting contempt" (Daniel 12:2).

"The hour cometh, in which all that are in the tombs shall hear his voice [the voice of the Son of man] and shall come forth; they that have done good, unto the resurrection of life; and they that have done evil, unto the resurrection of judgment" (John 5:28, 29).

"There shall be a resurrection both of the just and unjust" (Acts 24:15).

"The rest of the dead lived not until the thousand years should be finished . . . And I saw the dead, the great and the small, standing before the throne . . . And the sea gave up the dead that were in it; and death and Hades gave up the dead that were in them: and they were judged every man according to their works" (Rev. 20:5, 12, 13).

### 2. WHEN WILL THE SECOND RESURRECTION TAKE PLACE?

In the above texts, Daniel, Jesus, and Paul mention the two resurrections without making any distinction between them as to time. John, the last prophet of the Bible, completes the revelation by definitely stipulating that:

the first resurrection is to take place before the millennium, with a view to the kingdom reign; the second resurrection is to take place a thousand years later, with a view to the judgment (Rev. 20:5).

To anyone who objects that there ought to be more than one passage to establish such an important point, we might make this reply: In the Old Testament, the Jews made only one mention of the birth of the Messiah at Bethlehem (Micah 5:1); yet they quoted it with no hesitation whatever (Matt. 2:5, 6). Likewise only a single verse predicted that Jesus would be born of a virgin (Isa. 7:14; cf. Matt. 1:22, 23).

When the Lord has had His way down here in the granting of a thousand years of happiness and righteousness to men, He will raise up the unrepentant dead of all the ages and will bring them before Him for the last great judgment. These wicked ones will be taken out of the sojourn of the wretched dead, that place of provisional detention; and they will tremble at finding themselves before their Judge. (We shall come back later to this subject of the last judgment.)

### 3. WHAT DO WE KNOW ABOUT THE RESURRECTED BODIES OF THE CONDEMNED?

First of all, it is clear that these condemned will have bodies. In referring to the end of time, the Scriptures never present a resurrection except in a corporeal sense. Moreover, it would be absurd to speak of a spiritual resurrection of the wicked, for the following reasons:

a. The souls of the unrepentant do not need a resurrection in order to exist. In the abode of the dead, they are fully conscious and in torment (Luke 16:19-31; see also p. 42.)

b. The spiritual resurrection (i.e. regeneration) imparts eternal life (John 5:24). By definition, this eternal life is exactly what unbelievers do not possess (John 3:36).

It is plainly stated that the wicked and the unbelievers will be raised from the dust of the earth and that they will come out of their graves (Dan. 12:2; John 5:28, 29). Though we know a good deal about the new bodies of the elect, it is true that we do not find any description of the resurrected bodies of unbelievers.

Jesus speaks of "him who is able to destroy both soul and body in hell" (Matt. 10:28). Thus there will be a body which can undergo the punishment of hell. (See farther on the meaning of "able to destroy.")

Returning to what Paul has to say about the new bodies of believers, we can, by antithesis, apply the opposite terms to the bodies of the condemned.

| | |
|---|---|
| Believers will have incorruptible bodies; they will inherit incorruption (I Cor. 15:42, 53). | The wicked, raised corporeally, will of the flesh reap corruption (Gal. 6:8); they will not inherit incorruption (I Cor. 15:50). |
| They will have glorious bodies (I Cor. 15:43). | They will be raised to shame and everlasting contempt (Dan. 12:2). |
| They will come out of their graves unto the resurrection of life (John 5:28, 29). | They will experience the second death, the eternal torment of the lake of fire (Rev. 20:14, 10). |

### 4. For whom is this second resurrection reserved?

The texts cited above tell us: for those who have done evil (John 5:29); for the unjust (Acts 24:15); for those not worthy of having a part in the first resurrection (Rev. 20:5); for those who, not saved by faith, are to be judged according to their works (Rev. 20:13).

After having described the glorious resurrection, Paul adds: "Flesh and blood cannot inherit the kingdom of God; neither doth corruption inherit incorruption" (I Cor. 15:

50). The expression "flesh and blood" means unregenerate human nature. Those who become children of God by faith in Jesus are regenerated, "born, not of blood, nor of the will of the flesh, nor of the will of man, but of God" (John 1:12, 13). The man born only "of the flesh" and not " of the Spirit" cannot enter into the kingdom of God (John 3:5-8). This means that no unconverted person can ever go to live with Christ.

Our hearts are saddened when we reflect on these things. If John declares happy and holy those who have part in the first resurrection, how miserable, on the contrary, are those whose sins have not been washed away, those who will have to be raised again for judgment!

# Chapter XIV

# THE LAST JUDGMENT

## 1. WHAT IS THE LAST JUDGMENT?

IT IS THE TREMENDOUS final reckoning which will take place at the close of the millennium, the great assize where all the wicked from the beginning of time will appear. After that, there will never be anything more but the eternal state: heaven and hell.

The span of the patience of God will be ended. Since the revolt of the angels in heaven and the fall of man in the Garden of Eden, the Lord has held back the manifestation of His righteous judgment. He has waited long for sinners to repent and accept His grace. With incomprehensible long-suffering He has allowed the wicked to pursue their way and continue their revolt against Him. Now the time has come for the last judgment. For a long time righteousness has been mocked at, and the anguished cries to heaven of the victims of wickedness have apparently been all in vain (Rev. 6:10). At last there sounds the hour of the great accounting.

## 2. WHO WILL BE THE JUDGE AT THE LAST JUDGMENT?

"And I saw a great white throne, and him that sat upon it" (Rev. 20:11). This august Personnage is none other than Christ, whose reign and judgment were announced so long ago by the prophets: "The sceptre shall not depart from Judah . . . until Shiloh come [the One to whom the sceptre belongs]; and unto him shall the obedience of the peoples be" (Gen. 49:10). "Exalt that which is low, and abase that which is high. I will overturn, overturn, overturn it: this also shall be no more, until he come whose right it is; and I will give it him" (Ezek. 21:26, 27).

"The Father . . . hath given all judgment unto the Son . . . he gave him authority to execute judgment, because he is a son of man" (John 5:22, 27). "God shall judge the secrets of men by Jesus Christ" (Rom. 2:16). For "he hath appointed a day in which he will judge the world in righteousness by the man whom he hath ordained; whereof he hath given assurance unto all men, in that he hath raised him from the dead . . . He [Jesus] charged us . . . to testify that this is he who is ordained of God to be the Judge of the living and the dead" (Acts 17:31; 10:42; see also II Tim. 4:1.)

### 3. THE DESTRUCTION OF THE EARTH AND OF HEAVEN

". . . From whose face [the face of the Lord] the earth and the heaven fled away; and there was found no place for them . . . the first heaven and the first earth are passed away" (Rev. 20:11; 21:1).

The earth has known too much of sin and drunk too much blood: it will have to be destroyed. Likewise, heaven, sullied by the revolt of the angels, must be completely renewed.

This will be a judgment of fire. Whereas the world that once was perished in the waters of the deluge, "the heavens that now are, and the earth, by the same word have been stored up for fire, being reserved against the day of judgment and destruction of ungodly men . . . The day of the Lord will come as a thief; in the which the heavens shall pass away with a great noise, and the elements shall be dissolved with fervent heat, and the earth and the works that are therein shall be burned up. Seeing that these things are thus all to be dissolved, what manner of persons ought ye to be in all holy living and godliness, looking for and earnestly desiring the coming of the day of God, by reason of which the heavens being on fire shall be dissolved, and the elements shall melt with fervent heat?" (II Peter 3:7, 10-12). "Heaven and earth shall pass away" (Matt. 24:35). "Lord . . . the heavens . . . shall perish, but thou continuest; and they all shall wax old as doth a garment; and as a mantle shalt thou roll them up, as a garment, and they shall be changed" (Heb. 1:10-12; Ps. 102:26-28).

"The heavens shall vanish away like smoke, and the earth shall wax old like a garment" (Isa. 51:6).

Do not recent atomic discoveries help us to understand how the blazing heavens can some day melt and be dissolved: If God, by a formidable explosion, unleashes all the energy contained in the universe, is He not powerful enough to utilize it again for the creation of another world? "The fashion of this world passeth away" (I Cor. 7:31). That is, its form, its appearance passes away. But this has slight importance, since the Creator remains forever the same!

### 4. THE SUMMONS SERVED ON THE WICKED DEAD

"And I saw the dead, the great and the small, standing before the throne . . . The sea gave up the dead that were in it; and death and Hades gave up the dead that were in them" (Rev. 20:12, 13). As all believers must appear before the judgment seat of Christ for the evaluation of their service (II Cor. 5:10), even so all the unrepentant must give an account to their Judge: "We shall all stand before the judgment seat of God. For it is written, As I live, saith the Lord, to me every knee shall bow, and every tongue shall confess to God" (Rom. 14:10, 11). "The time is come for judgment to begin at the house of God: and if it begin first at us, what shall be the end of them that obey not the gospel of God: And if the righteous is scarcely saved, where shall the ungodly and sinner appear?" (I Peter 4:17, 18).

"If we sin wilfully after that we have received the knowledge of the truth, there remaineth no more a sacrifice for sins, but a certain fearful expectation of judgment, and a fierceness of fire which shall devour the adversaries . . . of how much sorer punishment [than that of the law of Moses], think ye, shall he be judged worthy, who hath trodden under foot the Son of God, and hath counted the blood of the covenant wherewith he was sanctified an unholy thing, and hath done despite unto the Spirit of grace? For we know him that said, Vengeance belongeth unto me, I will recompense . . . It is a fearful thing to fall into the hands of the living God" (Heb. 10:26-31) .

All who have denied the Lord down here will find themselves, then, in the presence of their Judge. Even during the final chastisements on earth, men's hearts will be "fainting for fear, and for expectation of the things which are coming on the world"; and they will lament when they see Christ appearing in the clouds (Luke 21:26; Matt. 24: 30) . What, then, will the last judgment be like when each one's eternal fate will be irrevocably sealed!

### 5. EVERY ONE TO BE JUDGED ACCORDING TO HIS WORKS

"Books were opened . . . and the dead were judged out of the things which were written in the books, according to their works" (Rev. 20:12, 13) .

a. *God keeps an exact record of our works.*

The word "books" is no doubt picture-language, for the Lord's perfect memory precludes the necessity of any actual writing down of all He wants to recall. But it is terrible to think that for the sinner nothing, absolutely nothing, is forgotten by God. "I will never forget any of their works" (Amos 8:7). The Lord in one instant will be able to bring before every sinner's eyes a "film strip" of his life (as was done at Nuremberg—and a good deal more effectively still!) This recollection will be entirely sufficient to make every one bow his head in shame—and sufficient to insure the strictest justice.

In a terrible way will be accomplished the prophet's warning: "Be sure your sin will find you out!" (Num. 32:23).

b. *Every work without exception will come into judgment.*

God will judge:

1). *Men's secret acts* (Rom. 2:16).

2). *Their evil words:* "Every idle word that men shall speak, they shall give account thereof in the day of judgment. For . . . by thy words thou shalt be condemned" (Matt. 12: 36).

3). *All their ungodly works:* "The Lord came with ten thousands of his holy ones, to execute judgment upon all, and to convict all the ungodly of all their works of ungodliness which they have ungodly wrought, and of all the hard things which ungodly sinners have spoken against him" (Jude 14, 15).

4). *Youthful sins:* "Rejoice, O young man . . . let thy heart cheer thee in the days of thy youth, and walk in the ways of thy heart, and in the sight of thine eyes; but know thou, that for all these things God will bring thee into judgment" (Eccl. 11:9).

5). *All works, with no exception:* "God will bring every work into judgment, with every hidden thing, whether it be good, or whether it be evil" (Eccl. 12:14).

c. *All those who have not believed will be lost.*

"A man is not justified by the works of the law [those works commanded by the law of God] . . . for it is written, Cursed is every one who continueth not in all things that are written in the book of the law, to do them" (Gal. 2:16; 3:10). We have all deserved this curse, having transgressed the law innumerable times; and even our best actions are inevitably imperfect before God: "All our righteousnesses are as a polluted garment" (Isa. 64:6).

"After thy hardness and impenitent heart treasurest up for thyself wrath in the day of wrath and revelation of the righteous judgment of God: who will render to every man according to his works . . . unto them that are factious, and obey not the truth, but obey unrighteousness, shall be wrath and indignation, tribulation and anguish, upon every soul of man that worketh evil, of the Jew first, and also of the Greek" (Rom. 2:5-8).

d. *Every mouth shall be stopped.*

Since every one is to be judged strictly "according to his works," written down in books, no one will be able to clear himself of the charge. It will be just as impossible to deny the facts as it will to put the blame on someone else or on God. John 16:8-11 will then have its ultimate accomplishment: the unbelievers will be convicted of sin, for not having believed on Christ, and of judgment, for having followed the prince of this world, who with them will be cast down into hell. As Paul says: Every mouth shall be stopped, and all the world will be recognized as guilty before God . . . "There is none righteous, no, not one . . . There is none that doeth good, no, not so much as one . . . there is no distinction; for all have sinned and fall short of the glory of God" (Rom. 3:19, 10, 12, 22, 23).

6. HOW WILL THOSE WHO HAVE NEVER HEARD THE GOSPEL BE JUDGED?

People have, indeed, often wondered about the responsibility and fate of those who lived before Christ, or of those who have never heard the Gospel. The Scriptures are not silent on this subject.

a. *Each one will be judged according to the light he has received.*

"As many as have sinned without the law shall also perish without the law: and as many as have sinned under the law shall be judged by the law" (Rom. 2:12). What Paul says here of the law is even more true of the Gospel. Those who have heard it God considers infinitely more responsible than

those who have not: the generation which rejected the message and the miracles of Jesus Christ will be condemned in
the day of judgment by the queen of the South (the Queen
of Sheba) and by the men of Nineveh (Luke 11:31, 32).

"That servant who knew his lord's will and made not
ready, nor did according to his will, shall be beaten with
many stripes; but he that knew not and did things worthy
of stripes shall be beaten with few stripes. And to whomsoever much is given, of him shall much be required: and to
whom they commit much, of him will they ask the more"
(Luke 12:47, 48). "Woe unto you, scribes and Pharisees,
hypocrites! for ye devour widows' houses, even while for a
pretence ye make long prayers: therefore ye shall receive
greater condemnation" (Matt. 23:14). "Woe unto thee,
Chorazin! Woe unto thee, Bethsaida! for if the mighty
works had been done in Tyre and Sidon which were done
in you, they would have repented long ago . . . But I say
unto you, it shall be more tolerable for Tyre and Sidon in
the day of judgment than for you." And Jesus went on to
say to His disciples: "Whosoever shall not receive you, nor
hear your words, as ye go forth out of the house or that city,
shake off the dust of your feet. Verily I say unto you, it
shall be more tolerable for the land of Sodom and Gomorrah
in the day of judgment than for that city" (Matt. 11:20-24;
10:14, 15).

b. *Still, even without the Gospel, the heathen are responsible before God.*

According to Paul, the Lord has given three revelations
to men:

1). *the creation,* where the invisible things of Him, His
everlasting power and divinity, are clearly seen (Rom. 1:19,
20);

2). *conscience,* on which God has imprinted the great
principles of the law, by the realization of good and evil
(Rom. 2:14, 15);

3). *the Scriptures,* the supreme revelation, in which God's love and righteousness and His salvation and condemnation are proclaimed to sinners (Rom. 2:17-20).

Now, all the heathen without exception have the benefit of the first two revelations. All have disobeyed revealed light and are without excuse before God (Rom. 1:20, 21). Of course, the Jews and the professing Christians, who possess the Word of God, are even more inexcusable if they have not made it their own in experience (Rom. 2:1).

c. *God does not let any of His creatures be lost without in His own way first seeking to win them.*

Jesus teaches us that the three Persons of the Trinity all work together to lead *all* men to salvation.

*The Father:* "They shall all be taught of God" (John 6: 45).

*The Son:* "And I, if I be lifted up from the earth, will draw all men unto myself" (John 12:32). "Behold, I stand at the door and knock: if any man hear my voice and open the door, I will come in to him" (Rev. 3:20).

*The Holy Spirit:* "He . . . will convict the world in respect of sin, and of righteousness, and of judgment" (John 16:8).

We thoroughly believe that in the life of every man there comes the moment when if sincere, he is obliged to exclaim, as did the magicians of Egypt: "This is the finger of God" (Exod. 8:19). Nature has spoken to him, his conscience has convicted him of sin, and the Holy Spirit has kept knocking at his heart's door to create in him a longing for eternal life. The tragedy is that, having come up to that point, most men choose to continue walking in darkness rather than to give up their sins (John 3:19).

To sincere souls (of whom, fortunately, there are always some) there is directed a beautiful promise: "Unto the upright there ariseth light in the darkness" (Ps. 112:4). In ways sometimes miraculous, God especially reveals Himself to them, or sends across their path one of His messengers, as

He did for Cornelius and for the Ethiopian (Acts 10:19, 20; 8:26-29). Thus, when the time comes to leave this world, every man has had enough light to have accepted or rejected God, so that he is fully responsible to Him.

d. *Can a heathen, ignorant but sincere, be saved?*

What will happen to a heathen, convicted of his sins and sincerely repentant, who has never had the chance to hear the Gospel clearly presented? We believe that the omniscient God knows perfectly whether that man, confronted with the truth, would have accepted it or not. And we can not know all that the Lord may do, before that sinner's death, to accomplish in his favor the above-mentioned promises: John 6:45 and 12:32. At any rate, if such a man does obtain God's pardon, it will not be merely because of his sincerity, but because of Jesus Christ, the atoning Substitute sufficient for the sins of the whole world (I John 2:2).

In like manner, the repentant sinners under the Old Covenant were pardoned because of the Messiah who was one day to come to die in their place. David, an adulterer and a criminal, found that his transgression was put away from him (Ps. 32:1-5). This, from a legal point of view, was unjust; and some might have asked if God was not thus making Himself an accomplice to evil. But later, in permitting His own Son to die for all men on the cross, God fully manifested His justice: He was thus making atonement also for "the sins done aforetime," which He had passed over with forbearance (Rom. 3:25). If the sacrifice of Christ could save the relatively unenlightened men of the Old Covenant, could it not also bring something to such ignorant heathen as obey with all their hearts what light they have?

Someone then will perhaps say: "If that's the way it is, what is the good of evangelizing the heathen? The ones that are sincere will be saved anyway." To reason like this is to misconstrue two things:

1). Since they live in such appalling darkness, how many

of those heathen are "sincere"? Their bodies are defiled, their consciences seared, and their hearts dominated by evil spirits. Let us have pity on their suffering and their spiritual abandonment, and let us hasten to take them the light! We have received so very much that of us there shall be much required. Let us take care not to brush aside Paul's pathetic appeal: "How then shall they call on him in whom they have not believed? and how shall they believe in him whom they have not heard? and how shall they hear without a preacher? . . . So belief cometh of hearing" (Rom. 10:14, 17). How shall we escape if we neglect to make known so great a salvation?

2). Is not the life of a heathen, even a sincere one, so crushed by the weight of personal and environing sin that he is quite deprived of any heavenly assurance at all? How could this man, knowing nothing of the Gospel, come to taste that which he can just vaguely long for, namely the peace and joy of salvation? And to think that we could selfishly revel in these blessings without feeling a burning desire to share them with him! No, nothing could excuse us from evangelizing the souls of all who are held under Satan's sway and the threat of eternal punishment.

## 7. THE BOOK OF LIFE

Let us come back to the scene of the last judgment: "And another book was opened, which is the book of life . . . And if any was not found written in the book of life, he was cast into the lake of fire . . . He that overcometh . . . I will in no wise blot his name out of the book of life . . . And all that dwell on the earth shall worship him [the beast], every one whose name hath not been written from the foundation of the world in the book of life of the Lamb that hath been slain" (Rev. 20:12, 15; 3:5; 13:8). "And at that time thy people shall be delivered, every one that shall be found written in the book" (Dan. 12:1).

Paul speaks of his fellow-workers, "whose names are in the book of life" (Phil. 4:3).

Moses, interceding for his people, cries out: "If thou wilt forgive their sin—and if not, blot me, I pray thee, out of thy book which thou hast written. And Jehovah said unto Moses, Whosoever hath sinned against me, him will I blot out of my book" (Exod. 32:32, 33). And the psalmist, speaking of the wicked, adds: "Let them be blotted out of the book of life, and not be written with the righteous" (Ps. 69:28). "Ye are come . . . to the general assembly and church of the first-born who are enrolled in heaven" (Heb. 12:22, 23).

Finally, Jesus declares: "In this rejoice not, that the spirits are subject unto you; but rejoice that your names are written in heaven" (Luke 10:20).

So, then, God inscribes in His book all those who are saved by faith. But at the last judgment it will be too late for anyone to start believing. The book of life will then be opened, and whosoever is not found written in it will be declared forever lost. God uses a second test, so to speak, before condemning sinners according to their works. He is seeking in this way to make them understand that had they not despised His grace, they could have escaped hell.

God knows everything in advance, so that from the foundation of the world He could write in His book the names of those who would believe on His Son. "For whom he foreknew he also foreordained"; He elected them according to His foreknowledge (Rom. 8:29; I Peter 1:2). But, however paradoxical this may seem to our limited understanding, we are exhorted to believe today, to accept the Savior now (II Cor. 5:20, 6:2; Heb. 3:12-15). Then we shall know that our names are written in heaven, and the joy of heaven will fill our hearts.

How foolish of men to refuse the only means of salvation, a means so readily accessible, too! Let us imagine that bandits come bursting into a meeting, announcing that at midnight everyone present will be shot down. "But," they add, "we have a notebook here; and all who ask us to put their names in it will be spared." Wouldn't the company all, without exception, hurry to be registered among those to be spared? And is it not incomprehensible that so few sinners, though deeply guilty before God, make an effort to be freely saved from eternal perdition?

We were saying that when the last judgment comes, it will be too late for anyone to be inscribed in the book of life. But it seems also that none of those so inscribed are to appear at that time before the Judge (except perhaps those of the elect who will have come out of the millennium, those who will not yet have been raised but who will, nevertheless, have been saved by faith). At the rapture of the Church, the Lord will examine the service of every believer, to know what reward he is to have; but his salvation is assured and he "cometh not into judgment," because "there is . . . no condemnation to them that are in Christ Jesus" (John 5: 24; Rom. 8:1). Since at the great white throne, every man is judged "according to his works," it is evident that, on those grounds, no one can be saved. Then is the Church going to be absent at the last judgment? Certainly not, for all human beings will necessarily be present at the great assize of our race, some to be glorified with their Savior and the rest to be condemned by Him. At the beginning of the millennium, judges will be seated on thrones at the right hand of Jesus Christ (Rev. 20:4). It is a legitimate supposition that, on the occasion of the last accounting, the saints will participate with their Lord in the judgment of the world and also of angels (I Cor. 6:2, 3).

## 8. THE END OF DEATH AND HADES

"And death and Hades gave up the dead that were in them . . . And death and Hades were cast into the lake of fire. This is the second death, even the lake of fire" (Rev. 20:13, 14).

The first death is the physical death by which we leave this world; the second is that which awaits the unrepentant in the other world. (We shall define this farther on.)

Since this life on earth is to be followed by the other world, it is only logical that the first death will give place to the second death. Those once "mortals" will forever after find themselves in either heaven or hell. Then will be brought to pass this word of the Apostle Paul: "For he must reign, till he hath put all his enemies under his feet. The last enemy that shall be abolished is death" (I Cor. 15:25, 26).

The "Hades" just mentioned is a place of provisional detention, as it were, where the unrepentant are held until the last judgment. At that time everything temporary will disappear, and the inhabitants of Hades itself will be "cast into the lake of fire"; that is, they will be thrown into eternal hell.

## 9. THE VERDICT

"If any was not found written in the book of life, he was cast into the lake of fire" (Rev. 20:15).

We must explain here an apparent contradiction: Jesus came to save guilty men, by atoning for the sins of the whole world. People are therefore not lost because of their sins, but because of their refusal of divine grace: "He that believeth on him is not judged: he that believeth not hath been judged already, *because he hath not believed* on the name of the only begotten Son of God . . . He [the Holy Spirit] will convict the world in respect of sin . . . *because they believe not on me*" (John 3:18; 16:8, 9). Thus men are saved by faith or are lost by the absence of it—by the refusal to be inscribed in the book of life. But he who rejects faith remains on the ground of law, and on that ground one can be judged only on the basis of his works. As we have seen, he will receive precisely what he deserves, and the law will condemn him without mercy.

How important it is then to be written in the book of life! It seems that right up to the end many deceive themselves on this subject, for on that day they will say: "Lord, Lord, did we not prophesy by thy name, and by thy name cast out demons, and by thy name do many mighty works?" And the Lord will say to them openly: "I never knew you: depart from me, ye that work iniquity" (Matt. 7:22, 23).

Then "the fearful [i.e. the timid, those who cannot make up their minds and who lack the courage to break with sin], and unbelieving [near the top of the list, as they should be, since the ultimate in sin is the refusal of salvation] and abominable, and murderers, and fornicators, and sorcerers, and idolators, and all liars, their part shall be in the lake that burneth with fire and brimstone, which is the second death" (Rev. 21:8).

Lest you one day incur such a condemnation, "as though God were entreating by us, we beseech you on behalf of Christ, be ye reconciled to God! . . . Behold, now is the acceptable time, now is the day of salvation" (II Cor. 5:20; 6: 2). Accept His grace today, for tomorrow may perhaps be too late!

# Chapter XV

# HELL

### 1. WITH WHAT BIBLICAL LANGUAGE IS HELL PICTURED?

HELL IS SOMETIMES SPOKEN of as "the infernal regions," *infernal* being etymologically related to the word *inferior* (i.e. *lower*). As such, it is not found in our versions of the Bible, but it is nevertheless certainly the idea in Ephesians 4:9: "He [Christ] also descended into the lower parts of the earth." It is in fact under the earth that the ancients located the abode of the dead. Today we reserve the expression "infernal regions," as we do the word "hell," for the place, not of the dead, in a general sense, but of the wicked dead condemned to eternal suffering in the other world.

This place is depicted in an impressive number of passages and expressions in the Bible. Let us attempt to pick out the most striking ones.

a. *The fire of God's anger*

"A fire is kindled in mine anger and burneth unto the lowest Sheol" (Deut. 32:22).

In a passage dealing with the fate reserved for Israel's great enemy, the Assyrian (and perhaps also for the Antichrist), Isaiah says: "For a Topheth is prepared of old; yea, for the king it is made ready; he hath made it deep and large; the pile thereof is fire and much wood; the breath of Jehovah, like a stream of brimstone, doth kindle it" (Isa. 30:33).

b. *The eternal flames*

"The sinners in Zion are afraid; trembling hath seized the godless ones: Who among us can dwell with the devour-

279

ing fire? who among us can dwell with everlasting burn-
ings?" (Isa. 33:14).

"Have mercy on me . . . for I am in anguish in this flame!"
(Luke 16:24).[1]

"The Lord Jesus [will appear] from heaven . . . in flaming
fire, rendering vengeance to them that know not God, and to
them that obey not the gospel of our Lord Jesus" (II Thess.
1:7, 8).

c. *The worm that never dies*

At the close of a chapter which deals with the glories of the
millennium, Isaiah adds: "And they shall go forth, and
look upon the dead bodies of the men that have transgressed
against me: for their worm shall not die, neither shall their
fire be quenched; and they shall be an abhorring unto all
flesh" (66:24).

Jesus takes the same expression, applying it beyond all
question to the punishment in the other world: He speaks
of Gehenna, "where their worm dieth not and the fire is not
quenched" (Mark 9:48).

d. *Shame, everlasting contempt*

"Many of them that sleep in the dust of the earth shall
awake, some to everlasting life, and some to shame and
everlasting contempt" (Daniel 12:2).

e. *The fire which is not quenched, or the eternal fire*

This expression already alluded to in Isaiah 66:24 is taken
up by John the Baptist and by Jesus: "the chaff he [the Son
of God] will burn up with unquenchable fire" (Matt. 3:12).
"It is good for thee to enter into life maimed, rather than
having thy two hands to go into hell, into the unquenchable
fire" (Mark 9:43, 45, 48). "It is good for thee to enter into
life maimed, or halt, rather than having two hands or two
feet to be cast into the eternal fire . . . Depart from me, ye
cursed, into the eternal fire which is prepared for the devil

---

[1]The passage in Luke 16:19-31 has to do with Hades; but what it says
about the torment there will be even more true of hell itself.

and his angels" (Matt. 18:8; 25:41). "If we sin wilfully after that we have received the knowledge of the truth, there remaineth no more a sacrifice for sins, but a certain fearful expectation of judgment, and a fierceness of fire which shall devour the adversaries" (Heb. 10:26, 27).

f. *Gehenna, or the fire of Gehenna*

"It is profitable for thee that one of thy members should perish, and not thy whole body be cast into hell [Gk. Gehenna]" (Matt. 5:29 and vss. 22 and 30). "Rather fear him who is able to destroy both soul and body in hell [Gehenna]" (Matt. 10:28). "To be cast into the hell [Gehenna] of fire" (Matt. 18:9).

This word *Gehenna* requires an explanation. It is the transcription of the Hebrew noun *Gé-Hinnom*—Valley of Hinnom—which designated the cursed place where Israel and her unfaithful kings burned their sons and their daughters in honor of Moloch (II Kings 23:10). It seems that in Jesus' time the sewage of Jerusalem was burned there. Christ uses this word *Gehenna* to speak of the fire of hell, just as the Scriptures employ in the same sense the metaphors of darkness, of brimstone, etc.

g. *Perdition (or Destruction)*

"Whose end is perdition" (A.V. "destruction"—Phil. 3: 19).

"Wide is the gate, and broad is the way, that leadeth to destruction, and many are they that enter in thereby" (Matt. 7:13). God "endured with much longsuffering vessels of wrath fitted unto destruction" (Rom. 9:22).

"The time of the dead to be judged [came], and the time to give their reward to thy servants . . . and to destroy them that destroy the earth" (Rev. 11:18).

h. *The furnace of fire*

"Them that do iniquity . . . [the angels] shall cast them into the furnace of fire" (Matt. 13:41, 42, 50).

i. *The place of weeping and gnashing of teeth*

"They . . . shall cast them into the furnace of fire: there shall be the weeping and the gnashing of teeth" (Matt. 13: 42, 50; 22:13) .

j. *Eternal punishment*

"And these shall go away into eternal punishment: but the righteous into eternal life" (Matt. 25:46) .

"Sodom and Gomorrah . . . are set forth as an example, suffering the punishment of eternal fire" (Jude 7) .

k. *Darkness*

"Bind him hand and foot, and cast him out into the outer darkness; there shall be the weeping and the gnashing of teeth" (Matt. 22:13 and 8:12) .

"If God spared not angels when they sinned, but cast them down to hell, and committed them to pits of darkness, to be reserved unto judgment . . . These [people] are springs without water . . . for whom the blackness of darkness hath been reserved" (II Peter 2:4, 17. See also Jude 6 and 13) .

l. *The wrath to come*

"Ye offspring of vipers, who warned you to flee from the wrath to come?" (Luke 3:7) . "After thy hardness and impenitent heart treasurest up for thyself wrath in the day of wrath and revelation of the righteous judgment of God . . . unto them that are factious, and obey not the truth, but obey unrighteousness, shall be wrath and indignation, tribulation and anguish, upon every soul of man that worketh evil . . . Much more then, being now justified by his blood [the blood of Christ] shall we be saved from the wrath of God through him" (Rom. 2:5, 8, 9; 5:9. See also I Thess. 1:10) .

m. *Exclusion*

"When once the master of the house . . . hath shut to the door, and ye begin to stand without, and to knock at the door . . . he shall answer and say to you, I know you not whence ye are . . . There shall be the weeping and the gnashing of teeth . . . and yourselves cast forth without" (Luke

13:25, 28). "Without are the dogs, and the sorcerers, and the fornicators, and the murderers, and the idolaters, and every one that loveth and maketh a lie!" (Rev. 22:15).

### n. *Torments*

"In Hades he lifted up his eyes, being in torments, and seeth Abraham afar off . . . That he [Lazarus] may testify [these things] unto them, lest they also come into this place of torment" (Luke 16:23-28). "The smoke of their torment goeth up for ever and ever; and they have no rest day or night . . . and they shall be tormented day and night for ever and ever" (Rev. 14:11; 20:10).

### o. *Eternal destruction*

"[They] shall suffer punishment, even eternal destruction from the face of the Lord" (II Thess. 1:9).

"The heavens that now are, and the earth . . . have been stored up for fire, being reserved against the day of judgment and destruction of ungodly men" (II Peter 3:7).

(We shall explain farther on the terms "ruin" and "destruction.")

### p. *Eternal judgment*

The passage in Hebrews 5:11 to 6:1 puts the doctrine of eternal judgment with "the first principles of Christ"; for the author, these "principles" are so simple and so self-evident that to "fullgrown men" there is no need of making any lengthy explanation.

### q. *Damnation (or Condemnation)*

"Whose sentence now from of old lingereth not, and their destruction [A.V. "damnation"] slumbereth not" (II Peter 2:3). "For there are certain men crept in privily, even they who were of old written of beforehand unto this condemnation" (Jude 4).

"Then shall be revealed the lawless one, whom the Lord Jesus shall slay with the breath of his mouth, and bring to nought by the manifestation of his coming" (II Thess.

2:8. See also, farther on, the explanation of the terms "destruction" and "bringing to nought.")

r. *Denial*

"Whosoever shall deny me before men, him will I also deny before my Father who is in heaven . . . I never knew you: depart from me!" (Matt. 10:33; 7:23).

"Whosoever shall be ashamed of me and of my words . . . the Son of man also shall be ashamed of him" (Mark 8:38).

"If we shall deny him, he also will deny us" (II Tim. 2:12).

s. *Anathema, curse*

"If any man loveth not the Lord, let him be anathema!" (I Cor. 16:22). "If any man preacheth unto you any gospel other than that which ye received, let him be anathema!" (Gal. 1:19).

"Cursed is every one who continueth not in all things that are written in the book of the law, to do them" (Gal. 3:10). "Depart from me, ye cursed!" (Matt. 25:41). "Children of cursing" (II Peter 2:14).

t. *Retribution*

"Whose end shall be according to their works" (II Cor. 11:15). "He that doeth wrong shall receive again for the wrong that he hath done" (Col. 3:25).

"The Lord is an avenger in all these things" (I Thess. 4:6). "It is a righteous thing with God to recompense affliction to them that afflict you, and to you that are afflicted rest with us" (II Thess. 1:6, 7). "Alexander the coppersmith did me much evil: the Lord will render to him according to his works" (II Tim. 4:14). "Render unto her even as she rendered, and double unto her the double according to her works . . . Behold, I come quickly; and my reward is with me, to render to each man according as his work is" (Rev. 18:6; 22:12).

u. *Woe*

"Woe unto that man through whom the Son of man is betrayed! good were it for that man if he had not been born" (Matt. 26:24). "It is impossible but that occasions of stumbling should come; but woe unto him through whom they come! It were well for him if a millstone were hanged about his neck, and he were thrown into the sea, rather than that he should cause one of these little ones to stumble" (Luke 17:1, 2). "Woe unto thee, Chorazin! woe unto thee, Bethsaida! . . . Woe unto you, scribes and Pharisees, hypocrites!" (Matt. 11:21; 23:13).

v. *Breaking to pieces*

"He that falleth on this stone [on Jesus, the corner stone] shall be broken to pieces: but on whomsoever it shall fall, it will scatter him as dust" (Matt. 21:44).

w. *Privation*

"From him that hath not, even that which he hath shall be taken away" (Matt. 25:29). It is a question of a wicked and slothful servant who has hidden his talent in the earth: it is not to be wondered at that he will be deprived of what he has. "Take heed therefore how ye hear: for whosoever hath, to him shall be given; and whosoever hath not, from him shall be taken away even that which he thinketh he hath" (Luke 8:18). Those who, listening, refuse to believe and to obey will cease even to hear the Word of God.

x. *Fire and brimstone*

"He also shall drink of the wine of the wrath of God, which is prepared unmixed in the cup of his anger; and he shall be tormented with fire and brimstone in the presence of the holy angels, and in the presence of the Lamb" (Rev. 14:10).

y. *The lake of fire, the lake that burneth*

"They two were cast alive into the lake of fire that burneth with brimstone . . . If any was not found written in the book of life, he was cast into the lake of fire" (Rev. 19:20; 20: 15, etc.).

z. *The second death*

"This is the second death, even the lake of fire . . . their part shall be in the lake that burneth with fire and brimstone, which is the second death" (Rev. 20:14; 21:8). What does this last expression mean? The first death is that by which sinners leave this earth; the second is that which awaits the unrepentant after the last judgment: in the Scriptures, it is a synonym of eternal hell. But if the first death carries with it the decomposition of the body, does not the second death entail the annihilation of the unrepentant soul? Let us leave the answer to the Scriptures: the Revelation twice sets forth this equivalency: the second death *is* the lake of fire (20:14; 21:8). Now we shall see shortly that souls in the lake of fire, far from being annihilated, are tormented day and night for ever and ever (Rev. 14:10, 11; 20:10). That also explains the expression "hurt of the second death" (Rev. 2:11).

2. OF WHAT DOES HELL CONSIST?

a. *The reality of hell*

There stands out from all the above passages the truth that hell is a terrible reality. Some people become indignant over the severe judgments which struck men, as recorded in the Old Testament: those of the deluge, Sodom and Gomorrah, Canaan, and even Israel; these people declare that they do not see in these the God of love shown in the Gospels. But they forget that the judgments of the New Testament are far more severe than those of the Old: "A man that hath set at nought Moses' law dieth without compassion on the word of two or three witnesses: *of how much sorer punishment,* think ye, shall he be judged worthy to fall into the hands of the living God" (Heb. 10:28-31). The Old Testament chastisements that are criticized so much were bodily and earthly, and therefore temporal; they frequently allowed the sinner the chance to repent as he was dying and thus to save his soul (which did not, however, prevent the hardened unbeliever from becoming eternally lost). But the chastisements that the New Testament particularly emphasizes are essentially spiritual and eternal; they are therefore infinitely more formidable.

b. *The metaphors that represent hell*

Fire: of the twenty-six designations of hell selected above, seven evoke the idea of a fire: the pile of fagots, the flames, the eternal fire, Gehenna, the furnace, fire and brimstone, and the lake of fire.

But there are other metaphors used:

the gnawing worm
the eternal shame
the weeping and gnashing of teeth
the darkness
the destruction
the "exclusion," etc.

The Scriptures of necessity employ human language to give us an idea of the other world. But how different is its description of the future from the crude representations of the Middle Ages! In the Bible there are none of those grotesque scenes that depict hell as a great pot in which the damned are boiled, as devils with horns derisively poke pitchforks into them as a means of torture. It is none the less true that the Biblical expressions, however metaphorical they may be, give unmistakable glimpses of a hideous reality. If the fire, the gnawing worm, the darkness, etc., are more spiritual than material, they imply all the more the concept of bitter suffering, remorse, misery, groping in darkness, and separation from God. Moreover, if there is a resurrection of the body even for the wicked, there will be in their torment some element of bodily pain.

c. *In short, what does hell consist of?*

We have just said that in all the Biblical expressions there is predominantly the fact that unrepentant sinners will be eternally separated from God. The most exact definition of hell, it seems to us, is that given in II Thessalonians 1:9: "Who [those that know not God] shall suffer punishment, even eternal destruction from the face of the Lord."

Eternal life is the knowledge and the presence of God. Eternal death, the second death, is final separation from God. This definition is in agreement with all that the Scriptures teach about the torment and duration of hell.

## 3. THE SUFFERING OF HELL

a. *How is it described?*

Let us take up once more the passages cited in Part I, the allusions made there:

The wicked "shall awake . . . to shame and everlasting contempt" (Dan. 12:2). "Their worm dieth not" (Mark 9:48). "There shall be the weeping and the gnashing of teeth" (Matt. 13:42). They will be cast "into the outer darkness" (Matt. 22:13), and they shall "go away into eternal punishment" (25:46). "Being in torments . . . he [the rich man] cried . . . Have mercy on me . . . for I am in anguish in this flame" (Luke 16:23, 24).

"Tribulation and anguish upon every soul of man that worketh evil" (Rom. 2:8, 9). "Suffering the punishment of eternal fire" (Jude 7).

They will be "tormented with fire and brimstone, in the presence of the holy angels, and in the presence of the Lamb: and the smoke of their torment goeth up for ever and ever; and they have no rest day and night . . . for ever and ever" (Rev. 14:10, 11; 20:10).

"There is no peace . . . to the wicked" (Isa. 57:21).

b. *What does such suffering consist of?*

What we have seen of the state of the wicked rich man

in Hades (Luke 16) gives us an idea of this; the condemned man was separated from the place of felicity by an uncrossable gulf. He was in full possession of his conscience and his memory. He distinctly realized the salvation that he had lost. His suffering was as keen as it was devoid of all hope. The reply of Abraham to his cries was a downright negative: no one from heaven could go down to help him, and no soul can ever leave the place of torment to rise to a higher sphere.

Some people have said: How can a God of love take pleasure in tormenting creatures for ever, even rebellious ones? The Bible does not anywhere say that God is the one who is to torment them. He will not even have anything to do with their suffering. They have obstinately and willfully spurned the Lord and all His grace. They have rejected Him, and their torment will consist precisely of this: the absence of the happiness, joy, pardon, and peace which the Lord alone can give. Let us quote here A. Matter: "The essential element in the punishment will consist of the divine reprobation, of the bitterness, the fury, and the despair of an unjustifiable and vain rebellion, a continuous torture to the condemned, since nothing can distract his attention from it" (*Etude de la Doctrine Chrétienne*) Fischbacher, Paris, 1892, p. 431).

The Lord said to the king of Tyre, a type of Satan: "I brought forth a fire from the midst of thee; it hath devoured thee" (Ezek. 28:18). It is indeed within himself that the hardened sinner finds his punishment. His empty heart, his conscience smitten with remorse, and his perturbed mind will be the cause of a great part of his anguish.

Furthermore, he will suffer from a terrible feeling of being abandoned. Speaking to the Israelites who, because of unbelief, had refused to enter into the Promised Land, God declared what their punishment for forty years in the wilderness would consist of: "Ye shall know my alienation" (Num.

14:34). One could not express any better the torment of hell: to be for ever deprived of the presence of God.

God has done His utmost to save men. For them He has given His Son; He has spoken to them by the triple revelation of nature, conscience, and the Scriptures (Rom. 1:20, 21; 2:14-16). He has convicted them by His Spirit and has entreated them to give themselves to Him. If they stubbornly run away from Him, He finally goes away and leaves them to themselves. That is what hell is. When Jesus exclaimed on the cross: "My God, why hast thou forsaken me?" He was experiencing hell; He endured its torment in our stead.

What terror and suffering will characterize those to whom the Lord will have to say some day: "Depart from me, ye cursed, into the eternal fire!" (Matt. 25:41).

### 4. THE DURATION OF HELL

What has just been said is awful, but the most horrible has yet to be expressed. Suffering is always hard; but, no matter how great it may be, the hope of deliverance helps a person to endure it. Now in regard to the duration of hell, we are convinced that the Bible is very explicit: it will never end. We shall see later on the objections that have been made to such a doctrine. But first of all, let us look at the texts.

a. *Where is there an affirmation of the eternal duration of the distresses of hell?*

1). Isaiah speaks of the everlasting burning of the fire that shall never be quenched and of the worm which shall never die (Isa. 33:14; 66:24).

2). Daniel said that some would awake unto eternal life and others unto shame and everlasting contempt (Dan. 12:2).

3). John the Baptist and Jesus spoke, both of them, of the unquenchable fire (Matt. 3:12; Mark 9:43, etc.)

We shall show a little later on that God Himself is a consuming fire. That is, His absolute holiness and righteousness can do nothing else but condemn the impenitent sinner. This attribute of God is as immutable as His Person; and the fire of His righteousness, according to Christ's own words, will never go out.

4). The Lord will say: "Depart from me . . . into the eternal fire . . . And these shall go away into eternal punishment: but the righteous into eternal life" (Matt. 25:41, 46).

5). "Whosoever shall blaspheme against the Holy Spirit hath never forgiveness, but is guilty of an eternal sin" (Mark 3:29). "Whosoever shall speak against the Holy Spirit, it shall not be forgiven him, neither in this world, nor in that which is to come" (Matt. 12:32).

We believe that, essentially, the sin against the Holy Spirit is the obstinate refusal of His work of conviction and regeneration. If the Lord declares Himself ready to fully pardon all repentant sinners, the refusal of salvation is the only sin that cannot be forgiven. We believe that only those will go to hell who have committed the unpardonable sin. Hell, then, for them will have no end, because there they will never find pardon.

6). They "shall suffer punishment, even eternal destruction from the face of the Lord" (II Thess. 1:9).

7). The "eternal judgment" is one of the most rudimentary and self-evident doctrines, according to Hebrews 6:2.

8). "And angels that kept not their own principality . . . he hath kept in everlasting bonds under darkness unto the judgment of the great day . . . Sodom and Gomorrah . . . are set forth as an example, suffering the punishment of eternal fire . . . These [men] are . . . wandering stars, for whom the blackness of darkness hath been reserved for ever" (Jude 6, 7, 13).

"The smoke of their torment goeth up for ever and ever; and they have no rest day and night . . . And her smoke goeth up for ever and ever . . . And they shall be tormented day and night for ever and ever" (Rev. 14:11; 19:3; 20:10).

Anyone reading these texts, just as they are, gets the inescapable impression from them that the torment of hell will
never end. Still, such a thought seems to our minds so
ghastly that many objections have been brought up in an
attempt to overcome any such conviction.

b. *What are the objections to the eternal duration of the
distresses of hell?*

1). It is pointed out that in the Old Testament the words
*forever, eternal,* and *everlasting* do not necessarily have the
absolute sense that we give to them now. For example: "Ye
have kindled a fire in mine anger which shall burn for ever
. . . to make their land an astonishment, and a perpetual hiss-
ing . . . I will punish . . . the land of the Chaldeans; and I will
make it desolate for ever . . . Return ye . . . and dwell in the
land that Jehovah hath given unto you and to your fathers,
from of old and even for evermore" (Jer. 17:4; 18:16; 25:12,
5).

To this one might add, for one thing, that we too sometimes use such expressions in a hyperbolic sense; and, moreover, that God, speaking in this way, may have in view the
truly eternal repercussions of His threats and His promises.
However, there is no doubt that these words, when referring
to the Lord and to everlasting life, take on their absolute
sense. How could it be otherwise in that which concerns
perdition, then?

"Thy throne, O God, is for ever and ever" (Ps. 45:6).

"Even from everlasting to everlasting, thou art God" (Ps.
90:2). "I will make an everlasting covenant with you" (Isa.
55:3).

Finally, it is significant that Daniel 12:2 twice employs
the same word: "everlasting," to qualify the endless life of
the elect (and there is no dispute on this point), as well as
to characterize the shame of the condemned.

2). They claim that, in the New Testament, the Greek
word "eternal"—aiōnios—means only: of a long duration, in

keeping with the "aeons" to come. (The word "aiōn" is translated by "age.") That there is a relationship between the "eternal" and the ages to come no one can doubt. But the New Testament takes care not to leave us uninstructed as to the sense in which it employs this term, one that it uses seventy-one times. It applies it sixty-four times to the divine and blessed realities of the other world: the eternal God, His eternal power, the eternal spirit, life eternal, the eternal Gospel, the eternal kingdom, eternal salvation, eternal redemption, the eternal covenant, the eternal heritage, the eternal glory, eternal consolation, the eternal tabernacles, eternal time, and the invisible things which are eternal. In all these cases, it is beyond all doubt a question of a duration without end. Seven times, on the other hand, the same word is applied to perdition—Matthew 18:8; 25:41; Jude 7: eternal fire; Matthew 25:46: eternal punishment; Mark 3:29: eternal sin (or judgment) ; II Thessalonians 1:9: eternal destruction; Hebrews 6:2: eternal judgment. How could it be that a word which sixty-four times means "eternal" would seven other times mean something entirely different? Moreover, Jesus employs the same expression, in Matthew 25:46, for eternal life and for eternal punishment. If the first is to last for ever, why not the second?

3). The same objection is raised regarding the expression "for ever and ever"; it is claimed that this means "a certain number of ages," but not eternity. Let us see what meaning is given to this word in the Revelation, where it is constantly found. Jesus Christ and God on His throne live for ever and ever (1:18; 4:9). They are adored for ever and ever (5:13; 7:12). God will reign for ever and ever (11:15). Likewise, the elect will reign with Him for ever and ever (22:5). Up to this point, beyond all doubt whatever, this expression signifies *always*. Why would it take on a different sense when it is applied to hell? "The smoke of their torment goeth up for ever and ever" (14:11; 19:3). "They shall be tormented day and night for ever and ever" (20:10).

Let us notice, finally, that the expression "for ever and ever" in the Revelation is found twelve times in the Greek as "eis tous aiōnas tōn aiōnon" and just once as "eis aiōnas aiōnon," in Revelation 14:11. We do not believe that there is any difference in meaning here, and all of the arguments in the above paragraph concur to show that this locution, so many times repeated, means of an eternal duration. (See, specifically, the two Greek forms of the expression in Revelation 14:11 and 19:3, which have absolutely the same meaning.)

4). Exactly the same thing can be said of the words "forever" and "for evermore." The New Testament unquestionably uses them in the absolute sense: "The law . . . appointeth a Son, perfected for evermore . . . He [Jesus Christ] abideth for ever . . . Jesus Christ is the same . . . for ever" (Heb. 7:28, 24; 13:8). "Perhaps he was . . . parted from thee for a season, that thou shouldest have him for ever" (Philemon 15). How could these same words suddenly change in meaning when Jude applies them to hell? (vss. 6, 13).

5). The worm that never dies and unquenchable fire, they say too, are only figures of speech. When everything is gnawed through, the worm dies; when everything is burned up, the fire is extinguished. In the Valley of Hinnom (Gehenna, in the Hebrew), near Jerusalem, refuse was burned; the fire lasted only as long as it was kept kindled. This seems like very logical reasoning for earthly fire and for that which it burns. But this does not at all go with what the Bible says about the future life. If souls and if torment both last forever, how could it be that the fire would be extinguished? We see that the beast and the false prophet are thrown alive into the lake of fire and brimstone after the Battle of Armageddon (Rev. 19:20). A thousand years later these two (who are men) are still there; and we read that they, with the devil, will be tormented day and night and for ever and ever (Rev. 20:10). Thus the lake of fire also will certainly be of perpetual duration.

(Since we are here considering only the duration of the suffering, we shall not discuss until later the question of "annihilation.")

We are very much aware of the fact that the affirmations of the Bible regarding eternity and the torments of hell are doubtless among the most difficult concepts to accept. But, once the texts are before us, we have no alternative but to accede to them and to follow the example of Adolphe Monod, whose experience reads as follows: "I did," declared this great preacher, "everything I could to avoid seeing eternal suffering in the Word of God, but I did not succeed in it . . . When I heard Jesus Christ declare that the wicked would go away into eternal punishment and the righteous into eternal life, and that therefore the sufferings of the one class would be eternal in the same sense that the felicity of the other would be, . . . I gave in; I bowed my head; I put my hand over my mouth; and I made myself believe in eternal suffering" (*Première Série de Sermons,* p. 391).

## 5. CONSIDERATION OF SOME QUESTIONS IN REGARD TO HELL

a. *Is an eternal hell compatible with the love of God?*

We have already mentioned popular opinion, which would make God too good to punish sinners for ever. As for this, let us clear up right away one gross error: we must declare that "the good God" does not exist! A God who is weak and indulgent, who spends His time pardoning anything and everything, and who never manifests any severity, is in reality just an idol. This is a *false god,* conjured up by those who take pleasure in their sins, without knowing the God of the Bible. The Scriptures reveal to us One who is at the same time the God of both love and holiness. In His love, the Father gave His Son for us; and in His holiness, He cursed

Him in our stead (I John 4:8-10; Gal. 3:10-13). That man who tramples under foot the Son of God and who spurns His love will eventually become acquainted with the terrible fire of God's justice. "It is a fearful thing to fall into the hands of the living God!" (Read Hebrews 10:26-31, the whole passage).

The entire story of humanity and that of Israel shows that the judgments of God are formidable. The same One who struck the generations living at the time of the deluge, of Sodom, of Egypt, of Babylon, and of Jerusalem; the One who, in our own day, permitted the death of millions of human beings and the devastation of our proud "civilization" by a scourge of fire, that God is not the "good God." He is simply the God who has sought, with incomprehensible love and longsuffering, to save all His creatures, but who does come to the time when He carries out His threats. And His severity, alas, is all the greater in proportion to the length of time that men have held His grace in derision. Hell will be nothing but the prolongation of what we already see down here.

The best proof that the judgment of hell will not be contrary to the holy love of God is that Christ Himself will be the One to carry it out. He will in fact say to the condemned, those on His left hand: "Depart from me, ye cursed, into the eternal fire!" (Matt. 25:41). And the lost will be tormented with fire and brimstone "in the presence of the holy angels and in the presence of the Lamb" (Rev. 14:10). In the parable of the pounds, Jesus exclaims: "But these, mine enemies, that would not that I should reign over them, bring hither and slay them before me!" (Luke 19:27).

Let us not forget, finally, that our God is Himself "a consuming fire" (Heb. 12:29; Deut. 4:24). In Daniel's vision "his throne was fiery flames . . . A fiery stream issued and came forth from before him" (7:9, 10). "Jehovah reigneth . . . A fire goeth before him and burneth up his adversaries" (Ps. 97:1, 3). "Behold, Jehovah will come with fire . . . to render his anger with fierceness, and his rebuke with flames of fire. For by fire will Jehovah execute judgment" (Isa. 66:15, 16. See also Isaiah 30:27, 28, 30 and II Thessalonians 1:7, 8.) Here we get an entirely different conception of the love and the righteousness of God from that which most of our contemporaries have.

b. *Won't the impenitent sooner or later be annihilated, in the other world?*

This is what the partisans of the doctrine of "conditionalism" try to claim. They say that God only has immortality (I Tim. 6:16). He indeed wants to communicate it to men, but on *the express condition* that they believe. "He that believeth on the Son hath eternal life; but he that obeyeth not the Son shall not see life, but the wrath of God abideth on him" (I John 5:12).

The same people add that, according to the Bible, the soul that sins shall die (Ezek. 18:4); therefore that soul will be annihilated in the other world, just as down here the body becomes decomposed. The destruction of the wicked is spoken of as their perdition and their destruction (Rev. 11:18; Matt. 7:13; II Thess. 1:9).

Correctly understood, the Scriptures refute every one of these statements.

1). We have seen, indeed, that God alone possesses life that is truly life and that He communicates it only to believers, for what eternal life means is knowing the Father and the Son (John 17:3); not to know God is to be plunged into spiritual death. But we have also seen that when men are overtaken by "the second death," far from being annihilated, they are on the contrary tormented for ever and ever in the lake of fire and brimstone (Rev. 20:14, 10).

2). It is certain that the idea of the survival of the soul is universal and is found in all heathen religions, including that of the Greeks, along with the concepts of a supreme God, of good and evil, of the necessity of a substitutionary atonement, of a judgment in the life beyond, etc. But the Bible alone teaches plainly that, by the resurrection, the whole human personality, the body as well as the soul, will go on living in the other world. It also affirms that there will be a resurrection of the unjust the same as of the just (John 5:29; Dan. 12:2).

3). When the Scriptures mention the destruction, perdition, and ruin of the wicked, one must understand the sense given to these expressions. The Revelation speaks of "destroying them that destroy the earth" (11:18). It is evident that the wicked are not annihilating the earth; they are ruining it, spoiling it; and that is also what God will do to them. (The same Greek word "diaphtheirō" is found in I Timothy 6:5, where it is translated "corrupted" in mind.)

Paul says that the wicked shall have as punishment "eternal destruction," separation from the face of the Lord (II Thess. 1:9). The word "ruin" (in Greek *olethros*) does not necessarily carry with it the idea of annihilation (see also I Cor. 5:5, I Thess. 5:3; and I Tim. 6:9); and the text adds that this state of misery will endure for ever. The "destruction" of the flesh, in I Cor. 5:5, will not hinder the bodily resurrection of the wicked as well as that of the believers.

Let us mention too the expression found in Matthew 10:28: "Fear him who is able to 'destroy' both soul and body in hell." In Greek, the word "apollumi" also means "to lose," and it is applied in the same chapter to the "lost" sheep of the house of Israel (vs. 6); likewise, to the "lost" sheep, the "lost" coin, and the "lost" son (Luke 15:6, 9, 24). Jesus came to save that which was "lost" (Matt. 18:11). Now the prodigal son before his return home existed perfectly well; but he was far from his father, broken in spirit, and miserable. It will be the same for sinners in hell.

4). Let us examine, finally, different words which, in the opinion of some people, seem to convey the idea of the annihilation of the wicked. Let us begin with the Old Testament. *I Samuel 2:9:* "The wicked shall be put to silence in darkness" (A.S.V.) Berkeley says "the godless perish." Darby translates: "the wicked are silenced in darkness." The same Hebrew word "damam" is found in Jeremiah 8:14: "puts us to silence"; in Ps. 30:12: "be silent"; and in Ps. 31:17: "be silent."

*Job 30:22:* "Thou dissolvest me in the storm"; the Hebrew word "mug" is translated by Young's Concordance: "dissolvest." Job is still alive when he uses the expression. *Ps. 92:7:* "all the workers of iniquity do flourish; they shall be destroyed forever." Berkeley says "eternally destroyed." Young's Concordance translates the Hebrew word "shamad" by "destroy," "cut off," "waste." (Jer. 48:8: "The plain shall be destroyed.")

*Ps. 94:23:* "He . . . will cut them off in their own wickedness." (See also Ps. 101:5: "Him will I destroy." Also Darby: "Him will I destroy." Young translates the Hebrew word "tsamath" as "cut off," "destroy." (*Ps. 119:39:* "My zeal hath consumed me.") *Hosea 8:8:* "Israel is swallowed up: now are they among the nations. This is what Berkeley translates: "Devoured is Israel." Darby: "Israel is swallowed up." Young gives the word "bala" the sense of "to swallow up," "to devour."

It is evident that none of these verbs express our philosophic notion of annihilation, cessation of existence.

*Obadiah 16* is likewise cited to support the idea of annihilation. But it is necessary to read verses 15 and 16 together: "The day of Jehovah is near upon all the nations: as thou hast done, it shall be done unto thee . . . so shall all the nations drink continuously . . . they shall drink and swallow down [the wine of the wrath of God], *and shall be as though they had not been.*" If one reads the analagous passage in Jeremiah 25:15-17 and 27:29, one sees this has to do with an earthly destruction of the nations at the return of Christ.

Let us now go over to the New Testament.

*Philippians 2:7:* "Christ . . . emptied himself" (A.S.V. and Berkeley). J. B. Phillips says "He stripped himself." The Greek word "kénoō" means literally "to empty." Having thus "emptied" Himself, the Lord was able to accomplish the marvelous work of our redemption.

According to another Greek expression (*katargéō*), the princes of this age are going to be "brought to nought" and Christ will give the kingdom back to His Father, after having "destroyed" all dominion, authority, and power, including death itself (I Cor. 2:6; 15:24, 26). But the same word here translated to "bring to nought" or to "destroy" is applied, for example, to the "body of sin," which was potentially destroyed at the cross (that is, made inoperative through faith), although it is still terribly active in every one of us (Rom. 6:6). It is also said that when Jesus died, He "brought to nought" the devil (Heb. 2:14). And yet we know that even if this enemy has had to let go of some of his victims, he has not for a moment desisted from his activities, which are still going on today. His being "brought to nought" consists of the breaking down of his control and the fact that he is to be tormented for ever and ever in the lake of fire and brimstone (Rev. 20:10). The Williams translation has a better rendering of Hebrews 2:14: "He put a stop to the power of him who has the power of death." In like manner, the Lord "will bring to nought" Antichrist by the brightness of His coming, after which this individual will be subjected to the same eternal torment in hell as the devil himself (II Thess. 2:8; Rev. 20:10). See also the use of the same Greek word in Ephesians 2:15: "having abolished in his flesh the enmity [the law]"; Luke 13:7: "Why doth it also cumber the ground?" (That is, why does it make the earth useless?) I Corinthians 13:8: "they [prophecies] shall be done away," knowledge "shall be done away"; each time the literal meaning is to render inoperative, or useless.

5). From all the preceding there comes this: even if, at

first sight, certain biblical expressions, taken out of context and found in a single place, seem to raise a question as to the annihilation of the unrepentant, one is most definitely obliged to answer negatively, on looking at all the passages and at the general idea in each of the essential words. This is altogether normal, for the doctrine of annihilation is completely the opposite of all the Scriptures cited above, which speak of the eternal torments of hell. The idea of some conditionalists is that the rebellious have not in themselves the strength to keep on living and that, separated from God, they die out. But in that case, the worst reprobates ought to be annihilated the fastest! It is said that the worst punishment for a reprobate would be annihilation. But don't we often see where a person commits suicide so as to escape the consequences of his evil deeds? Such an argument is basically an affront to reason.

6). *As to the question of the time of annihilation,* the conditionalists are not in agreement among themselves, since the Bible contains nothing on the subject. Some believe that the wicked cease to exist as soon as they leave this world. That would be all that unbelievers could wish: "Let us eat and drink, for tomorrow we die"! The account of the rich man and Lazarus militates against this view (Luke 16:19-31). Others claim that the annihilation will take place at the last judgment, at the time when sinners will be cast into the lake of fire and brimstone. But we have seen that there is no basis for this idea. Furthermore, it would be a supreme injustice if Cain had to suffer for thousands of years in the "place of torments" whereas the rebellious at the end of the millennium and the devil himself would stay there only a few instants. Man, they say, would be like a biennial plant, which lives after it is buried, but not forever! But it is plain that no text speaks of temporary stages in a hell where everything is eternal.

c. *Will there not come a day when all creatures will be saved?*

Another doctrine, called *Universalism*, claims that after certain punishments made necessary by man's sin and God's holiness, everyone will be saved at last. According to the Universalists, the Lord is too good to allow the eternal suffering in hell of creatures who have sinned such a short time on earth. Moreover, they quote: "As in Adam *all* die, so also in Christ shall *all* be made alive . . . that God may be all in *all*" (I Cor. 15:22, 28). Christ has been highly exalted "that in the name of Jesus *every* knee should bow . . . in heaven and . . . on earth and . . . under the earth, and that *every* tongue should confess that Jesus Christ is Lord, to the glory of God the Father" (Phil. 2:10, 11). "God hath shut up all unto disobedience, that he might have mercy upon *all*" (Rom. 11:32). "It was the good pleasure of the Father . . . through him [Jesus Christ] to reconcile *all* things unto himself, having made peace through the blood of his cross" (Col. 1:19, 20).

They take these texts to mean that the day will come when all creatures, even those in hell, will turn to the Savior and receive His grace—these including the devil and the demons. For, they add, the triumph of Jesus Christ would not be complete and God would not be all-powerful if a single one of His creatures, even the most hardened sinner, were to remain in hell, this being an indication that He had not been able to bring that one to Himself. E. F. Ströter, one of the most fervent partisans of Universalism, claims that it is exactly through and by (German: "durch") the infernal fire, the death and ruin and damnation, that God finally does save men. Thus understood, he explains, hell is a manifest and inexpressibly precious proof of His holy love—and that author can "without a particle of mental reservation thank, praise, and worship God with all his heart for this sort of hell . . . Thus the way of the restitution of all things does not bypass hell, but rather goes right through it" (*Die Hölle, ein Erweis der Liebe Gottes,* pp. 2-4). In that case redemption would be effected, not by the blood of Christ alone, but by the sufferings endured by men in the purifying fire of this new type of hell.

E. Pétavel, D. D., theologian of a similar persuasion, writes: "Jesus urges us to 'strive to enter in at the strait gate'; he tells us that the broad way leadeth to destruction. The Universalists, however, say: No, that way also leads to life; longer, but easier than the narrow way, it leads to the same end" (*The Problem of Immortality,* p. 300). The Lord said of Judas: "It would have been good for that man if he had not been born." If a blessed eternity lay ahead of Judas at last, Jesus would surely not have said this to him. It is a matter of record that the Baroness of Krudener offered prayers to God for the conversion of the devil. What did she, then, make of such a text as Revelation 20:10?

Let us now examine more closely some of the other arguments of the Universalists:

1). They claim that it would be unjust to punish for eternity those who have sinned only in time. But we must understand that sin is of infinite gravity: it offends an infinite Person; and furthermore, it is committed by man, created in the image of God, a creature who even now exists in the perspective of eternity. Do not these two brief events in time, the fall of Adam and the cross of Christ, themselves have infinite consequences? (Rom. 5:17-19). It is also plain that the doctrine of Universalism contradicts all the passages which speak of eternal suffering in the other world. Moreover, it is easy to explain quite differently and in harmony with the whole import of the Scriptures those passages on which the Universalists depend for their arguments.

2). In order to understand I Corinthians 15:22, one must also read verse 23: the *all* who "shall . . . be made alive" in

Christ are limited to those "that are Christ's." Likewise it is only to that number that God will be "all in all," since "flesh and blood cannot inherit the kingdom of God" (vss. 28, 50). Paul declares, moreover, that "Christ is all and in all" already; but, of course, he shows that this is only as regards those who make up the true Church, in which "there cannot be Greek and Jew . . . bondman [and] freeman" (Col. 3:11).

3). The fact that in heaven, on earth, and under the earth every knee shall bow and every tongue confess that Jesus is Lord does not necessarily mean that all men will be converted. After the first coming of Christ, the demons were the first to proclaim who He was and to obey Him (Mark 1:24, 27). So, too, the moment will come when, in the other world, all the enemies of the Lord will be required to recognize His authority with trembling and will be compelled to bow before Him. But that will, alas, be too late for their salvation.

4). One might cite many other texts which attest that it is God's will to save all men by the fully sufficient sacrifice of the cross. (See also I Timothy 2:4; I John 2:1, 2; II Peter 3:9; Matthew 18:4, etc.) But, despite this desire, the Lord will never force salvation on those who stubbornly reject it. Jesus cried out: "Jerusalem . . . how often *would I* have gathered thy children together . . . *and ye would not!*" (Matt. 23:37). If men go to hell, it will be because God respects their liberty and their rebellious will and because He has no other salvation to offer them (Heb. 10:26-31). Salvation is obtained only by faith (Rom. 1:17; 3:23, 28, etc.). In the other world, unfortunately, it will no longer be possible to receive it, for sight will have taken the place of faith.

5). According to the words of Christ in Luke 16:26, there is a great gulf fixed between the place of torment and the place of rest; this gulf makes impossible any passage from the one sphere to the other. How then could the condemned ever get into heaven?

6). However appealing Universalism may seem, we are therefore obliged to insist that it is not in accord with the Bible. Its ideas of a universal reintegration are really a good deal more akin to the doctrines of Pantheism.

Finally, let us add that if there were any possibility of redemption after death, it could come about in only one of these two ways:

> *either* men would have to decide for Christ, in the sense of being compelled to do it. In that case, what would become of their liberty, and of what moral value would their decision be?

> *or* it would be the way it is here on earth, a situation in which there would be the possibility of a refusal. Then, what good would that repetition do, and to how many such repeated tests should the unrepentant sinner be submitted?

No, the whole Bible tells us that the decision is to be made *today*. Tomorrow it will be too late.

> The warnings of the prophets,
> the tears of Jesus,
> the appeals of the apostles,
> the impassioned arguments of Paul,
> the overwhelming pictures in the Revelation—
> all cry out to us: *Today!*

> "*Today*, if ye shall hear his voice, harden not your hearts!"
> "Take heed . . . so long as it is called Today, lest any one of you be hardened by the deceitfulness of sin."

Let us fear therefore lest haply a promise being left of entering into his rest, any one of you should seem to have *come short* of it . . . God (in the New Covenant) again defineth a certain day—*today!*

"How shall we escape if we neglect so great a salvation"!
(Heb. 3:7, 8, 13; 4:1, 7; and 2:3).

"We entreat also that ye receive not the grace of God in
vain, for he saith, At an acceptable time I hearkened unto
thee, and in a day of salvation did I succor thee: Behold,
*now* is the acceptable time. Behold, *now* is the day of salvation!" (II Cor. 6:1, 2).

"Choose you *this day* whom ye will serve!" (Joshua 24:
15).

"Seek ye Jehovah while he may be found; call ye upon
him while he is near" (Isa. 55:6).

After the day of salvation there will come that of judgment; and the door of heaven will be shut, as was of old the
door of the ark. Then "many . . . shall seek to enter in and
shall not be able." They will knock and entreat in vain,
they will at that time repent of their ways, when at last they
see their perdition; but it will be too late. The Lord will
say to them: "I know you not whence ye are . . . depart from
me, all ye workers of iniquity. There shall be the weeping
and the gnashing of teeth" (Luke 13:24-27 and Matt. 25:
10-12).

Who, then, reading these solemn declarations, would dare
to put off his conversion to God, counting on a possibility
which does not exist of salvation after death? The Bible
shows us, alas, that repenting just as the hour of punishment
is sounding does not do a bit of good:

"If we sin wilfully after that we have received the knowledge of the truth, there remaineth no more a sacrifice for
sins, but a certain fearful expectation of judgment and a
fierceness of fire which shall devour the adversaries . . . Looking carefully lest there be any man that falleth short of the
grace of God . . . lest there be any fornicator, or profane person, as Esau, who for one mess of meat sold his own birth-
right. For ye know that even when he *afterward* desired to
inherit the blessing, he was rejected; for he found no place

for a change of mind [in his father] though he sought it diligently with tears" (Heb. 10:26, 27; 12:15-17).

The repentance in hell, the weeping and the gnashing of teeth, can do no good whatsoever. Down here, at the opportune time, let us seize the offer of grace before it is too late.

d. *What are we to think about purgatory?*

The Roman Church teaches in a very orthodox way that there is an eternal hell, from which one can never get out; but it adds that between heaven and hell there is an intermediate place called "purgatory." To it there go, at death, all who are saved by Jesus Christ from everlasting chastisement, but who are not pure enough to be taken directly to heaven. One cannot be certain of the presence of any individual in paradise unless that one has been canonized, and masses are still being said today for the repose of the souls of popes who died centuries ago.

A look at the Scriptures gives sufficient proof that purgatory is wholly imaginary. All the clear passages about the world beyond present only two possibilities:

| | |
|---|---|
| the broad way leads to destruction, | the narrow gate leads to life (Matt. 7:13, 14); |
| the tares are cast into the fire, | the wheat is gathered into barns (Matt. 13:30); |
| the wicked are thrown into the furnace of fire, | the righteous shine forth in the kingdom of their father (Matt. 13:41-43; 49, 50); |
| the foolish virgins stay outside, | the wise virgins enter into the marriage feast (Matt. 25:10, 11); |
| the unprofitable servant is cast into the outer darkness, | the faithful servant enters into the joy of his lord (Matt. 25: 21, 30); |

| | |
|---|---|
| the cursed, on the left hand, go away into the fire of eternal punishment, | the blessed, on the right hand, receive the kingdom and eternal life (25:33-46) ; |
| the wicked rich man is in torments, | Lazarus is comforted in Abraham's bosom (Luke 16:22, 23) ; |
| some are raised for judgment, | others are raised for life (John 5:29) ; |
| some awaken to everlasting shame, | others awaken to everlasting life (Dan. 12:2) ; |
| the wicked are cast into the lake of fire and brimstone, etc., etc. | the elect are brought into the heavenly Jerusalem (Rev. 21: 1-4, 8) . |

There is nowhere a question of any other place than heaven and hell. The texts brought forth by Rome to uphold the doctrine of purgatory are irrelevant or do not say what they are made to say.

1). ". . . the fire itself shall prove each man's work . . . If any man's work shall be burned, he shall suffer loss; but he himself shall be saved, yet so as through fire" (I Cor. 3:13, 15) . This is a question of people who are saved, having built their lives on Jesus Christ, the one foundation (vss. 11, 12) . Paul is speaking of the reward which the children of God will receive in heaven: it will vary according to their love and their zeal; some may even suffer loss. But if they have had a close attachment to the Savior, in spite of all, the unmerited, free grace of the Lord will carry them, even as through fire. There is in this passage no reference to a purification of sins by the undergoing of any atoning sufferings. Such a thought is entirely contrary to the teaching of the Bible. The sufferings of Christ are alone expiatory—and sufficient. He died saying "It is finished!" (John 19:30) . Man is justified "freely by his grace . . . by faith, apart from . . . works . . . To him that worketh not, but believeth on him that justifieth the ungodly, his faith is reckoned for righteousness" (Rom. 3:23, 28; 4:5) . Thus our merits, our efforts, and our sufferings can never in any way atone for our sins. But when we believe in the complete pardon of Calvary, we are by God's Spirit made capable of producing works which glorify God, and He will reward them (Eph. 2:8-10. See all that we have to say about rewards, p. 221.)

Furthermore, what would there still be to atone for, since our sins, though red like crimson, have been made as white as snow (Isa. 1:18)? The blood of Jesus cleanses us from all sin, and God is faithful and just to forgive us our sins and to cleanse us from all unrighteousness (I John 1:7-9) . The Savior has abolished sin by His sacrificial death; and we are sanctified once for all by that offering up of His body, even to the point where God Himself no longer remembers our sins (Heb. 9:26; 10:10; 8:12) .

According to the New Testament, there is nothing of "saints" having to finish purifying themselves in purgatory so as to be declared safe in heaven after a solemn "canonization." They are simple believers still living on earth, as the Ephesians were, once dead in their trespasses and sins, but now raised up spiritually and by faith made to sit with Christ "in the heavenly places," children of God, sealed by His Spirit (Eph. 1:1, 13; 2:1, 6, etc.) . There are even the saints of Corinth (I Cor. 1:2; 6:11), of Philippi (Phil. 1:1, 6), of Colosse (1:2, 27), etc. What need have those believers of a purgatory? Jesus Christ is sufficient for them, as for us, for He can abundantly save those who come unto God by Him, who ever liveth to make intercession for them.

"Agree with thine adversary quickly . . . lest haply . . . thou be cast into prison. Verily I say unto thee, Thou shalt by no means come out thence, till thou have paid the last farthing" (Matt. 5:25, 26). The master of the unmerciful servant "delivered him to the tormentors, till he should pay all that was due" (Matt. 18:34) . These two passages, first of all, speak of the strictness of human justice. The first warns against law suits and their consequences, implying that it is much better to avoid them, even at the cost of a humiliating reconciliation. The text about the merciless servant shows that earthly judges can be inexorable too in the inflexible application of the law. Even so God will manifest no leniency in the execution of His righteous sentence. Moreover, the two passages considered are to be understood in the light of very many other texts which allow for only two solutions to the problem of the other world and which speak emphatically of eternal hell. If the idea of purgatory were biblical, it would at least be mentioned somewhere in a crystal clear way, but this is not the case. It therefore is untenable because it contradicts every definite passage there is.

2). "Whosoever shall speak against the Holy Spirit, it shall not be forgiven him, neither in this world nor in that which is to come" (Matt. 12:32). If one certain sin cannot be forgiven in the other world, declares the Roman Church, does that not imply that others will be forgiven there? The text, at any rate, does not say so. We believe, moreover, that there is only one unpardonable sin, the sin against the Holy Spirit, which consists of the obstinate refusal of divine grace (Matt. 13:13-15; John 12:37-40; 16:8, 9. See R. Pache, *The Person and Work of the Holy Spirit*, p. 60.) God would save the whole world, and Christ died to atone for every sin; the only sin which will never be pardoned is the rejection of that very pardon, which God will never force anyone to accept. All who find themselves in hell, then, have committed that sin and canont be absolved from it. This is even the denial of a purgatory.

3). Not finding in the canonical books of the Scriptures any support for its doctrine, attacked by the Reformers, the Roman Church was obliged to go hunt for texts in Jewish apocryphal books: she declared them "canonical," then, at the Council of Trent in 1546. According to II Maccabees 12:39-46, the Jews pray and offer an atoning sacrifice for their comrades who have died in battle. This fact would justify today the prayers and masses said for the dead and would demonstrate the existence in the other world of a place where sinners complete their purification. It is surprising that, to dogmatically affirm such things, Catholicism had to wait until fifteen centuries after Jesus Christ, to suddenly proclaim as inspired some books which had not been so regarded up to that time by the Jewish Synagogue and the Church. A simple reading of these books quickly convinces us, moreover, that they are of a truly inferior quality. The text cited above, therefore, does not impress us in the least. On the contrary, we are not surprised that it contradicts the Scriptures themselves.

4). In the encouragement of the faithful to pay for prayers and masses for the souls in purgatory, one comes, in spite of oneself, on something immoral. Is it fair that a not-very-scrupulous rich man, for whom impressive sums are paid, goes to heaven sooner than does a poor man whose family can pay nothing? We have known cases where people have bequeathed fabulous sums to the Church for masses to be said to perpetuity for the repose of their souls. Anyway, where in the Gospels does it say that money can purchase that which is, by its very definition, a gift? Let us, on the contrary, cite some texts showing the marvelous gratuity of eternal salvation.

"Ho, every one that thirsteth, come ye to the waters . . . without money and without price!" (Isa. 55:1). "Freely ye received; freely give" (Matt. 10:8). The king said to his guests: "All things are ready: come to the marriage feast!" (Matt. 22.4). The entrée into such a banquet occasion is certainly not one to be paid for! "Thy silver perish with thee, because thou hast thought to obtain the gift of God with money!" (Acts 8:20). "Being justified freely by his grace . . . the free gift of God is eternal life in Christ Jesus our Lord" (Rom. 3:24; 6:23). "By grace have ye been saved through faith; and that not of yourselves; it is the gift of God" (Eph. 2:8). "Ye were redeemed, not with corruptible things, with silver or gold . . . but with precious blood . . . [even the blood] of Christ" (I Peter 1:18, 19). Speaking of heaven, the Lord said, in the Revelation: "I will give unto him that is athirst of the fountain of the water of life freely . . . He that is athirst, let him come; he that will, let him take the water of life freely" (Rev. 21:6; 22:17).

Yes, let us bless the Lord for His ineffable gift, and let us thank Him for His promise: "He that heareth my word and believeth him that sent me hath eternal life, and *cometh not into judgment*, but hath passed out of death into life" (John 5:24).

Before the language—and the silence—of the Scriptures, both of them so eloquent, one comes to understand the mortal danger that men risk from the doctrine of purgatory. Most people know that they are not holy enough to go to heaven; but they do not believe themselves bad enough, either, to go to hell. They comfort themselves with the thought that all they will need is a time in purgatory to put themselves in order. And thus they delay until the other world the decision to become converted to God; and they neglect here below the only means of salvation which will ever be offered to them, namely cleansing from their sins by faith in the blood of Christ and a completely changed life. They come up to death without being saved; and, headlong, with their eyes shut, they rush into perdition. In our days, many Protestants are also allowing themselves to be dragged into this woeful error. They do not use the word "purgatory," but it amounts to the same thing: they persuade themselves that after a time of purification beyond the grave they will all go to heaven. Let us pray that the number may not increase of those who daily lead happy, careless lives but who will wake up forever in the place of torment (Luke 16:19-23). Such a situation is so tragic that, without wanting to enter into any controversy, we feel obliged to shout these things from the house tops.

e. *What does "limbo" represent?*

According to the Roman catechism, that is the place where unbaptized dead babies go for all eternity. Jesus declares that unless a man is born of water and the spirit, he cannot enter into the kingdom of God. To Nicodemus, who was astonished at hearing this, He added that it is by faith that one receives eternal life and that therefore one must be born again (John 3:5, 9, 16. See also John 5:24 and John 1:13.) The Roman Church teaches, on the contrary, that the rite of baptism regenerates even an innocent baby—that infants who die without having been baptized will thus never get into heaven. The catechism adds: "But it is permissible to think that they will not go to hell. This is the opinion of St. Augustine, generally followed by the doctors and accepted as probable. They would be put into an intermediate place called *limbo,* where they would never see God, but where they would not suffer. Under those circumstances, according to the judgment of St. Augustine, their fate would still be better than non-existence" (*Dictionary of Dogmatic Theology,* Pietro Parente, trans. by Emmanuel Doronzo, O.M.I., S.T.D., Ph.D. The Bruce Pub. Co., Milwaukee, p. 165). In the above text, the repeated use of the conditional and the total absence of any biblical confirmation shows that limbo, like purgatory, is a purely imaginary place. What would an existence in the after-life be if separated from God? And would it not be most unfair for such a frightful deprivation to be imposed for eternity on poor innocent little babies just because other people did not have them baptized? Moreover, the Church shows itself to be less exacting in the case of adults. It does say that baptism is necessary for the eternal salvation of those who are acquainted with Christianity. But as for adults still plunged in the darkness of unbelief and heathenism, "they will be judged according to their works.

*God could not require of them a baptism that they know*
*nothing about;* and if they have been faithful to the duties of
their conscience and their religion, they can be saved" *(The*
*Meaning of Grace,* Charles Journet, P. J. Kennedy & Sons,
N. Y., p. 104). Fortunately no such flagrant injustice has any
foundation in the Word of God.

We see, on the contrary, that each one will be judged according to his works and the light he has received (Rom. 2:12;
Rev. 20:12). Men are without excuse when, having known
God, they have not worshiped or served Him (Rom. 1:20,
21); they sin when they transgress His law (I John 3:4). Now
innocent children have neither received light nor had the
capacity to act. It is true that from birth they have a sinful
nature which will one day lead them to a wrong use of their
will (Eph. 2:3). But as long as their consciences are not
awakened and especially if they have not yet been able either
to accept or refuse grace, it is clear that the Scriptures do not
hold them responsible. Jesus said that we must become like
little children if we are to enter into the kingdom of God
(Matt. 18:3). Is it not strange that it is the only real in-
nocents that they wish to shut out of heaven for ever? Let us
bless God, rather, for the certainty we have that the Good
Shepherd Himself takes in His arms the most tender of His
little lambs!

f. *Was not the Gospel preached to the dead?*

"Christ also suffered for sins once . . . being put to death
in the flesh, but made alive in the spirit; in which also he
went and preached unto the spirits in prison, that aforetime
were disobedient, whom the longsuffering of God waited in
the days of Noah, while the ark was a preparing" (I Peter 3:
18-20). One has wondered if this text (one of the most difficult of explanation in the Scriptures) alludes to an activity of
Christ in Hades between His death and His resurrection.
Would it then be that He brought a message to those under
the Old Covenant, who up to that time had not known the

Gospel? But, in that case, why would Peter have said that this preaching was addressed only to the generation of the deluge?

Another explanation seems much more plausible to us: Instead of saying "He went," an equally legitimate translation would be "He had gone." One may suppose that Peter is here referring to an intervention of Christ at the time of Noah, to save if possible the unbelievers threatened by the flood. Such an action would not be at all surprising to us, for the Old Testament already shows us Jesus Christ at work on several occasions. For example, He participated in the creation of the world and showed Himself to the patriarchs in the guise of Melchizedek and of the angel of the Lord. But He could have spoken to the people at the time of the flood in a still different way. Peter declares, at the beginning of his epistle, that the prophets of old spoke by the Spirit of Christ which was in them (I Peter 1:10, 11); and it is he also who calls Noah "a preacher of righteousness" (II Peter 2:5). In the passage before us he may mean that the Spirit of Christ made known by Noah a message to the unbelievers of his time, those who are now in prison.

At any rate, it is a question here of an action in the past; and nothing in this text permits the interpretation that the Gospel is being preached now to unbelievers in the other world.

How then can the following text be explained: "They [the wicked who falsely accuse the Christians] shall give account to him that is ready to judge the living and the dead. For unto this end was the gospel preached even to the dead, that they might be judged indeed according to men in the flesh, but live according to God in the spirit" (I Peter 4:4-6). At His return, Jesus Christ will require all humanity to give an account: the dead whom He will raise up and the living whom He will find still on earth. The dead also are responsible, since the Gospel had been preached to them. But the text does not say either where or when, and we think that it is during their existence on earth. Anyway, it again has to do with an action in the past, and Peter does not say here either that the Gospel *is* now being announced to the dead or that it will be later on.

Furthermore, one must realize that this question does not directly concern us, because those who have heard the Gospel (such as all of us who are reading these lines) no longer have any excuse before God and, according to the Bible, will not have any other opportunity for salvation after death. "For if we sin wilfully after that we have received the knowledge of the truth, there remaineth no more a sacrifice for sins, but a certain fearful expectation of judgment, and a fierceness of fire which shall devour the adversaries . . . It is a fearful thing to fall into the hands of the living God" (Heb. 10:26, 27, 31).

g. *Can we be happy in heaven thinking of the condemned in hell?*

Some are persuaded that they could have no rest in heaven if they did not find there all those whom they have loved on earth. To this grave question let us again bring a reply from the Scriptures:

1). We shall be happy in heaven in the same way that the Lord is happy. Paul calls Him the "blessed" God, in spite of the terrible realities of sin, death, and perdition (I Tim. 6:15). Do we think enough about the terrible power of death? Approximately fifty million people die every year, more than a hundred thousand a day. Even as death exists, hell can also exist. Since it is God who has permitted death and ordained judgment, the redeemed, when they are brought into His presence, will necessarily accept them also.

2). On the other hand, God solemnly declares that "he shall wipe away every tear from our eyes" (Rev. 21:4 and 7:17). Thus all grief and torment will be banished from our hearts.

3). It is certain that, in the other world, the elect and the condemned will no longer have anything in common one with the other. Even down here the regenerated become children of God, partakers of the divine nature; they soon will even be made like the Lord (II Peter 1:4; I John 3:1, 2). The wicked, on the contrary, seemingly undergo something of a conversion in reverse: by sin they are children of the devil, and they will increasingly come to resemble their father (I John 3:8). "They . . . became abominable like that which they loved" (Hosea 9:10).

In speaking of Judas, Jesus declares not that he "has a demon," but that he "*is* a devil" (John 6:70). When the Lord separates the just from the unjust, He uses the comparison of sheep and goats, that is of animals which are of different species; and He sends the unjust "into the eternal life which is prepared for the devil and his angels" (Matt. 25:32, 41), thus comparing the condemned to demons. Is this not a terrible thing? Paul declares that already, here on earth, there is nothing in common between the faithful and the unfaithful, between righteousness and iniquity, between the temple of God (which we are) and idols, or between Christ and Belial, i.e. Satan (II Cor. 6:14-17).

But what will that separation be in the other world, when there shall be completed the transformation of the one group into the image of God and that of the others into the image of Satan! It seems evident, then, that certain ties will be entirely sundered.

4). Since, in heaven, we shall love God in a perfect, entire way, how could we still feel attached to those who, right to the end, sought to remain His enemies? Again, the words of Jesus will be accomplished: "He that loveth father or mother more than me is not worthy of me . . . If any man cometh unto me and hateth not his own father, and mother, and wife, and children . . . he cannot be my disciple" (Matt. 10:37; Luke 14:26). When our love for God and our love for the condemned become irreconcilable, the latter must cease to exist. In the countries occupied by the military forces during the war, terrible things took place at the time of the liberation. Recognized traitors were spewed out of the mouth of the national community; people no longer considered them their fellow citizens. How much less will the citizens of heaven be able to fellowship with the condemned in hell! Sometimes if a single fact about the moral character of a person has been made known to us, we suddenly lose all confidence in him and esteem for him. And our affection too can be considerably strained. What will become of our judgments of men when we shall see them in the light of the divine holiness?

## 6. CONCLUSION

Even a cursory study of the collection of passages relating to hell leaves us utterly overwhelmed. From these texts we are obliged to say that the eternal torment of hell is a horrible reality. We do not, however, claim that we can solve all the grave questions raised by such a fearful affirmation. But we do believe that we can add this:

a. *God will make us to understand later on that which still troubles us about His judgments.*

In fact, it is always impossible for us on earth to truly understand God. "As the heavens are higher than the earth, so are my ways higher than your ways, and my thoughts than your thoughts" (Isa. 55:9). I cannot understand God as Creator: His works are infinite; and my eyes can scarcely fathom them, much less explain them. Nor do I understand God as Savior: His love is inconceivable, and His mercy toward us surpasses all our imagination. How then could I understand Him as Sovereign Judge! As Paul said: "How unsearchable are his judgments and his ways past tracing out!" (Rom. 11:33). Still, the moment will come when we shall know even as also we are known (I Cor. 13:12). Then what seems bewildering in the plan of God will be perfectly clear to us. All that God will do will be entirely in harmony with His absolute righteousness and love. "Judgment shall return unto righteousness; and all the upright in heart shall follow it" (Ps. 94:15). "Jehovah of hosts is exalted in justice, and God the Holy One is sanctified in righteousness" (Isa. 5:16). "They shall know that I am Jehovah, when I shall have executed judgments . . . and shall be sanctified . . ." (Ezek. 28:22).

We shall admire, rather, the great patience with which God has endured the "vessels of wrath fitted unto destruction" (fitted thus, it goes without saying, by themselves); and we shall praise Him for having willed to "make known the riches of his glory upon vessels of mercy, which he afore prepared unto glory" (Rom. 9:22, 23).

Here on earth we are still sunk deep in sin and are accomplices of all those who do evil. We have much difficulty in accepting the severity of God. But John shows us that, in heaven, all creatures praise the Lord for His great judgments and even expect them of Him. "Righteous art thou, who art and who wast, thou Holy One, because thou didst thus judge . . . yea, O Lord God, the Almighty, true and righteous are thy judgments . . . Hallelujah! Salvation, and glory, and power belong to our God: for true and righteous are his judgments; for he hath judged the great harlot . . . And a second time they say, Hallelujah! And her smoke goeth up for ever and ever" (Rev. 16:5-7; 19:1-3. See also Rev. 6:10; 11:17, 18; 18:20.) This is certainly what our reaction will be when we find ourselves in the presence of God.

b. *In the meanwhile we are not to worry about our dead, for only God knows where they are.*

It is plain, normally, that a true believer will be recognized as such by his friends; his life and words ought to testify clearly of his faith. Those who mourn him after his departure will at least have the sweet consolation of knowing that he is in the presence of the Lord. But appearances are sometimes deceiving, and it is probable that we shall have some surprises in heaven. One whom we might surely have counted on as being there will not be; another whom we never should have expected to find there will be there. Saving faith need be only a matter of a minute, and we do not know what can take place at the last moment between a soul and God. The father of one of our friends, a prominent preacher, was a close acquaintance of an unbelieving sailor who one day fell into the ocean. Seeing himself lost, the man in his despair yielded his life to the Savior. Pulled out of the water unconscious and brought back to life, he thereafter proved that he had been truly converted. Now, had he stayed in the water, would not some people have considered him as among those in hell? So let us not attempt to lift the veil that hides from us those we have lost. God loves them more than we do; and He knows where they are, for He knows them that are His (II Tim. 2:19). Let us then put our confidence in His righteousness and at the same time in His mercy, awaiting the great day which will reveal all things. In no other way can we have any peace of soul, without mentioning the fact that all our restlessness in regard to the dead cannot do a thing to change their fate. And let us not have the audacity to speak as did a lady who said to us one time: "My husband died unsaved; and if he is not going to be in heaven, I don't want to go there either!" To express oneself like this is to insult God and to prefer His creature to Himself. Also that attitude may lead a person into a very serious mistake. What would that woman say if her husband had been converted without her knowing it and if she would be going to hell by herself? And the husband could, besides, be thinking just the same as the wicked rich man, who feared above everything else seeing his loved ones join him in his torments (Luke 16: 27, 28).

This being said, let us not have the idea either that we can surely become converted at the last minute. Death can strike us down like lightning; and the Bible several times mentions men who hardened their hearts so much that when they came to die, they found that they could not believe (Matt. 13:13-15; John 12:39, 40). Let us not then allow the day of salvation to pass us by.

Finally, we quote what the great historian Guizot had to say on the subject of his dead loved ones: "For a long time I wore myself out trying to figure out where they had gone. I got nothing out of my efforts but dark conjectures and worry . . . But since by faith I have given it all over to God, since I have thrown down at His feet all the pretentiousness of my intellect and even the premature strivings of my soul, I go on in peace, even though in the dark; and in simply accepting my ignorance, I have finally experienced assurance."

c. *The condemned would be miserable in heaven.*

The unrepentant man trembles before God. Rejecting the Savior, he sees in Him only a Judge. Paradise for Adam and Eve was no longer paradise after the fall; gripped by fear, they hid when God drew near to them (Gen. 3:10). If put in heaven, in the immediate presence of the Lord, hardened sinners would have only one desire: to flee as far as possible from the One whom they were never willing to love on earth. They know only too well that "it is a fearful thing to fall into the hands of the living God" (Heb. 10:31). Besides, as we have seen, that bewildered flight—that eternal separation——will be their principal punishment.

d. *The denial of eternal hell marks the first step toward religious unbelief and infidelity.*

In spite of the overwhelming affirmations of the Scriptures, a very great number of so-called Christians do not for all practical purposes believe in hell any more.

From the beginning of time the devil's big argument has been to deny perdition. God had seriously warned Adam and Eve, but the serpent impudently said to them: "Ye shall not

surely die; . . . your eyes shall be opened and ye shall be as
God" (Gen. 3:4, 5). He holds out the same reasoning to
the men of our generation. Our contemporaries find it
more convenient not to believe in the severity of God. They
claim, as we have mentioned, either that the unrepentant
will be annihilated (exactly what they wish for) or else
that all will be saved. This seems to us the first step toward
religious liberalism. The reasoning is continued as follows:
since an eternal hell does not exist, there is no need of a
divine Savior to deliver us from it. Jesus can be only a simple
man, the son of Joseph, quite sufficient for showing us the
good way which is leading man to salvation by his own
efforts . . . Besides, is there still a need of salvation, since
there is no longer any perdition? As for the Bible, which
teaches those old-fashioned things, how can it be taken literally? The "conscience of modern man" knows better than
what it can tell about what will happen in the other world.
And, in fact, those who deny eternal suffering often hunt
for extra-biblical arguments, based on reason and feeling:
"A God of love ought to . . . He ought not to . . . His glory
would be greater if . . . In His place, we would lose no time
in forgiving . . .; sin is not serious; the time of testing on
earth is so slight in comparison to an eternity of suffering . . .
*Therefore,* hell cannot exist; there is need of another possibility of salvation after death," etc., etc. We have heard
this kind of talk ad infinitum.

A remarkable fact: the acceptance of the doctrine of perdition, as the Bible teaches it, is one of the touchstones of
true faith. When it is not present, the other doctrines are
imperceptibly shaken and the whole edifice totters. It
seems to us that there is but one question for us believers to
raise: Even if the doctrine of hell does not please us, is it
taught in the Bible—yes or no? We have seen the answer
which an impressive number of texts give to this single

question. And since God has so emphatically revealed such things to us in His Word, we unreservedly acquiesce.

e. *The reality of eternal perdition is one of the most powerful motives that impel us to preach the Gospel.*

If perdition does not exist, if some day all the unrepentant are to be saved—even the devil, what is the good of going to such lengths to persuade them beforehand? If all will necessarily come to salvation, let us leave them alone and everything will come out just fine. But if eternal hell really threatens them, then let us not give ourselves any rest. Let us imitate our Lord who, knowing the abyss about to swallow us up, came down to snatch us from it. Let us give of ourselves, let us preach, let us exhort in season and out of season, let us urge sinners to repent, let us shout these truths from the house tops, let us pray night and day that a greater number of souls may be saved. If we believe in perdition, it is a crime if we just lounge around at home. The fact that such a large number of so-called Christians are content to do nothing proves that they have neither love for the perishing nor any realistic notion of their condition. Let us learn to imitate Paul, who said: "Woe is unto me if I preach not the gospel . . . I have great sorrow and unceasing pain in my heart. For I could wish that I myself were anathema from Christ for my brethren's sake"! (I Cor. 9:16; Rom. 9:2, 3). Let us surge forward along the paths marked out by William Carey, Hudson Taylor, John G. Paton, and the many other great pioneers, who were pushed irresistibly on by the call of the multitudes destined to eternal perdition. Then, in the great day of the Lord, we shall not appear alone before God, our hands made red by the blood of sinners.

f. *Are we really sure of escaping hell ourselves?*

To be lost, man need do nothing; he is a sinner, condemned by the law of God; and he need simply stay as he is to go directly to hell. No need, for that, to have "killed or stolen," as it is sometimes put.

"Cursed is every one who continueth not in all things that are written in the book of the law, to do them" (Gal. 3:10).

"For whosoever shall keep the whole law, and yet stumble in one point, he is become guilty of all" (James 2:10).

"There is none righteous, no, not one . . . There is no distinction; for all have sinned, and fall short of the glory of God" (Rom. 3:10-23).

"He that obeyeth not the Son shall not see life, but the wrath of God abideth on him" (John 3:36).

Still, as we have said, all that God asks for is to deliver man from the perdition where his sin is dragging him. In His love, He has given His only Son that we should not perish. But for that to be actualized in our experience, we must believe on Christ and accept Him with all our hearts; apart from this we shall continue to be lost. In such a case, man is not lost by his sins, but by his refusal of pardon—by his *unbelief.* That is why the fearful and the unbelievers are at the top of the list of those who are going to hell (Rev. 21: 8): the cowards, who never have the courage to decide for Christ and to bear His shame; and the unbelievers, who deliberately deprive themselves of salvation, since they thus commit the unpardonable sin.

Yet it is so easy with God's help to escape perdition. The Savior finished the work of our redemption on the cross, and all God asks of us is to accept His grace: "I will give unto him that is athirst of the fountain of the water of life freely" (Rev. 21:6; 22:17).

If you desire salvation, come to Christ, who rejects no one. Make your decision today. For the Bible says:

> *those who want to* will go to hell;
> *those who want to* will go to heaven.

Thus you alone would be responsible for your eternal perdition, with no other chance of redemption in the other world. *Seize* grace then; possess salvation by an act of faith. "For by grace have ye been saved through faith; and that not of yourselves; it is the gift of God" (Eph. 2:8). So take this gift of God, and thank Him beginning this moment for having saved you for time and for eternity. "He that believeth on him is not judged . . . He that heareth my word and believeth him that sent me hath eternal life and cometh not into judgment, but hath passed out of death into life" (John 3:18; 5:24). "There is therefore now no condemnation to them that are in Christ Jesus" (Rom. 8:1).

Then, as soon as you have by faith taken hold of the marvelous assurance of the salvation of your soul, realize that God is entrusting to you the task of warning and of winning others:

"So thou, son of man, I have set thee a watchman . . . Hear the word at my mouth, and give them warning from me. When I say unto the wicked, O wicked man, thou shalt surely die, and thou dost not speak to warn the wicked from his way, that wicked man shall die in his iniquity; but his blood will I require at thy hand. Nevertheless, if thou warn the wicked of his way to turn from it, and he turn not from his way, he shall die in his iniquity, but thou hast delivered thy soul" (Ezek. 33:7-9).

"He who converteth a sinner from the error of his way shall save a soul from death, and shall cover a multitude of sins" (James 5:20).

"For God so loved the world that he gave his only begotten Son, that whosoever believeth on him should not perish, but have eternal life" (John 3:16).

# PART SIX
# HEAVEN

## Chapter XVI

## HEAVEN

IT IS MORE DIFFICULT to speak about heaven than about any other subject. These are pre-eminently heavenly things that "eye hath not seen, nor ear heard, neither have entered into the heart of man." Paul, carried away into Paradise, heard there "unspeakable words, which it is not lawful for a man to utter" (II Cor. 12:4). Here below no one can see God and live (Exod. 33:20). Let us not be surprised, then, that the Bible, in order to describe heaven for us, is limited to terms of our poor human language; again, on our part, we can catch only a glimpse of the glory of the eternal realities. Still, if we simply allow ourselves to be led by the Spirit, we shall not fail to be amazed and edified by all that the Lord wants even now to reveal to us.

1. HOW IS HEAVEN DESCRIBED?

Let us see what expressions the Scriptures employ to make us understand what it will be like.

a. *The new heavens and the new earth*

A completely new dwelling place is reserved for us: the first heaven and the first earth have passed away, and God makes all things new (Rev. 21:1, 5). It is the great re-establishment of all things announced by the prophets and to which Peter alludes (Isa. 65:17; Acts 3:21). The earth has already been partially renewed during the millennium; but it is now destroyed, and heaven is also, in order that all trace of the former revolt may disappear. "According to

329

his promise, we look for new heavens and a new earth, where-in dwelleth righteousness" (II Peter 3:13).

It is told us that at the creation of the world "the morning stars sang together, and all the sons of God [the angels, no doubt] shouted for joy" (Job 38:7). Since then, this joy has become dimmed by the fall and by the curse of sin, so that the whole creation groans and suffers the pains of travail. When, at last, the new heavens and the new earth appear, the whole universe will resound with praise. Myriads of myriads and thousands upon thousands of beings around the heavenly throne have already sung of the God of creation, of redemption, and of judgment (Rev. 4:11; 5:11-14; and 15:3, 4). Alleluias have resounded for the marriage of the Lamb (19:6, 7). They will certainly burst forth again when, all things having become new, there will be seen descending out of heaven from God the new Jerusalem, prepared as a bride adorned for her husband (21:1, 2).

b. *The New Jerusalem*

Jerusalem represented to the Israelites the dwelling place of the Lord and the place of profoundest blessings. As for us, we shall have the privilege of entering into the heavenly Jerusalem, the city of the living God, which He has prepared especially for us (Heb. 12:22; 11:16). John gives us a description of that city in graphic terms, meaningful even to the most simple (Rev. 21:10-27).

The *Builder* and the *Maker* of that city is God Himself (Heb. 11:10).

The *materials* which compose it are pure gold, pearls, and precious varicolored stones, symbols of beauty and of inalterable wealth (see also Isa. 54:11, 12). Strikingly, it is with these same materials, according to Paul, that we are to build our lives down here, for these alone will resist the judgment fires (I Cor. 3:12-14).

A *wall* of jasper surrounds the city, a hundred and forty-four cubits high (Rev. 21:17, 18). It assures the perfect security of the city and likewise its separation from all that would be unworthy of entering in. "For I, saith Jehovah, will be unto her [Jerusalem] a wall of fire round about, and I will be the glory in the midst of her" (Zech. 2:5).

The twelve *foundations* of the wall bear the names of *the twelve apostles* (not of one alone), guaranteeing solidity (Rev. 21:14). This brings to mind the word of Paul: "Built upon the foundation of the apostles and prophets, Christ Jesus Himself being the chief corner stone" (Eph. 2:20).

The dimensions of the city are considerable: they form a transparent cube twelve thousand furlongs on each side (Rev. 21:16). The holiest place in the Jewish temple was likewise a cube (I Kings 6:20). Such an immense city is obviously not of our material universe—but it is big enough to contain all the generations of all time.

There are *twelve gates,* three on each side, signifying that an abundant access is provided for those who come from all points on the horizon (Rev. 21:13, 14). On the gates are inscribed the names of *the twelve tribes of Israel.* John indicates here that "salvation is of the Jews"—and moreover that heaven is opened to the believers of both the Old and the New Covenants. We have just mentioned Paul, according to whom the church is founded on the apostles and the prophets (Eph. 2:20). Before the throne of God are seated the twenty-four elders—doubtless twelve patriarchs and twelve apostles (Rev. 4:4). Among the servants of God of whom John has a glimpse in Revelation 7 there are a hundred and forty-four thousand of the twelve tribes of Israel and the great multitude which no man could number coming out of all nations (vss. 4, 9). Each gate is formed of one single *pearl,* symbolizing unity, purity, beauty, and worth (21:21). At each gate stands an *angel* to watch over the elect admitted into the city and to keep anything defiled from entering in (vss. 12, 27). Finally, the gates are *never closed:* there is no enemy to be feared, and free access into the presence of God is always assured (vs. 25).

The *street* of the city is also of pure gold (vs. 21). All its traffic and all its activity are in harmony with its glory and its perfection. There, all is as transparent glass (vs. 21): graft, riotings, and accidents are outlawed.

There is no *temple* in the city (vs. 22). In the earthly Jerusalem, the temple was essential; and in our holy cities, churches and other places of worship are innumerable. Here, on the contrary, no more temple—rather, the city has itself become a sanctuary: the Lord God Almighty is its temple, as is the Lamb. He is "all in all"; His presence fills both the whole city and every heart: what need is there any more for a temple as in former times?

On the other hand, the *throne* of God and of the Lamb is there (22:3). This indicates that the Lord rules unrivaled over the holy city; there is no longer either revolt or disorder. On this throne the redeemed themselves are called to sit (Rev. 3:21).

Who are the *inhabitants* of the heavenly city? Only those whose names are written in the Lamb's book of life (21:27). "Blessed are they that wash their robes [in the blood of the Lamb, 7:14], that they may have the right to enter in by the gates into the city" (22:14).

The new Jerusalem is *illuminated by the glory and the presence of God.* It has "no need of the sun, neither of the moon, to shine upon it; for the glory of God did lighten it, and the lamp thereof is the Lamb. And the nations [of them which are saved] shall walk amidst the light thereof . . . And there shall be no night there; and they need no light of lamp, neither light of sun; for the Lord God shall give them light" (Rev. 21:23; 22:5). The whole city shines even like a jasper stone, clear as crystal, and its pure gold is like unto transparent glass (21:11, 18, 21). This seems to us both normal and glorious: could the illumination of the dwelling place of Him who is the light of the world be otherwise?

Let us notice, finally, that the new Jerusalem is *made to the measure of the redeemed ones* that it is to receive. If the number "seven" is the number of God (Rev. 4:5; 5:6), the number "six" with its compounds is that of man (Rev. 13: 18). Now in Revelation 21:12 to 22:2, the numbers "twelve," "144," and "12,000" occur twelve times in all, evidently to indicate that the "measure of man" characterizes the heavenly city. No other place could better assure the happiness and the perfect unfolding of the human personality and of the human race.

Such is the "bride, the wife of the Lamb," the holy city which is soon to descend out of heaven from God (Rev. 21: 9, 10). The Jews had—and still have—an exclusive love for the earthly Jerusalem. In their captivity they cried out: "If I forget thee, O Jerusalem, let my right hand forget her skill. Let my tongue cleave to the roof of my mouth if I remember thee not; if I prefer not Jerusalem above my chief joy" (Ps. 137:5, 6). We who are citizens of a place infinitely more glorious, ought we not to love it and to desire it even more? In order constantly to keep the sanctifying vision of it before us, let us learn to lift up our spirits, as John did, unto the high mountain of faith (Rev. 21:10). Let us not think merely of earthly things, for "our citizenship is in heaven" (Phil. 3:20). Let us await, as did the patriarchs, "the city which hath the foundations, whose builder and maker is God." Like Bunyan's famous Pilgrim, let us proceed all our lives toward the glorious city which God Himself has prepared for us (Heb. 11:10, 16).

c. *Paradise*

The terrestrial Eden, sojourn of innocent man directly in touch with God, remains the type of the heavenly felicity. The Jews early called "paradise"—or "Abraham's bosom"— the abode of the believing dead, until the resurrection of

Christ (Luke 23:43; 16:22). But the Scriptures particularly call "paradise" heaven itself, where God waits for us. It is there that Paul was transported in ecstasy (II Cor. 12:4). And Christ gives us this promise: "To him that overcometh, to him will I give to eat of the tree of life, which is in the paradise of God" (Rev. 2:7). Let us study the remarkable parallel that the Bible establishes between Genesis 2 and Revelation 22:1-5, and let us measure the distance which separates Eden from the heavenly paradise.

*The river of the water of life* flows, not only from Eden, but also from the throne of God and of the Lamb (22:1). Ezekiel had already seen the living water issue forth from the altar and bring life everywhere it went (47:9). On the new earth there will be completely fulfilled the word of the psalmist: "There is a river, the streams whereof make glad the city of God . . . God is in the midst of her: she shall not be moved" (Ps. 46:4, 5).

*The tree of life* is found "in the midst of the street thereof [of the city] and on either side of the river," sufficing for the maintenance of life of all the elect (Rev. 22:2). The *fruits* of the tree are yielded *every month,* a sign of fecundity and of constantly renewed freshness. On the earth it was necessary to wait for the maturity until after the flowering and to wait for the fulfillment until after the promise. Here, the divine food is always available, and *the leaves* of the tree are enough to assure perpetual health. "To him that overcometh, to him will I give to eat of the tree of life, which is in the Paradise of God . . . To him that overcometh, to him will I give of the hidden manna . . . Blessed are they that wash their robes, that they may have the right to come to the tree of life" (Rev. 2:7, 17; 22:14). Let us also note that "the way of the tree of life" is again freely opened. After the fall, the flaming sword of the cherubim denied access to it (Gen. 3:24). In heaven, there is no more curse, neither is there any prohibition for the elect (Rev. 22:3, 4).

Whom then does this tree of life represent? One may say that it is the Lord Himself, already symbolized in the Bible by the manna, the rock of Horeb, the living water, the Paschal Lamb, etc. The eternal life which nourishes our souls is the Lord Himself, communicating Himself to us (Rev. 2:7). "He that eateth *me* [said Jesus], he also shall live because of me" (John 6:57). "And this is life eternal, that they should know thee the only true God, and him whom thou didst send, even Jesus Christ" (John 17:3).

The life of God will be for us the food and drink of paradise, the manna and the living water, the tree and the river; even as here below it is the bread and the wine, the body and the blood of the communion. What more could we hope for?

An interesting comparison can be made of the earthly paradise and the heavenly paradise. Here is what Erich Sauer writes in his remarkable book, *The Triumph of the Crucified*, p. 212: The beginning and the end blend in together; the first and the last pages of the Bible resemble each other: the Scriptures begin and end with paradise. But the end is more beautiful than the beginning, the omega grander than the alpha: the future paradise is not simply the old one restored; it is the heavenly paradise eternally glorified. The psalmist cries out: "Even from everlasting to everlasting, thou art God" (Ps. 90:2). It is He who is the point of departure, as He is the end of all things.

d. *The tabernacle of God with men* (Rev. 21:3)

In the Old Testament God had the tabernacle erected to permit His presence to reside in the midst of His people. He had expressly charged Moses to build it "according to the fashion" which was given to him on Mt. Sinai (Exod. 25:8; 26:30). The Epistle to the Hebrews adds that the tabernacle with its worship service was "a copy and shadow of the heavenly things." So then in heaven is found the true tabernacle . . . "the greater and more perfect tabernacle, not made with hands" (Heb. 8:2, 5; 9:11, 12). It is the very dwelling place of God. The earthly tabernacle was to be purified of encompassing sin by the blood of the sacrifices. The heavenly sanctuary, sullied by the revolt of men, had to be purified by the infinitely better sacrifice of Christ (Heb. 9:23, 24). Immediately after the cross, Jesus entered, with His own blood, "once for all into the holy place" . . . "into heaven itself . . . before the face of God for us." (He did not do it in 1844, "coming back to purify the sanctuary," as the Adventists ciaim!) There, our High Priest appears and pleads now for us. A picture of His body sacrificed on Calvary, the veil which barred access into the holy place (heaven) has been rent in two (Heb. 10:20-22; Matt. 27: 51). By faith, we can therefore come unto the very throne of God, while waiting for Jesus to appear to lead us finally into the abode of the great King (Heb. 4:14-16; 9:28).

The Lord Himself alludes to the "eternal tabernacles" and to those who will receive us there with Him (Luke 16: 9). To dwell in the midst of men and to admit them forever into His intimate presence—that is what the desire of the Lord has been from the beginning. After the repeated failures of the first paradise and the first tabernacle, "the Word [Jesus] became flesh and dwelt [tabernacled] among us . . . full of grace and truth" (John 1:14). Christ wanted to be Immanuel, God with us, in order to be able by the Spirit to put into us His divine presence. The body of the believer becomes His temple, and the Church itself is "a habitation of God in the Spirit" (I Cor. 6:19; Eph. 2:22).

In every detail the plan of God will be wonderfully worked out. Ezekiel saw something of what will be the essential blessing of the millennium, which will subsequently be prolonged in a total and eternal manner in heaven. "I will set my sanctuary in the midst of them for evermore. My tabernacle also shall be with them; and I will be their God, and they shall be my people" (37:26, 27). And John cries out at last: "Behold, the tabernacle of God is with men, and he shall dwell with them, and they shall be his peoples, and God himself shall be with them" (Rev. 21:3). The believer already has a foretaste of heaven, since the Lord lives in him (John 14:23). But what will it be when the ardent desire of the psalmist is realized for eternity: "Surely goodness and lovingkindness shall follow me all the days of my life: and I shall dwell in the house of Jehovah for ever! . . . How amiable are thy tabernacles, O Jehovah of hosts! . . . My King, and my God. Blessed are they that dwell in thy house!" (Ps. 23:6; 84:1-4).

In the earthly tabernacle only the priests were admitted to the service of God. In the heavenly tabernacle—as already in the Church here below—all believers are a part of the priesthood. We have been made kings and priests (Rev. 1:6); or, as Peter says: members of a royal priesthood (I Peter 2:5, 9). Jesus, moreover, declares in the Revelation: "He that overcometh, I will make him a pillar in the temple of my God, and he shall go out thence no more" (3:12). If the Lord Himself is the temple of the heavenly city (Rev. 21:22), that means that we shall all be in His presence—and in Him—for ever.

e. *The heavenly country*

The patriarchs were strangers and pilgrims in the earth. Abram and his family left Ur, then Haran. After a brief sojourn in Palestine, his descendants experienced the long servitude of Egypt. Having met God at Sinai, they stayed forty years more in the desert before at last taking possession of the Promised Land. This is what the Epistle to the Hebrews says of them: "These all died in faith, not having received the promises, but having seen them and greeted them from afar . . . They make it manifest that they are seeking after a country of their own. And if indeed they had been mindful of that country from which they went out, they would have had opportunity to return. But now they desire a better country, that is, a heavenly: wherefore God is not ashamed of them, to be called their God" (Heb. 11:13-16). Like the patriarchs, we are also "strangers and pilgrims" here below, according to I Peter 2:11. If, like them, we press on with all our being toward the heavenly country, God will not be ashamed to be called our God either.

f. *Mount Zion*

The Epistle to the Hebrews compares two mountains, Mt. Sinai and Mt. Zion. Sinai revealed the awful God of the law, surrounded by the cloud and the tempest of judgment. The people, and even Moses as well, were terrified; and the beasts which touched the mountain had to be stoned. "But ye [adds the text] are come unto mount Zion, and unto the city of the living God, the heavenly Jerusalem, and to innumerable hosts of angels, to the general assembly and church of the firstborn who are enrolled in heaven, and to God the Judge of all, and to the spirits of just men made perfect, and to Jesus the mediator of a new covenant, and to the blood of sprinkling, that speaketh better than that of Abel" (Heb. 12:18-24). That is the miracle produced on our behalf by the blood of the cross: we now approach the mountain of grace, no longer trembling before the Judge whom we have offended; there, we enter into the communion of the myriads of angels and of the assembly of all the redeemed of the Lord, who are the "firstborn" or the "first fruits" of humanity (Rev. 14:1, 4; James 1:18); there we join the spirits of just men made perfect, having ourselves become perfect like them.

Each one of us will shortly appear before the Lord. Do we not all want to make our choice to meet the God of grace on Mount Zion rather than to meet the God of judgment at Sinai?

g. *Heaven—or the heavens*

As opposed to the earth, heaven is the place of glory, where

God dwells and where He is making ready a reception for His own.

God the Father is in heaven, where His will is perfectly done (Matt. 6:9, 10). Jesus left heaven; then He went back (John 3:13; Acts 1:11; 3:21). From there He will come again on the glorious day of His return (I Thess. 4:16).

Henceforth it is in heaven that we are to lay up our treasure (Matt. 6:20). It is there that God will reward us (Matt. 5:12), there also that we await the eternal dwelling destined to replace our earthly house of this tabernacle (II Cor. 5:1, 2). Our names are written in heaven (Luke 10:20); and we shall soon enter into our city, which is in heaven (Phil. 3:20).

It is evident that the word "heaven" has various meanings in the Scriptures. The Jews distinguished three principal ones:

1). *the heaven of the atmosphere* over our heads, where the clouds and the birds pass by. This has to do with the rain from heaven (Deut. 11:11), the birds of the air (Luke 9:58), etc.

2). *the heaven of the stars,* the firmament, the immensity which our eyes cannot fathom (Gen. 15:5). But however great it may be, "the heaven of heavens" of the physical universe cannot contain God (I Kings 8:27). Then we have

3). *the third heaven,* which is even the presence of God. It is there that Paul was snatched away in ecstasy, where he heard that which it is not lawful for a man to utter (II Cor. 12:2-4). This same heaven opened before the eyes of the dying Stephen, to permit him to see Jesus standing in glory on the right hand of God (Acts 7:55, 56). Soon we shall all be like the angels of God in that heaven, being sons of the resurrection (Matt. 22:30).

### h. *The heavenly kingdom*

If our faith is sincere, we can say with Paul: "The Lord will deliver me from every evil work, and will save me unto his heavenly kingdom" (II Tim. 4:18). There we shall be seated at the table in the kingdom of God, which it has pleased the Lord to give to His little flock (Luke 13:28; 12:32). "Wherefore, receiving a kingdom that cannot be shaken, let us have grace, whereby we may offer service well-pleasing to God with reverence and awe, for our God is a consuming fire" (Heb. 12:28, 29).

### i. *Above*

"Seek the things *that are above*, where Christ is seated on the right hand of God. Set your mind on the things that are above, not on the things that are upon the earth" (Col. 3: 1, 2). Jesus said to the Jews: "Whither I go, ye cannot come . . . Ye are from beneath; I am from above: Ye are of this world; I am not of this world" (John 8:21, 23).

This language is very plain. We are acquainted only too well with demoralizing and vile things, which so easily can drag us down, to end in the bottomless pit. Let us turn toward that which is above, to our treasure in heaven. Soon we shall be forever up there, seated at the right hand of the Father with Christ, who will have put all His enemies under our feet.

### j. *The Father's house*

"In my Father's house are many mansions. If it were not so, I would have told you, for I go to prepare a place for you . . . I come again, and will receive you unto myself" (John 14:2, 3). What a marvelous message! Heaven is not going to be to us the vast palace of a far-off God, where we would feel lost. It is the house of our Father in Jesus Christ, the home where His love and His solicitude will surround us. What can these "many mansions" be? Jesus means first of all this: in His Father's house there ought normally to be room just for the only Son, at best for the faithful angels

as well, those perfect servitors. But in pleading now before
His Father with His own blood, Jesus assures our entrance
there. And He does not want simply to introduce us into
the quarters set aside for the servants: He receives us as His
Bride in the nuptial chamber of the most beautiful apart-
ment. Moreover, in the Father's house a place is being prepared, not only for the believing Israelites and the first
disciples, but for all the pagans gained by the Gospel. The
Jews had much difficulty in seeing that truth. Therefore
Jesus emphasizes it in these words: "Other sheep I have,
which are not of this fold; them also I must bring . . . and
there shall become one flock, one shepherd" (John 10:16).

You who never have had a real home, or who are suffering at seeing your home broken up, would you miss the
wonderful welcome of the Father's house?

(It seems difficult for us to draw any more from this verse,
John 14:2—to speculate, for example, on the different stages
that the believers in heaven are to go through. As for the
various degrees of rewards, see p. 231.)

k. *The dwelling place of the Most High*

The men of the Old Testament had the vision of the
august majesty of the Lord. They keenly sensed the distance
which separated them from His holiness and the difficulty
which sinful men, even believers, experience in penetrating
into His sanctuary. It is with all the more reverence and
adoration that they accepted the signal grace by which they
were admitted into the palace of the great King. May such
a sentiment always fill our hearts! "There is a river, the
streams whereof make glad the city of God, the holy place
of the tabernacles of the Most High" (Ps. 46:4). "Thus
saith the high and lofty One that inhabiteth eternity, whose
name is Holy; I dwell in the high and holy place, with him
also that is of a contrite and humble spirit . . . Look down
from heaven, and behold from the habitation of thy holiness
and of thy glory" (Isa. 57:15; 63:15). "In his temple every-

thing saith, Glory . . ."! (Ps. 29:9). The psalmist several times asks this question: "Who shall ascend into the hill of Jehovah, and who shall stand in his holy place?" (Ps. 24:3). Then, having appropriated the grace which flows down from the altar of sacrifice, he cries: "Jehovah, I love the habitation of thy house, and the place where thy glory dwelleth" (Ps. 26:8).

1. *Before the throne*

Heaven is pre-eminently the place where God reigns, from which He governs the universe. In the visions of the prophets the Lord is seated on His throne, surrounded by His heavenly court: "I saw Jehovah sitting on his throne, and all the host of heaven standing by him on his right hand and on his left" (I Kings 22:19). "Jehovah hath established his throne in the heavens; and his kingdom ruleth over all" (Ps. 103:19). "I saw the Lord sitting upon a throne, high and lifted up . . . Above him stood the seraphim . . . And one cried unto another, and said, Holy, holy, holy, is Jehovah of hosts: the whole earth is full of his glory" (Isa. 6:1-3). "And one that was ancient of days did sit: . . . his throne was fiery flames, and the wheels thereof burning fire. A fiery stream issued and came forth from before him: thousands of thousands ministered unto him, and ten thousand times ten thousand stood before him" (Dan. 7:9, 10).

In the midst of all the upheavals of the Revelation, the apostle John keeps ever before us the unshakable throne of God; and whenever he transports us to heaven, he places us before that throne: "Straightway I was in the Spirit; and behold, there was a throne set in heaven, and one sitting upon the throne . . ." (Rev. 4:2). Everything is in terms of the throne, as these expressions indicate:

about the throne
of the throne
before the throne
in the midst of the throne

All the worship and prayers of heaven converge on the throne (Rev. 4:10; 5:13; 8:3; 14:3; and 19:4). From it there emanate judgments, directives, and life (6:16; 20:11; 22:1). Heaven, in short, is this: "The throne of God and of the Lamb shall be therein [in the city]: and his servants shall serve him; and they shall see his face; and his name shall be on their foreheads" (Rev. 22:3).

What security and stability the throne of the Lord brings to the universe! May we always live as "before the throne," by our faithful service hastening the establishment of this absolute and glorious reign!

m. *With the Lord*

"Whilst we are at home in the body, we are absent from the Lord . . . and [we] are willing rather to be absent from the body and to be at home *with the Lord*" (II Cor. 5:6, 8).

"Having the desire to depart and be *with Christ;* for it is very far better" (Phil. 1:23). "We . . . shall together with them be caught up in the clouds, to meet the Lord in the air: and so shall we ever be with the Lord" (I Thess. 4:17).

Jessu promised the thief on the cross, about to go down with Him to the abode of the blessed dead: "Today shalt thou be *with me* in Paradise" (Luke 23:43). And He promised all His disciples that the Holy Spirit, the Comforter, would be *with them* forever (John 14:16).

The fact that God dwells with us and we with Him is in itself heaven, for eternal bliss does not depend upon a given place or even upon a particular condition.

To be forever united to Him who is the source of life and perfect happiness—this is all that any creature could wish for. On the other hand, to be separated from God is to know hell and all its torment. The choice is ours as to whether we want to go to heaven to enjoy the divine Presence or whether we want to find out what it is to be deprived of it forever (Num. 14:34).

## 2.  GOD IN HEAVEN

We have just said that heaven is the Presence of God.
There, more than anywhere else, He occupies the preeminent place. When the Bible—and especially the Revelation—carries us to heaven, it gives us a vision of the Lord.

*God the Father,* as we have just seen, is often shown to us
as governing the universe: "Thrones were placed, and one
that was ancient of days did sit: his raiment was white as
snow, and the hair of his head like pure wool . . . A fiery
stream issued and came forth from before him: thousands
of thousands ministered unto him, and ten thousand times
ten thousand stood before him" (Dan. 7:9, 10). "Jehovah
hath established his throne in the heavens, and his kingdom ruleth over all" (Ps. 103:19). "Jehovah reigneth; he is
clothed with majesty . . . The world also is established, that
it cannot be moved. Thy throne is established of old (Ps.
93:1, 2). Around that throne, whereby all things are sustained and governed, the Bible gives us a glimpse of a
great multitude of angels and of redeemed ones adoring,
praising, and serving the Lord. (See, for example, Revelation 4:4-11; 5:8-14; 7:9-12; 14:1-3; 15:2-4; 19:1-7; and 22:
3-5).

In the following terms Paul sums up some of the attributes
of the Lord and of the universe:

> the blessed and
> only Potentate,
> the King of kings and Lord of lords;
> who only hath immortality,
> dwelling in light unapproachable;
> whom no man hath seen, nor can see:
> to whom be honor and power eternal.
> Amen!  (I Tim. 6:15, 16).

It is this great unapproachable God who desires to admit

us for ever into His Presence and to have us participate in His reign.

*Jesus Christ* fully shares with His Father the preeminent place in heaven. Daniel adds: "Behold, there came with the clouds of heaven one like unto a son of man; and he came even to the ancient of days . . . And there was given him dominion, and glory, and a kingdom; that all the peoples . . . should serve him: his dominion is an everlasting dominion" (7:13, 14). It seems to us that the prophet Ezekiel had already seen a vision of the Son of God incarnated and then glorified when he wrote: "And above the firmament . . . upon the likeness of the throne was a likeness as the appearance of a man upon it above. And I saw as it were glowing metal, as the appearance of fire within it round about . . . As the appearance of the bow that is in the cloud . . . This was the appearance of the likeness of the glory of Jehovah. And when I saw it, I fell upon my face" (Ezek. 1:26-28). We are not surprised that the only begotten Son shares in the government of the universe since, as shown in so many passages, He participated in its creation (John 1:3; Col. 1:16; Heb. 1:2, 10, etc.).

The Apocalypse—the revelation of Jesus Christ—has much to say of His role in heaven. It also shows Him to us there on the throne: "I . . . overcame and sat down with my Father in his throne" (3:21). "And I saw in the midst of the throne . . . a Lamb standing as though it had been slain, having seven horns, and seven eyes, which are the seven Spirits of God, sent forth into all the earth." (That is to say that He has all the power, the omniscience, and the fullness of Deity.) Jesus is exalted and adored even in the eternal glory because of the death He suffered: "Worthy is the Lamb that hath been slain to receive the power, and riches, and wisdom, and might, and honor, and glory, and blessing . . . Unto him that sitteth on the throne [God the Father] and unto the Lamb be the blessing, and the honor, and the glory, and the dominion, for ever and ever! . . . And the elders fell down and worshipped" (Rev. 5:6-14).

Not only is Christ exalted in heaven because of His atoning sacrifice, but also He has kept the marks of His glorified humanity. As for His resurrected body, we have seen that John, in the first chapter of the Revelation, still represents Him as a Son of man. His head, hair, eyes, feet, voice, hand, mouth, and face are all depicted. What blessedness for redeemed men to be welcomed into heaven by one of their own, by that One who chose to become a member of their race! "The Lamb that is in the midst of the throne shall be their shepherd and shall guide them unto fountains of waters of life: and God shall wipe away every tear from their eyes" (Rev. 7:17). It is He who will seat us on that same throne which He shares with His Father (Rev. 3:21). And we shall be united throughout eternity to Christ, our heavenly Bridegroom.

When Christ shall have gathered all of His own into the glory of heaven, the cycle of His redemptive work will be finished. He went out from His Father, so as, through death, to put an end to the revolt of sinners and to reestablish God's universal kingdom. After the conversion and the resurrection of all the elect, the sublime triumph of the millennium, the great judgments, and the victory over all His enemies—death included—"then cometh the end, when He [Jesus] shall deliver up the kingdom to God, even the Father; when he shall have abolished all rule and all authority and power . . . And when all things have been subjected unto him, then shall the Son also himself be subjected to him that did subject all things unto him, that God may be all in all" (I Cor. 15:24, 28).

The *Holy Spirit,* intimately united to the Father and to the Son, continues to act with Them throughout all eternity. Let us emphasize, in particular, what He will do in behalf of the redeemed. The fact that we received in this world the first-fruits, or the earnest, of the Spirit (Rom. 8:23; II Cor. 1:22) signifies that upon our entrance into heaven, He will take complete possession of us. Then we shall be by the Spirit "filled unto all the fulness of God" (Eph. 3:19). For the present, He is the pledge of our eternal inheritance (Eph. 1:14); soon He will actualize the whole of it for us.

To summarize, if we wish to depict heaven in a word, we can say again that it will be the Presence of the Lord,

## GOD ALL AND IN ALL.

It has been put something like this:

The light of heaven will be the face of God and of the Lamb,
the joy of heaven, the Presence of the Lord,
the beauty of heaven, the perfection of God,
the duration of heaven, the eternity of God,
the warmth of heaven, the love of the Lord,
the harmony of heaven, the praise of the Lord,
the melody of heaven, the name of Jesus,
the theme of heaven, the work of Jesus,
the activity of heaven, the service of Jesus,
the fullness of heaven, the unsearchable God in Person.

(Adapted from Capt. R. Wallis,
*Heaven, Home of the Redeemed*)

## 3. THE CHARACTERISTICS OF HEAVEN

From all the Biblical descriptions of heaven the following points stand out clearly. The dwelling place of the redeemed will be characterized by:

a. *Glory*

"In his temple everything saith, Glory" (Ps. 29:9). "Father, I desire that they also whom thou hast given me be with me where I am, that they may behold my glory" (John 17:24). "The sufferings of this present time are not worthy to be compared with the glory which shall be revealed to usward" (Rom. 8:18). "When Christ, who is our life, shall be manifested, then shall ye also with him be manifested in glory" (Col. 3:4). "God . . . calleth you into his own kingdom and glory" (I Thess. 2:12). "That the proof of your faith . . . may be found unto praise and glory and honor at the revelation of Jesus Christ" (I Peter 1:7). "And the city hath no need of the sun, neither of the moon, to shine upon it: for the glory of God did lighten it" (Rev. 21:23). And the redeemed themselves will be clothed with incomparable splendor: "They that are wise shall shine as the brightness of the firmament; and they that turn many to righteousness as the stars for ever and ever" (Dan. 12:3). "Then shall the righteous shine forth as the sun in the kingdom of their Father" (Matt. 13:43). As Jesus was transfigured before His disciples, "his garments became glistening, exceeding white, so as no fuller on earth can whiten them" (Mark 9:3). "His face did shine as the sun, and his garments became white as the light" (Matt. 17:2). When John had the vision of the glorified Savior, he observed that "his countenance was as the sun shineth in his strength" (Rev. 1:16). Now this same splendor will be communicated to us, since the Lord "shall fashion anew the body of our humiliation, that it may be conformed to the body of his glory" (Phil. 3:21). Thus will be perfectly consummated the work of which Paul speaks: "We all, with unveiled face beholding as in a mirror the glory of the Lord, are transformed into the same image from glory to glory, even as from the Lord the Spirit" (II Cor. 3:18).

One extraordinary thing is that as the Lord clothes us with His glory, we shall also contribute to His. Man, indeed, was created to be "the image and glory of God" (I Cor. 11:7). The perfect redemption of believers, the masterpiece of the divine power and love, will contribute above all else to the exaltation of the name of the Savior, "when he shall come to be *glorified in his saints, and to be marvelled at in all them that believed*" (II Thess. 1:10) . Is there any higher perspective than that?

b. *Holiness*

God said: " I dwell in the . . . holy place." Before Him the seraphim cry unceasingly: "Holy, holy, holy, is Jehovah of hosts!" (Isa. 57:15; 6:3) . "Follow after ... the sanctification without which no man shall see the Lord" (Heb. 12:14) . "There shall in no wise enter into it [the celestial city] any thing unclean" (Rev. 21:27) . What a relief, after all the uncleanness which has constantly surrounded us and contaminated us on this earth! Speaking of death, Wesley said one time: "Oh, to dwell in a country where we shall sin no more and where we shall see no more sin!" And we too shall exclaim with the psalmist: "We shall be satisfied with the goodness of thy house, thy holy temple!" (Ps. 65:4) .

c. *Beauty*

The works of God were magnificent even back in creation: "The heavens declare the glory of God . . . How excellent is thy name in all the earth!" (Ps. 19:1; 8:1) . But the spiritual creation is far more beautiful still: "His work is honor and majesty; and his righteousness endureth for ever" (Ps. 111:3). The holy city of Revelation 21 and 22 is resplendent in beauty, although it is only a reflection. For that which makes the splendor of heaven is the glory of God Himself, the source of all magnificence: "Out of Zion, the perfection of beauty, God hath shined forth" (Ps. 50:2) . "Thou that sittest above the cherubim, shine forth! . . . Cause thy face to shine, and we shall be saved" (Ps. 80:1, 3) . "Of the glorious majesty of thine honor and of thy wondrous works will I meditate" (Ps. 145:5) . "Thine eyes shall see the king in his beauty" (Isa. 33:17) .

This beauty, moreover, will be written on our foreheads. Satan himself, in Eden before the fall, was perfect in beauty, the epitome of perfection (Ezek. 28:12) . Adam and Eve, fresh from the hand of the Creator, were certainly entirely faultless, a condition superior even to that of Absalom (Gen. 1:31; II Sam. 14:25). When all believers have become glorious, "not having spot or wrinkle or any such thing" (Eph. 5:27), it is legitimate to suppose that not only will their spirits attain moral perfection, but also their new bodies will have radiant beauty. Is not the body to be raised in incorruption, in glory, and in power (I Cor. 15:43)?

d. *Immortality*

God "only hath immortality" (I Tim. 6:15). He delivers all believers from the second death, which is endless hell, and communicates to them eternal life (Rev. 20:6). Their sinful souls are raised again by regeneration (John 5:24), and their mortal bodies will receive immortality at the coming of the Lord (I Cor. 15:53). Thus the first death is no more, for it has been swallowed up in victory (I Cor. 15:26, 54). For the inhabitants of heaven there will never again be mourning or any separation at all (Rev. 21:4). They are henceforth not only free from death, but also not subject to time, as those on whom has been put the stamp of eternity.

e. *Light*

"Arise, shine; for thy light is come, and the glory of Jehovah is risen upon thee. For, behold, darkness shall cover the earth . . . but Jehovah will arise upon thee, and his glory shall be seen upon thee. And nations shall come to thy light, and kings to the brightness of thy rising . . . The sun shall be no more thy light by day; neither for brightness shall the moon give light unto thee; but *Jehovah will be unto thee an everlasting light,* and thy God thy glory. Thy sun shall no more go down" (Isa. 60:1-3, 19, 20).

"And the city hath no need of the sun, neither of the moon, to shine upon it; for the glory of God did lighten it, and the lamp thereof is the Lamb. And the nations shall walk amidst the light thereof . . . for there shall be no night there" (Rev. 21:23-25). How could it be otherwise in the place where God

is the light (I John 1:5) ; in the house of the Father of light
(James 1:17); in the realm of the One who has said: "I am the
light of the world" (John 8:12) ? On the first day of the physical creation, God said: "Let there be light, and there was
light." In Christ He has called us out of darkness into His
marvellous light (I Peter 2:9) , and He makes us meet to be
partakers of the inheritance of the saints in light (Col. 1:12) .
Once we were darkness, but now we are light in the Lord
(Eph. 5:8) .

All these affirmations mean, primarily, that in heaven
everything will be bright, pure, and transparent. There
will never again be anything which will or can be obscured
by darkness. At the same time, nothing will be left under the
shadow of ignorance. Human means of knowledge and in-
vestigation will be surpassed. "And there shall be night no
more; and they need no light of lamp, neither light of sun;
for the Lord God shall give them light" (Rev. 22:5) . "For
now we see in a mirror, darkly; but then face to face: now
I know in part; but then shall I know fully even as also I was
fully known (I Cor. 13:12) .

Thus, there will be no more unanswered questions, disturbing doubts, or unsolvable problems, no more anguished
"why's," no more ignorance, no more mistakes. At last we
shall see face to face the One who is Himself the Truth. Even
now we can make the dying words of Guizot our own: "At last
I am going to know!"

f. *Unity*

In God all is harmony and unity. The Father and the Son
are one, and the created universe forms an ensemble which is
wonderfully governed and held together. When the last
traces of revolt are put down, everything will again take the
shape of perfect order. The creation will be "delivered from
the bondage of corruption" (Rom. 8:9-22) . God will complete the execution of His eternal plan "to sum up all things

in Christ, the things in the heavens and the things upon the earth" (Eph. 1:10).

In heaven, no more division, no separation. The believers of the Old and of the New Covenant will be united in the heavenly city (Rev. 21:12, 14). All will share together in the banquet of the kingdom of God (Luke 13:28, 29). Earthly barriers will no longer exist, and anything which now separates true believers will be done away with. The body of Christ will be manifested in that day in its unity. But why should that state be reserved until the other world? Since we are to spend all of eternity together, is it not incumbent upon us that, beginning down here, we learn to love and understand one another, so that the world may see our oneness? Among the most serious sins is that against unity, for it is enough to ruin the temple of God, which we together make up (I Cor. 3:17). Must the Lord have recourse to the furnace of persecution and judgment in order to melt together so many separate nuggets and rid them of their dross?

g. *Perfection*

Since the fall of man, everything has been imperfect in this world. But soon that which is perfect shall come (I Cor. 13:10). The spirits of just men are being made perfect (Heb. 12:23). "He who began a good work in you will perfect it until the day of Jesus Christ" (Phil. 1:6). "The God of all grace . . . shall himself perfect . . . you" (I Peter 5:10). We are already children of God; but soon "we shall be like him, for we shall see him even as he is. And every one that hath this hope set on him purifieth himself, even as he is pure" (I John 3:2, 3).

It is not on earth that we are to attain this entire perfection, for here there is always some progress still to be made (Phil. 3:12-14). And then, God has not allowed the heroes of the Old Covenant to be made perfect apart from us (Heb. 11:39, 40). At the coming of the Lord, we shall all together receive this crowning of our spiritual lives. We believe the concept of perfection also implies that in heaven one's personality will attain its full maturity. On earth those who can make the most of all their gifts are very rare. How many intelligent children have never had the chance to study, and how many truly capable men have never had the opportunity to utilize all the resources lying dormant in them! Some day, for believers, all these riches will be fully manifested and appropriated. For the present, we are still only children; then we shall attain unto the fullgrown man and the "measure of the stature of the fullness of Christ." (See Eph. 4:13, 14; Col. 1:28.)

Let us answer at this point a question that is often raised: will children who die very young still be children in heaven? No text substantiates this—and the contrary even seems likely to us. Upon leaving this world, none of us can boast that we have already reached perfection, the measure of the stature of the fullness of Christ. We have just observed that what we lack for this full development will be granted us by divine grace at the return of Christ. We shall all be made like Him, because we shall see Him as He is. Every one will have a perfect body, like the body of His glory (Phil. 3:21). This miracle of complete physical and spiritual maturity will indeed be scarcely more to the Lord in the case of a young person than in that of an older person. God knows perfectly what He has put in germ form in each created individual, and He has promised to perfect His work until the day of Jesus Christ (Phil. 1:6). If something must be argued from the silence of Scripture, it is a fact that the Bible gives no description of children playing in the courts of heaven.

h. *Love*

Since heaven is the Presence of God, it will have all His perfections. In any case, it will be the place of perfect love. A little boy was asked one time what heaven is. His answer was this: "The place where everybody loves everybody!" Prophecies, tongues, and knowledge shall all be done away, but love will never fail (I Cor. 13:8). God Himself is love, and He will fill all of heaven with love. His Spirit will be given to help us understand the love of Christ, which passes knowledge, that we may be filled with all the fullness of God" (Eph. 3:18, 19). How wonderful it will be at last to be able to love God perfectly, when the prayer of Jesus will be wholly fulfilled: "I made known unto them thy name . . . that the love wherewith thou lovest me may be in them and I in them" (John 17:26)!

i. *Joy*

Even in this world the fruit of the Spirit is love, joy, and peace. How much more true will this be in the presence of God! Joy characterizes the believer, and a sad believer is a poor Christian. That is why we read: "I create new heavens and a new earth . . . Be ye glad and rejoice for ever in that which I create; for, behold, I create Jerusalem a rejoicing and her people a *joy*. And I will rejoice in Jerusalem and joy in my people . . . Jehovah delighteth in thee . . . so shall thy God rejoice over thee . . . The ransomed of Jehovah shall return, and come with singing unto Zion; and everlasting joy shall be upon their heads; they shall obtain gladness and joy, and sorrow and sighing shall flee away" (Isa. 65:17-19; 62:4, 5; and 35:10).

If such promises are in a large part realized after the earthly restoration of Israel, what will the heavenly Jerusalem be? "Sing, O daughter of Zion; shout, O Israel; be glad and rejoice with all the heart, O daughter of Jerusalem. Jehovah hath taken away thy judgments . . . Jehovah thy God is in the midst of thee, a mighty one who will save; he will rejoice over thee with joy; he will joy over thee with singing" (Zeph. 3:14-17). If the Lord's own joy bursts forth like this, could that of the elect be anything less than perfect?

Moreover, the Lord's will for us is this: "These things have I spoken unto you, that my joy may be in you and that your joy may be made full" (John 15:11).

It is not too much to say that joy is the very climate of heaven. After the creation, "the morning stars sang together, and all the sons of God shouted for joy (Job 38:7). "There is joy in the presence of the angels of God over one sinner that repenteth" (Luke 15:10). "In thy presence is fulness of joy; in thy right hand there are pleasures for evermore" (Ps. 16:11). Soon will dawn the day of eternal gladness, when at last we can exclaim: "Hallelujah: for the Lord our God, the Almighty, reigneth. Let us rejoice and be exceeding glad, and let us give the glory unto him: for the marriage of the Lamb is come" (Rev. 19:6, 7). "Make a joyful noise unto Jehovah . . . Serve Jehovah with gladness: Come before his presence with singing . . . Enter into his gates with thanksgiving" (Ps. 100:1-4). "Insomuch as ye are partakers of Christ's sufferings, rejoice; that at the revelation of his glory also ye may rejoice with exceeding joy" (I Peter 4:13). Down here, it is difficult for us to "rejoice in the Lord always," as the Apostle Paul enjoins us to do (Phil. 4:4). But in heaven our joy will be without fear or mental reservation. It will be just as perfect and eternal as that of God Himself.

j. *Consolation*

If we enjoy such bliss, it will be because our hearts will be completely comforted, after all the sorrows down here. This consolation is repeatedly promised us in the Scriptures. "Blessed are they that mourn: for they shall be comforted" (Matt. 5:4). God is called "the God of all comfort" (II Cor. 1:3). "Comfort ye, comfort ye my people, saith your God . . . Sing, O heavens; and be joyful, O earth; and break forth into singing, O mountains: for Jehovah hath comforted his people and will have compassion upon his afflicted . . . Ye shall be borne upon the side and shall be dandled upon the knees. As one whom his mother comforteth, so will I comfort you" (Isa. 40:1; 49:13; 66:12, 13). Carried by the angels to Abraham's bosom, the poor man Lazarus found instant solace (Luke 16:22, 25). And in the holy city, God "shall wipe away every tear from their eyes; and death shall be no more; neither shall there be mourning, nor crying, nor pain any more: the first things are passed away" (Rev. 21:4). How can we fail to be comforted now in our sufferings with such a consoling perspective before us?

k. *Perfect happiness*

Need we say that in heaven our every desire will be satisfied, and our hearts quite overwhelmed with felicity?

Nine times Jesus declared "blessed" those who suffer when they live in this world according to His law (Matt. 5:3-11); what will He say to the overcomers once they are introduced forever unto the presence of the Lord? "Blessed and holy is he that hath part in the first resurrection . . . he that sitteth on the throne shall spread his tabernacle over them. They shall hunger no more, neither thirst any more; neither shall the sun strike upon them, nor any heat: for the Lamb that is in the midst of the throne shall be their shepherd; and shall guide them unto fountains of waters of life: and God shall wipe away every tear from their eyes" (Rev. 20:6; 7:15-17).

l. *Eternity*

Everything here is limited by time. Everything has a beginning and an ending. We are saddened when we realize that the most treasured things last only for a little season—and we wish we might hold back the rapid flight of the hours. At other times, the opposite is true: we wish we might avoid the delays that plague our short lives; we should like to make the hands of the clock turn faster. On earth, especially in modern living, we are frustrated by the sense of a lack of time. Man has an insatiable urge for action, for pleasure, and for possession. If a day held forty-eight hours, he would immediately clamor for ninety-six! We are therefore obliged for now to accept philosophically this limitation and, for lack of time, simply let go a multitude of things that strongly appeal to us. The best we can do is to "redeem the time"—to "number our days" with care, since we have so few of them (Eph. 5:16; Ps. 90:12).

On the other hand, what a relief and what joy to know that in heaven there will be no more time: no more hurrying, no more delays, no more wasting of time or lack of it, and no more rude interruptions of the most beautiful of moments, for everything will have become patterned after the image of the eternal God.

The elect will enjoy eternal life (John 3:16).

They will reign for ever and ever (Rev. 22:5).

They will never again be separated from God (I Thess. 4:17; Rom. 8:38, 39).

## 4. THE REUNION IN HEAVEN

Many people are disturbed by the fear of not recognizing their loved ones in heaven. They suppose that the disappearance of the former body of flesh might be a hindrance to that recognition. But such a fear is absolutely groundless, and we believe that this can easily be proved by the Scriptures.

The essential element of personality is not the carnal envelope, destined to decrepitude and death; it is much more the spirit, that "inward man [which] is renewed day by day." A person can suffer and grow old in his body while his spirit stays just as young and alert as ever. That is the individual we shall meet again in the other world. Even here below we can recognize a person without seeing him. Mary Magdalene knew Jesus by His voice when, her eyes filled with tears, she did not think of turning toward Him (John 20:16). We know very well the one we are talking with on the telephone, and we are not deceived by the handwriting of someone we know.

It is plain that the angels, though they have no bodies, possess distinct personalities. We know by name Michael and Gabriel—and the same thing is true of Satan. In the visions of Daniel and John, the angels speak and act in an entirely personal way. On the other hand, the Bible mentions many personalities that continue to live in the beyond: Jacob said that he would go down to his son in the abode of the dead (Gen. 37:35). Samuel came back to speak to Saul (I Sam. 28:15). David declared that he would go to rejoin the child that he had lost (II Sam. 12:23). Moses and Elijah were recognized on the Mount of Transfiguration (Luke 9:28). Abraham, Lazarus, and the wicked rich man conversed in the other world ( Luke 16:23-28). God considered as alive Abraham, Isaac, and Jacob (Matt. 22:32). The risen Lord made Himself known to His disciples, some way, although He was clothed with His new body: "See my hands and my feet, that *it is I myself;* handle me and see . . ." (Luke 24:39). Moreover, Jesus said that we shall see Abraham, Isaac, and Jacob, and all the prophets, in the kingdom of God (Luke 13:28). Paul wrote to the Thessalonians: "For what is our hope, or joy, or crown of glorifying? Are not even ye, before our Lord Jesus at his coming?" (I Thess. 2:19). And he added, to the Corinthians, "We are your glorying, even as ye also are ours, in the day of our Lord Jesus" (II Cor. 1:14). How could Paul write like this if he had not been sure that he and his spiritual children would meet again and would recognize one another in the presence of God? On the other hand, to keep the Thessalonians from sorrowing as those who have no hope, Paul declared to them that God would bring back with Jesus, and by Him, those who had died (I Thess. 4:13, 14, 18). Now what consolation would the perspective have if there were no recognition possible? There is no worse solitude than that which one feels when he is lost in a big city, surrounded by a crowd of strangers. Wouldn't it be dreadful in the immense heavenly city, surrounded by the myriads of the redeemed, to be saying constantly to oneself: "Out in that multitude somewhere are my loved ones. I have possibly brushed against them any number of times without having recognized them! Now where can they be, and how can I get to them?" Such a situation would be as absurd as it would be hopeless. No, we shall know one another in the world to come; and we shall not only meet our dear ones, but make new acquaintances as well. What joy it will be to meet the patriarchs, prophets, and apostles who have done us so much good by their example and their writings! What a privilege to see David, Paul, John, and so many other heroes of the faith since the beginning of time! On earth we often have this experience: "Behold, how good and how pleasant it is for brethren to dwell together in unity! . . . For there Jehovah commanded the blessing, even life for evermore" (Ps. 133:1, 3). Reunion with the children of God is to us a foretaste of heaven. But, alas, difficulties come up sometimes —and at best we always have eventually to face the inevitable parting. The reunion of heaven will be perfect and eternal, just like the blessing associated with it.

## 5. WHAT WILL BECOME OF FAMILY RELATIONSHIPS?

The heart relationships will not be changed. We shall meet again our husbands and wives and our parents and children, and we shall love them even more than we did on earth. But it is clear that conjugal relations will not be the same. To mock at Jesus, the unbelieving Sadducees recounted to Him the ridiculous story of a woman who had supposedly married seven brothers, one after the other—and they wanted to know which one's wife she would be "in the resurrection." The Lord answered them: "They that are accounted worthy to attain to that world and the resurrection from the dead neither marry nor are given in marriage: for neither can they die any more: for they are equal unto the angels and are sons of God, being sons of the resurrection" (Luke 20:35, 36). It goes without saying that there will be no more need for procreation for the continuance of the race, which will then be immortal.

## 6. ACTIVITY IN HEAVEN

Some Christians not blessed with imagination—or with a knowledge of the Bible either—are very much troubled by this question. They are even tempted to think that they will be bored if they will have to "be good" during all eternity. The story is told of a little boy who was informed that by becoming a Christian, he would go to live forever in heaven, where he would sit on a stool playing a golden harp. The boy promptly declared emphatically that he didn't want to do anything of the kind! Then there is the one concerning the very devout old lady who, when dying, was apprehensive about leaving this world. Those standing by reminded her of heaven and asked her what she thought it would be like. She replied: "Oh, there must be chairs arranged the way they are in church. People sit on them and sing psalms during all eternity." No wonder that she preferred this earth to such a heaven as that! But is this the only impression the Scriptures give? Let us see, on the contrary, what glorious prospects they hold out to us. In heaven we shall find:

### a. *Adoration*

When the Bible takes us before the throne of God, it shows us the Lord surrounded by a multitude of creatures who are worshipping Him. It is inherent in the very nature of God to receive adoration. True worshippers worship the Father in spirit and in truth, for it is they whom the Father seeks. "God is a Spirit: and they that worship him must worship in spirit and truth" (John 4:23, 24). What else could created beings do in the presence of the divine Majesty but bow down, yield to Him, praise and serve Him, and give thanks to Him? Worship is the highest form of service, for by means of it we become occupied with God Himself and give Him the honor which is rightfully His. Down here we do not at all know how to worship aright. We present ourselves before the Lord and beg, ask for things, and complain;

but how hard it is for us to forget ourselves so as, above everything else, to seek God alone and His glory!

*Contemplation* is one of the forms of worship. In heaven, the servants of God "shall see his face; and his name shall be on their foreheads" (Rev. 22:3, 4). We shall cease to be in the position of Moses, to whom God declared: "Thou canst not see my face, for man shall not see me and live" (Exod. 33:20).

One finds over and over in the Scriptures the terror of the sinner in the presence of God. Samson's parents said: "We shall surely die, because we have seen God" (Judges 13:22). The devout prophet Isaiah cried out: "Woe is me! for I am undone . . . mine eyes have seen the King, Jehovah of hosts!" (Isa. 6:5). In heaven, however, grace will have done its perfect work. Man, washed in the blood of Christ and sanctified by the Holy Spirit, will be able to appear before the Lord, there to contemplate Him face to face. Here on earth we know what it is not to be able to take our eyes off a lovely sight: a wonderful flower, a magnificent panorama, or an unusual work of art can make us quite beside ourselves, so to speak. What will it be like when we shall see face to face the Author of all that is beautiful and perfect!

Furthermore, the consideration of the Lord changes us into His image: when the elect see His face, "his name shall be in their foreheads." After Moses had spent forty days in the presence of God, his face shone with God's glory (Exod. 34:29). And we also, beholding as in a mirror the glory of the Lord, are transformed into the same image from glory to glory, even as from the Lord the Spirit (II Cor. 3: 18). Soon our contemplation will be direct and immediate, and its results will be even more glorious. The secret of a victorious walk now is for us always to be "looking unto Jesus" (Heb. 12:2), but all too often we turn our gaze from Him. In heaven the eyes of all creatures will be fixed on the Lord, without cessation or distraction. Even in being thus taken up with the Lord, shall we ever be able to search Him out perfectly? Paul tells us that "the Spirit searcheth all things, yea, the deep things of God . . . the things of God none knoweth save the Spirit of God" (I Cor. 2:10, 11). Will it not take all eternity to come to know the infinite God in this way? We are frequently surprised at the reactions of a versatile and dynamic personality whom we thought we knew; shall we not also be constantly making new discoveries in the Person of Him who is at the same time unsearchable (Isa. 40:28) and yet desirous of having us know even as we are known?

From the first moment in heaven, believers—even those of the Old Covenant—will find their dearest wishes granted. Did not Job exclaim: "I know that my Redeemer liveth . . . Without my flesh shall I see God; whom I, even I, shall see, on my side, and mine eyes shall behold, and not as a stranger. My heart is consumed within me" (Job 19:25-27). The psalmists also considered that to see the Lord would be their greatest privilege: "One thing have I asked of Jehovah, that will I seek after: That I may dwell in the house of Jehovah all the days of my life, to behold the beauty of Jehovah, and to inquire in his temple . . . Blessed is the man whom thou choosest and causest to approach unto thee, that he may dwell in thy courts: We shall be satisfied with the goodness of thy house, thy holy temple" (Ps. 27:4; 65:4). "As for me, I shall behold thy face in righteousness; I shall be satisfied when I awake, with beholding thy form . . . My soul thirsteth for God, for the living God: When shall I come and appear before God? . . . Thou hast holden my right hand. Thou wilt guide me with thy counsel and afterward receive me to glory. Whom have I in heaven but thee? And there is none upon earth that I desire besides thee. My flesh and my heart faileth; but God is the strength of my heart and my portion for ever" (Ps. 17:15; 42:2; 73:23-26). It has been said that though God takes away from us all His gifts, He never takes

Himself away from us. Since He is our portion for ever, what more can we ever want?

*Praise and thanksgiving* are also essential to worship. "Whoso offereth the sacrifice of thanksgiving glorifieth me" (Ps. 50:23). Toward the end the Psalms magnify praise in an ever-increasing crescendo; they call on the whole universe, the angels, the saints, and all the works of creation to join in a triumphant alleluia. "Praise ye Jehovah; for it is good to sing praises unto our God; for it is pleasant, and praise is comely . . . Sing unto Jehovah with thanksgiving . . . Praise Jehovah, O Jerusalem; praise thy God, O Zion . . . Let the saints exult in glory: Praise God in his sanctuary . . . Let everything that hath breath praise Jehovah!" (Ps. 147:1, 7, 12; 149:5; 150:1, 6. See also Psalms 134, 135, 136, 148, etc.) We are called upon to offer to God by Jesus Christ "a sacrifice of praise continually, that is, the fruit of lips which make confession to his name" (Heb. 13:15). The Revelation, too, shows us, throughout, the host of angels and of the elect that praise and glorify the Father and the Son. "Unto him that loveth us . . . to him be the glory and the dominion for ever and ever . . . The four and twenty elders shall fall down before him . . . and shall worship him that liveth for ever and ever and shall cast their crowns before the throne, saying, Worthy art thou, our Lord and our God, to receive the glory and the honor and the power: for thou didst create all things, and because of thy will they were, and were created." (This refers to the hymn of praise addressed to the Creator, alluded to in Job 38:7.) "The four and twenty elders . . . sing a new song, saying, Worthy art thou to take the book, and to open the seals thereof: for thou wast slain, and didst purchase unto God with thy blood men of every tribe, and tongues, and people, and nation." This "new" song exalts the Redeemer, whose name merits all the more praise because of the significance of His cross. "I saw, and I heard a voice of many angels round about the throne and the living creatures and the elders; and the number of them was ten thousand times ten thousand, and thousands of thousands . . . And every created thing which is in the heaven, and on the earth, and under the earth, and on the sea, and all things that are in them, heard I saying: Unto him that sitteth on the throne, and unto the Lamb, be the blessing, and the honor, and the glory, and the dominion, for ever and ever. And the four living creatures said, Amen. And the elders fell down and worshipped" (Rev. 1:5, 6; 4:10, 11; 5:8, 9, 11-14; see also 7:9-12 and 11:16-18.)  Let us note that it is not only the God of creation and of redemption who is praised. The four-fold Alleluia of chapter 19, verses 1-6, exalts the God of judgment, who punished Babylon the Great, taking over the rule of it.

It pleases the Lord when praise is lifted up to Him by means of *music,* that daughter of heaven. In the temple of old, two hundred eighty-eight musicians were to enhance the divine service by singing and by playing on various instruments: cymbals, psalteries, and harps (I Chron. 25:1-8) . The Psalms, which are lyric poetry, also mention the trumpet, the timbrel, the pipe, and stringed instruments (Ps. 150). Hezekiah exclaimed: "Jehovah is ready to save me! Therefore we will sing my songs with stringed instruments all the days of our life in the house of Jehovah" (Isa. 38:20) . Jesus Himself sang with His disciples psalms, or the hymns which accompanied the Passover (Mark 14:26). And Paul says: "Speaking one to another in psalms and hymns and spiritual songs, singing and making melody with your heart to the Lord . . . with psalms and hymns and spiritual songs, singing with grace in your hearts unto God" (Eph. 5:19; Col. 3:16) . Then James adds: "Is any cheerful? Let him sing praise" (5:13). In fact, Christian nations are the only ones which have real music—and often the most remarkable and the most joyous composers have been vital Christians: Bach and Handel, to mention only two.  Is it not the heart delivered from all fear and filled with the joy of the Holy Spirit that can best express itself in song? Thus, we are not surprised to see the place that music occupies in the description of heaven. Freed from all evil, the redeemed can intone the new song to the glory of the Lamb that was slain. The elders sing, accompanying themselves on harps of gold (Rev. 5:8, 9). The voice that John heard was "as the voice of harpers harping with their harps." The hundred and forty-four thousand also sing the new song before the throne (Rev. 14:2, 3). Then the apostle sees all them that come off victorious from the beast, "standing by the sea of glass, having harps of God. And they sing the song of Moses, the servant of God, and the song of the Lamb" (15:2, 3). These two hymns have essentially the same inspiration: the song of Moses is perhaps that of Exodus 15, which the Israelites uttered after their marvelous experience of the Passover and the Red Sea, the symbol of our deliverance from the slavery and condemnation of a world given over to Satan. In Egypt, under the whip of Pharaoh, there were only cries and groanings to be heard. Redeemed by the blood of the Passover lamb and delivered from their enemies at the Red Sea, Moses and the Israelites raised a hymn of praise and triumph. In heaven this same song of redemption will resound, sung only by those who have received divine grace. Throughout all eternity, our praise and our anthems will mount up to Him who has saved us. And the perfect harmony of heaven will go far beyond the already sublime harmony of our earthly music.

b. *Rest*

Eden was a place of calm and blessing. Then after the fall, work became a burden, and the ground was cursed; and now our entire existence is carried on at the cost of wearisome effort. We all "labor and are heavy laden," are slaves of the inexorable laws of this world, and are pursued by the tempter. Jesus Himself had nowhere to lay His head. But His grace brings rest and freedom to any who will accept His light and easy yoke (Matt. 11:28-30). Still, we are saved only by hope;

and we have to "fight the good fight" until the very end. Soon we shall enter into a perfect rest, which neither temptation nor sin can ever trouble. After the forty hard years in the wilderness, the Israelites, thanks to Joshua, could at last settle down in the rest of the Promised Land. So at the end of our pilgrimage on earth, our heavenly "Joshua" will lead us to the full enjoyment of that heavenly rest, which even now we have entered into by faith (Heb. 4:8-11). Believers, on leaving this world, experience at once the rest of the elect, as we see in the case of Samuel and in that of Lazarus (I Sam. 28:15 and Luke 16:22 and 25). It is not necessary to go through endless litanies to implore the Lord to grant rest. "Blessed are the dead who die in the Lord from henceforth: yea, saith the Spirit . . . for their works follow with them" (Rev. 14:13). This rest will become eternal when, at the return of Christ, the whole Church will enter into glory: "It is a righteous thing with God to recompense . . . to you that are afflicted rest with us, at the revelation of the Lord Jesus from heaven" (II Thess. 1:6, 7).

c. *Service*

Heaven will not consist of contemplation and rest alone. Our God is a fountain-head imparting life and activity. Jesus said: "My Father worketh even until now, and I work" (John 5:17). It is written of the redeemed: "[They are] before the throne of God, and they serve him day and night in his temple . . . and his servants shall serve him" (Rev. 7:15; 22:3). Men take pride in occupying places of responsibility before kings or others who are much esteemed in this world. What an infinitely greater honor is ours when God allows us to have a place in His service! Even down here, this ministry is our highest privilege. We are saved "to serve a living and true God, and to wait for his Son from heaven" (I Thess. 1:9, 10). The blood of Christ has cleansed our conscience from dead works, that we may serve the living God (Heb. 9:14). But our service is far from being as faithful,

disinterested, and effective as it ought to be. In heaven we
shall work without fatigue, error, or disobedience, perfectly
accomplishing the will of our beloved Lord. The Queen of
Sheba, quite dazzled and beside herself at beholding the
wisdom and glory of Solomon, cried out: "Happy are thy
men, happy are these thy servants, that stand continually
before thee and that hear thy wisdom!" (I Kings 10:4-8).
Shall we ever find words to express our delight at being thus
for ever in the presence of the King of kings?

One thought more: Our sphere of activity here often
seems very limited. Our field of endeavor is small, our
strength gives out quickly, and both circumstances and the
enemy are against us. But there will be none of these limi-
tations in the land of perfection. And who knows in what
new capacity or in what undreamed-of ways the Lord may
be able to use us? As for us, we have made our choice. With
humility, but with confidence, we affirm as did Joshua: "As
for me and my house, we will serve Jehovah!" (Joshua 24:
15).

## d. *The kingdom*

Does not what has just been said seem sufficient? Is it not
marvelous enough that the Lord has snatched us from hell,
provided an entrance for us into His heaven, and given us a
place in His service? But He has still more for us: He is
to share His throne with us. He does this by associating us,
first with the judgment of the world and of the angels (I Cor.
6:2, 3), and then with the thousand-year reign on earth:
"He that overcometh . . . to him will I give authority over
the nations: and he shall rule them with a rod of iron, as the
vessels of the potter are broken to shivers; as I also have received of my Father . . . [Thou] madest them to be unto
our God a kingdom and priests: and they reign upon the
earth . . . They shall be priests of God and of Christ, and
shall reign with him a thousand years" (Rev. 2:26, 27; 5:10;

20:6). Jesus further indicates, in regard to His apostles: "Ye
are they that have continued with me in my temptation; and
I appoint unto you a kingdom, even as my Father appointed
unto me, that ye . . . shall sit on thrones judging the twelve
tribes of Israel" (Luke 22:28-30). The Lord says to all believers: "Fear not, little flock, for it is your Father's good
pleasure to give you the kingdom" (Luke 12:32). "Come, ye
blessed of my Father, inherit the kingdom prepared for you
from the foundation of the world" (Matt. 25:34). Indeed,
from the creation, God has destined man to have dominion
over all the creatures (Gen. 1:28). Here, as in so many other
ways, grace has reestablished and expanded what sin ruined.
"Did not God choose them that are poor as to the world to
be rich in faith and heirs of the kingdom which he promised
to them that love him?" (James 2:5). "If we endure, we
shall also reign with him" (II Tim. 2:12). After the thousand years, this reign will go on into eternity: "He that
overcometh, I will give to him to sit down with me in my
throne, as I also overcame and sat down with my Father in
his throne . . . And they shall reign for ever and ever" (Rev.
3:21; 22:5). "The saints of the Most High shall receive the
kingdom for ever, even for ever and ever" (Dan. 7:18; see
also vss. 22 and 27.)

This is truly enough to make one dizzy. Who could
comprehend the sovereignty of the King of kings and Lord
of lords? The discoveries of scholars in the domain of the
infinitely great leave us breathless; and we are no less impressed by the infinitely small. But all this is perhaps only
an infinitesimal part of God's universe, as glimpsed from the
limited perspective of pretentious humanity. How is it that
Christians can wonder what they will be doing in heaven?
It seems to us, on the contrary, that every minute of such a
rich eternity will be replete with the most thrilling significance. In sixty centuries we have scarcely explored our

own planet. How much time shall we need to fathom God and all His works?

As for the unmerited share in His reign, the wonder of it will probably never cease to cover us with confusion. The four and twenty elders will cast their golden crowns at the feet of Him who alone is worthy to receive glory and honor and power, the characteristics of royal authority (Rev. 4:10, 11). We shall follow their example, remembering with humility and adoration that He alone is the blessed and only Potentate, the King of kings and Lord of lords (I Tim. 6: 15).

## 7. THE THINGS WHICH WILL CEASE TO EXIST IN HEAVEN

Made wonderful by the presence of so many positive joys, heaven will also be a remarkable place because of the absence of that which otherwise might cast a gloom over it. From a negative point of view, we can further say this: In heaven there will be no more:

| | | | |
|---|---|---|---|
| sea, | Rev. 21:1 | sickness, | 22:2 |
| tears, | 21:4 | curse, | 22:2 |
| death, | 21:4 | light of sun, | 22:5 |
| mourning, | 21:4 | light of lamp, | 22:5 |
| crying, | 21:4 | deceiver, | 20:10 |
| pain, | 21:4 | hunger, | 7:16 |
| sun, | 21:23 | thirst, | 7:16 |
| moon, | 21:23 | heat, | 7:16 |
| insecurity, | 21:25 | condemnation, | Rom. 8:1 |
| night, | 21:25 | separation, | Rom. 8:38, 39 |
| sin, | 21:27 | time—since all will have become eternal | Rev. 10:6 |

It is not likely that anyone will regret the absence of any of these!

## 8. WILL THERE BE MANY PEOPLE IN HEAVEN?

This question, which haunts many people's minds, was

asked of Jesus Christ Himself: "Lord, are there few that are saved?" To which the Savior replied: "Strive to enter in by the narrow door: for many, I say unto you, shall seek to enter in and shall not be able" (Luke 13:23, 24). In one sense, then, this is an idle question; God alone knows how many belong to Him (II Tim. 2:9). Still, the Bible does not leave in the dark those who are sincerely troubled about the perdition of the multitudes.

It is true that Jesus says that there are many called, but few chosen (Matt. 22:14); that many will go to perdition by the broad way, whereas few will find life by the narrow way. And these words seem a true picture of the situation as we see it. But does that mean, as some think, that in all of the vast expanse of heaven there will be just a small number of redeemed ones? Certainly not, for the Bible tells us the opposite. In the parable of the wedding feast, the king was absolutely determined that his banquet might be well attended. He persistently sent his servants several times to bring in all those they could find, "and the wedding was *filled with guests*" (Matt. 22:10). The account as given by Luke is even plainer. After having brought in the poor, the maimed, the blind, and the lame, the servant reported, "Lord . . . yet there is room. And the master said to the servant: Go out into the highways and hedges, and constrain them to come in, *that my house may be filled*" (Luke 14:21-23). The hardened Jews had been rejected; but Paul declared that one day they would all be converted and that Israel (those living at that time) would thus be saved. The apostle also said that the hardening of Israel would last until all the heathen had entered in (to the Church) —that is, until the completion of the number of believers that would come out of paganism. So God will not leave behind any of His own. Jesus will be able to say to His Father at the last day: "I kept them in thy name which thou hast given me: and I guarded them, and not one of them perished . . . Behold, I and the children whom God hath given me" (John 17:12; Heb. 2:13). This is why the Scriptures often speak of the great throng that will make up the inhabitants of heaven. Daniel said of the Ancient of Days: "Thousands of thousands minstered unto him, and ten thousand times ten thousand stood before him" (Dan. 7:10). The reference is to "the host of heaven" surrounding the Lord and to the innumerable hosts of angels which make up the heavenly choir (I Kings 22:19; Heb. 12:22).

Apart from the hundred and forty-four thousand Israelites given the mark of God, John saw before the throne and before the Lamb a vast multitude which no man could number, out of every nation and of all tribes and peoples and tongues (Rev. 7:9). The apostle heard as it were the voice of "a great multitude in heaven, saying, Hallelujah!" That chorus of the great multitude was "as the voice of many waters, and as the voice of mighty thunders" (Rev. 19:1, 6). Thus it will be when all the redeemed shall lift their voices to praise God, the Savior. Yes, the enormous dimensions of the heavenly city (Rev. 21:16) indicate that God is preparing enough room for a crowd of chosen ones such as we cannot imagine. Did He not promise to Abraham, the father of them that believe, that his posterity would be as numberless as the sand which is upon the seashore and as the stars of the heavens? (Gen. 22:17).

We, in our time of apostasy, are perhaps not well enough placed in history to evaluate correctly the number of true believers. There have been epochs of revival and of vast conquests; for example, both those during the first centuries and those following the Reformation; in our own time, on some mission fields, the last are becoming the first, and people are thirsting for the truth. Moreover, it seems probable to us that the millennium will be a season of unparalleled harvest. First, because of the reduction of wars and of mortality, there will be a considerable population increase. Then again,

Satan being bound, the earth shall be full of the knowledge of Jehovah as the waters cover the sea, and the nations themselves shall seek Christ (Isa. 11:9, 10). Who knows to what extent this blessed victory may make up in some way for all the generations which have come short? (See R. Pache, *The Return of Jesus Christ*, p. 403.)

### 9. TO WHOM IS HEAVEN OPENED?

God "would have all men to be saved" (I Tim. 2:4). The Lord "is longsuffering to you-ward, not wishing that any should perish, but that all should come to repentance" (II Peter 3:9). His will, then, is unmistakable: all sinners are invited to heaven, through repentance and faith in Jesus Christ. The King has everyone, whether wicked or upright, told this: "All things are ready: come to the marriage feast." Those who accept the invitation are welcomed at once (Matt. 22:4, 10). The wise virgins are ready; they have oil in their lamps (the Holy Spirit in their hearts, Rom. 8:9); they are awake and prepared. As soon as the Bridegroom comes, they enter with Him into the marriage feast (Matt. 25:10). Jesus said: "I am the way, the truth, and the life; no one cometh unto the Father but by me." And He says, further, to those who have received Him as their personal Savior: "I go to prepare a place for you . . . I come again and will receive you unto myself, that where I am, there ye may be also" (John 14:6, 2, 3). On the last page of the Bible the appeal is made in an even more emphatic way: "I will give unto him that is athirst of the fountain of the water of life freely. He that overcometh shall inherit all things; and I will be his God, and he shall be my son."

"And he that *is athirst,*

let him *come;*
he that *will,*
let him *take* the water of life
*freely*" (Rev. 21:6, 7; 22:17).

Could anything be said more simply? *To thirst* for pardon and eternal life—*to come* to Jesus—*to will*, i.e., to make the decision to give oneself to Him—*to take* His salvation (not merely to beg or to wait for it)—and *to repudiate* any merit of one's own, as implied in the word "freely"—those are the five steps which lead to the appropriation of salvation. A child can comprehend them—and can experience them at once. What about you who are reading these lines?

At the risk of laboring the point, let us solemnly repeat once more that

> those who want to go to heaven go there
>    and, just as surely,
> those who want to go to hell go there.

Now let us quote one last time that pathetic exclamation of Jesus over Jerusalem: "How often *would I* have gathered thy children together . . . and *ye would not!*" (Matt. 23:37). So no one will ever be able to say to God, "Lord, I should like to have entered into Thy heaven, but Thou didst not let me enter!" The opposite is true, and in that lies our responsibility.

It is frightening to realize that so many people are deliberately depriving themselves of eternal bliss. In the parable, the first ones invited *"would not* come." The king insisted and sent more servants; but *"they made light of it* and went their ways, one to his own farm, another to his merchandise; and the rest laid hold on his servants and treated them shamefully, and killed them" (Matt. 23:3-6). According to Luke, *all with one consent began to make excuse."* Therefore, the master, indignant, declared: "I say unto you that none of those men that were bidden shall taste of my supper" (Luke 14:18, 24). For the time being, the door of grace is wide open and Jesus does not cast out those who come to Him. But the hour is coming when that door is going to be shut, and then it will be too late to be saved. The Bible emphasizes this terrible thought:

Noah entered into the ark with his family and even with some animals. He had seven days to wait in the ark, during which time many could have still been saved. Then *"Jehovah shut him in,"* and all the rest subsequently perished (Gen. 7:7, 10, 16). "Strive to enter in by the narrow door: for many . . . shall seek to enter in and shall not be able. When once the master of the house is risen up and hath *shut to the door,* and ye begin to stand without and to knock at the door, saying, Lord, open to us; and he shall answer and say to you, I know you not whence ye are . . . depart from me, ye that work iniquity. There shall be the weeping and the gnashing of teeth, when ye shall see Abraham, and Isaac, and Jacob, and all the prophets, in the kingdom of God, and yourselves cast forth *without"* (Luke 13:24-28).

"The Bridegroom came; and they that were ready went in with him to the marriage feast; and *the door was shut.* Afterward came also the other virgins, saying, Lord, Lord, open to us. But he answered and said, Verily I say unto you, I know you not" (Matt. 25:10-12).

"Today if ye shall hear his voice, harden not your hearts, as in the provocation . . . where your fathers tried me by proving me . . . As I sware in my wrath, *They shall not enter into my rest* [the rest of the Promised Land]! . . . And we see that they were not able to enter in because of unbelief. Let us fear therefore lest haply, a promise being left of entering into his rest, any one of you should seem to have *come short of it"* (Heb. 3:7-11, 19; 4:1). Indeed, it is still true that the only obstacles which can keep you from entering into heaven, the true Promised Land, are the voluntary hardening of your heart and unbelief.

"Blessed are they that wash their robes, that they may have the right to come to the tree of life and may *enter in by the gates* into the city! *Without* are the dogs, and the sorcerers, and the fornicators, and the murderers, and the idolators, and every one that loveth and maketh a lie!" (Rev. 22:14, 15).

Let us then see to it that we wash our robes in the blood of the Lamb (Rev. 7:14). Let us follow the advice of Peter, who wrote: "Adding on your part all diligence, in your faith supply virtue . . . knowledge . . . self control . . . patience . . . godliness . . . brotherly kindness . . . love . . . Give the more diligence to make your calling and election sure: for if ye do these things, ye shall never stumble: for thus shall be richly supplied unto you the entrance into the eternal kingdom of our Lord and Saviour Jesus Christ" (II Peter 1:5-12).

10. WHAT EFFECT WILL THE PROSPECT OF HEAVEN HAVE ON BELIEVERS?

Will it make us mere dreamers, that live in the clouds, quite incapable of keeping our feet on the ground? Certainly not! Just as in the case of our waiting for Christ's return, a correct understanding of the anticipation of heaven will produce a more virile and practical devotion than ever. Indeed, it will bring us:

> sanctification: "We shall be like him, for we shall see him even as he is. And every one that hath this hope set on him purifieth himself, even as he is pure" (I John 3:2, 3).

> joy: "When men shall hate you . . . and cast out your name as evil, for the Son of man's sake . . . Rejoice in that day, and leap for joy: for behold, your reward is great in heaven" (Luke 6:22, 23).

> consolation: "Ye . . . took joyfully the spoiling of your possessions, knowing that ye have for yourselves a better possession and an abiding one" (Heb. 10:34).

> endurance: Moses accounted "the reproach of Christ greater riches than the treasures of Egypt, for he looked unto

the recompense of reward . . . he endured, as seeing him who is invisible" (Heb. 11:26, 27).

*the ennobling of our affections:* "Lay up for yourselves treasures in heaven . . . for where thy treasure is, there will thy heart be also" (Matt. 6:20, 21).

*confidence:* "We are of good courage . . . and are willing rather to be absent from the body and to be at home with the Lord. Wherefore also we make it our aim, whether at home or absent, to be well pleasing unto him" (II Cor. 5:6-9).

*anticipation:* "Our citizenship is in heaven, whence also we wait for a Saviour, the Lord Jesus Christ, who shall fashion anew the body of our humiliation, that it may be conformed to the body of his glory" (Phil. 3:20, 21).

May we too be able to say with the Apostle Paul: "The Lord will deliver me from every evil work and will save me unto his heavenly kingdom: to whom be the glory for ever and ever! Amen!" (II Tim. 4:18).

"Now unto him that is able to guard you from stumbling, and to set you before the presence of his glory without blemish in exceeding joy, to the only God our Saviour, through Jesus Christ our Lord, be glory, majesty, dominion, and power, before all time, and now, and for evermore! Amen!" (Jude 24, 25).